BETWEEN
ANGER AND HOPE

BETWEEN
ANGER AND HOPE

South Africa's Youth and the
Truth and Reconciliation Commission

KARIN CHUBB
AND
LUTZ VAN DIJK

FOREWORD BY
ARCHBISHOP DESMOND M TUTU

WITWATERSRAND UNIVERSITY PRESS

Witwatersrand University Press
1 Jan Smuts Avenue
2001 Johannesburg
South Africa

ISBN 1 86814 363 5

First published in English in 2001

Originally published in the series 'rororo aktuell' under the title
DER TRAUM VOM REGENBOGEN
Copyright © 1999 by Rowohlt Taschenbuch Verlag GmbH, Reinbek bei Hamburg

Distributed in North America by:

Transaction Publishers
New Brunswick (U.S.A.) and London (U.K.)

Transaction Publishers   Tel: (732)445-2280
Rutgers University   Fax: (732)445-3138
35 Berrue Circle   For orders (US only):
Piscataway, NJ 08854   Toll free 888-999-6778

Cover photograph by: Motlhalefi Mahlabe © South Photographs
Typesetting and Cover Design by: Sue Sandrock
Printed and bound by: Clyson Printers, Maitland

for
KATHY CHUBB
1970-1994

THE AUTHORS

KARIN CHUBB teaches German language and literature at the University of the Western Cape. She was a Vice-President of the Black Sash for several years .

LUTZ VAN DIJK, PhD, is the author of several books. Among the awards he has received is the National Youth Literature Award of Namibia (1997). He was a staff member on the Anne Frank Foundation in Amsterdam from 1992 to 1999.

———— • ————

All royalties from this book go towards Reparations for Victims

CONTENTS

FOREWORD

THE VOICES OF OUR CHILDREN

It is often said that children and youth are our hope for tomorrow. This is true, but in South Africa they were also yesterday's heroes. Where would we have been were it not for the brave school children of 1976 in Soweto and elsewhere in the country? Children and young people paid an unbelievable price for our freedom. Many of them sacrificed their most precious years – years that should have been filled with joy and laughter – in order to participate in 'the struggle' Many not only believed the slogan 'liberation before education' but willingly sacrificed their future careers in fighting against apartheid. Others sacrificed their lives for the sake of their parents, their friends and generations yet to be born. Perhaps the greatest miracle of all is that so many triumphed over Bantu education which was designed to equip black children for no more than 'their place' within apartheid society. Equally amazing is that so many white children rejected the imposition of racist ideas which formed part of the brain washing in 'white' education and the military training intended to equip them for positions of *baasskap* (domination) over blacks. This resilience made some of them conscientious objectors and resulted in others going into exile.

The Truth and Reconciliation Commission sought to create a space within which the victims of apartheid could reclaim their human dignity by telling their stories of defiance, suffering and heroic struggle. We held children and youth hearings across the country. Some children told their stories *in camera*. Others told the world – all who would hear, that they were not victims, but survivors and soldiers. What terribly sad and yet incredibly brave testimony that was.

This wonderful book creates yet another space within which children and youth can be heard. Their first-hand testimony, the sensitive analysis of the two authors, and the excursions into German and South African history are deeply moving. We are gently – and yet at times roughly –

taken into the lives of young people who bore the brunt of suffering engineered and sustained by adult people. Some children and young people are indeed victims, some are survivors, some are heroes and some are perpetrators. And yet even the most cavalier, raucous and determined perpetrators among them were in one way or another victims of the apartheid past.

Some within this country should be taking responsibility for having contributed to the broken lives of these young people – some of whom persist in their self-defeating ways. Others of us need to recognise that, given a different set of circumstances, we too could have either directly contributed to the evil of apartheid or silently allowed it to continue.

Yet here is hope. As social forces have a capacity to create evil, social forces also have the capacity to create compassion, human decency and goodness. Now is the time for us to create a better society for our children and youth. Now is the time for us to share with them in creating a better society for us all. Now is the time to realise that each child, each youth and every person on God's earth, whether particularly nice or decidedly unpleasant is a child of God. Everyone – the good, the bad and the ugly – all have the potential to contribute to a better South Africa.

The authors of this book, Karin Chubb and Lutz van Dijk, have for many years each contributed to the quest for a better society and the healing of victims. Karin was an important member of the Black Sash movement of women in South Africa. Lutz, author of many books for young adults, has worked for human rights and against racism and discrimination on many educational projects in Europe and until recently in the Anne Frank House in Amsterdam. I am grateful to them for a splendid book. They tell a deeply human story that captures the many different voices of children and youth. I join with them and with you as readers in celebrating the lives of our children and young people.

God bless you all as you share in the journey forward to hope, renewal and reconciliation. May God give us the grace to forgive one another, to love one another and to be sisters and brothers together.

Rt Rev Desmond Mpilo Tutu
Archbishop Emeritus of Cape Town

PREFACE

THE MANDATE OF THE TRC

The preamble to the Interim Constitution of South Africa states:

'This Constitution provides a historic bridge between the past of a deeply divided society characterised by strife, conflict, untold suffering and injustice, and a future founded on the recognition of human rights, democracy and peaceful co-existence and development opportunities for all South Africans, irrespective of colour, race, class, belief or sex. The pursuit of national unity, the well-being of all South African citizens and peace require reconciliation between the people of South Africa and the reconstruction of society.'

Final Report Vol 1, chapter 5, page 103

The mandate of the TRC was established in the Promotion of National Unity and Reconciliation Act in May 1995. Its six main points were:

- To generate a detailed record of the nature, extent and causes of the human rights violations that occurred in South Africa during the period 1960-1994, and to document the context in which those violations occurred.
- To name the people, institutions, organisations, political parties and so on responsible for gross violations of human rights.
- To provide the victims of gross human rights violations with a public platform to express themselves in order to allow them to regain their human dignity.
- To make recommendations to the government to prevent human rights violations in the future.
- To make recommendations for reparations to victims of human rights violations.
- To facilitate the granting of amnesty to individual perpetrators of

human rights violations, conditional upon them making full disclosure of their involvement in such violations.

The last point particularly determined the central motto of the Commission, 'Truth – the Road to Reconciliation', which featured on the green and black banners above the podium while the hearings were in process.

This brief summary belies the inherent complexities and the implications which soon became apparent once the work of the Commission had commenced. A few of these are noted here:

- If the focus was to be on 'gross violations of human rights' (that is serious crimes such as murder, manslaughter or torture, which were in principle also outlawed in the apartheid state) would that not marginalise the essential illegality of apartheid and the structural injustice of racism as it was entrenched in a vast number of laws?
- What should happen with those perpetrators who refused to make a complete confession of their crimes and who could therefore not be granted amnesty?
- How could any form of reparation conceivably be realised for the millions who were disowned, displaced, tortured – or whose closest relatives had been murdered?
- Why should proposals for reparations be submitted only as 'recommendations', whereas decisions over the granting or refusal of amnesty were final?

There can, however, be no doubt about the immense significance of two of the crucial areas which were negotiated:

- A general, blanket amnesty, which had been demanded by the old regime, was rejected in favour of individual amnesty, the basis for which had to be carefully evaluated in each individual case. Without the proviso 'Amnesty for truthful and complete disclosure' a continuation of the civil war and a bloodbath would have been unavoidable. All participants in the negotiation process were in agreement on this point. The constitutionally entrenched task of the TRC – to help in the process of moral reconstruction and building democratic values in the new South Africa – could proceed on this contextually limited but deeply credible foundation.

- The witnesses were the central focus of all the human rights violations hearings. They and their stories were shown respect and were acknowledged in many ways during the proceedings. It is this respect which made the character and spirit of the South African Truth Commission unique and which characterised its image on the national and the international stage, perhaps more so than any of the findings which are so immensely significant to researchers and other experts.

What was achieved, visibly, publicly and accessibly, was a complete break with the 'scorning of others'. This ethic was extended to the perpetrators. When witnesses entered or left the hall, everyone stood up in silent tribute. Every witness could speak in her or his mother tongue, and psychological support and other assistance was offered as a matter of course. It was not required from the victims that they should render 'convincing proof' of violations and crimes. Instead, every witness had the right to tell her or his subjectively remembered truth. Both victims and perpetrators were assisted by an investigative unit which delivered forgotten or missing details.

INTRODUCTION

MORE THAN
HALF THE POPULATION

I t is one of the many hearings of the Truth and Reconciliation Commission held between 1996 and 1998 but it is a hearing with a difference: today is the turn of the youth. The witnesses who have been invited to testify are young adults, and the hall in Cape Town is filled with several hundred boys and girls, most of them in their school uniforms. There is a great deal of pushing and shoving at the entrance; in some rows there is more noise and restlessness than in others – pupils giggle, nudge each other; teachers do their best to maintain order – just a typical scene of a large gathering of children and youths.

Two hours later: The pupils in the hall are spellbound by the testimony being given on the stage. Here the stories are told of what happened to the witnesses when they were the age of most of today's audience. Vuyani Mbewu, for example, was only fourteen years old when, during an incident of spontaneous unrest, he was shot in the street and blinded in one eye. Vuyani was no political activist. He merely happened to be walking along the road and was unable to hide in time. His great dream had been to become a soccer star. Why did he choose to appear before the TRC? 'I am here to show that there is no sense in what happened to me ...' He speaks about the futility of violence, this boy who dreamed of being a great soccer player. Next to us three girls are clutching one set of headphones. There are not enough of those today. Two of the girls have tears in their eyes. The third holds one earphone tightly against her head, her eyes fixed on the floor.

Riefaat Hattas was fifteen when he first became involved in the political struggle. At seventeen he was arrested several times and tortured cruelly. He breaks down as he recounts how, under torture and because of a tragic misunderstanding, he was led to betray a friend. At the end of his testimony he pleads with the children in the hall: 'We were destroyed ... Please, I beg you, make the most of your life. You owe it to us!' There is a moment of complete silence. Then the three girls next to us jump to their feet, most of the other children in the hall follow suit, and there is warm, sustained applause.

We feel on this day that something quite extraordinary is happening. However, it takes a while before we grasp its full extent and magnitude. What we are hearing is not only another devastating report of the horrors endured by children and young people in the flash points and crisis areas of our world. There is something more, something which makes the stories of these children and youths unique: it is their potential to create communication, both with adults and with the youth. While the stories are being told, the Commissioners of the Truth and Reconciliation Commission (TRC) and the children in the hall become part of an extraordinary event. Here a new reality is being created – that social truth made up of individual dreams and hopes and of the simple wish to be respected as one is or would like to see oneself, be it as soccer player or freedom fighter. This is human rights in concrete terms.

We decide to obtain and study the testimony of youths and children, not only at this hearing but at those hearings which we have not experienced personally. Many hundreds of pages of transcript are available from the TRC at the conclusion of the hearings. Reading all these stories is immensely moving and disturbing and, at times, unbearable. But through it all there is a continuing engagement with life. Pitted against the reality of horror and darkness are shining individual beacons of survival, of endurance, of new directions being sought.

Sandra Adonis who, like Riefaat, had been politically active since the age of fifteen and had also suffered detention and torture, makes a telling point: 'I have never ever heard anybody say anything in recognition to the youth of that time. In fact, this is the first time that I have seen ... some people who are interested in who we were and who we are now.'

The figures tell some of the story. During apartheid sixty percent of all those who died as a result of political violence were younger than twenty-five, and a quarter were under eighteen. About 100 000 youths were detained for resistance activities of various kinds, or on the merest unfounded suspicion of such activities. In crisis areas at times whole schools, even primary schools, were taken into custody. And today? What has become of them? What are their perspectives on the future? How does the past impinge on the present for them in spite of a new democratic dispensation? Already, there is a new generation growing to maturity. More than half of South Africa's population today is below the age of sixteen.

With very few exceptions, all those who became involved in the liberation struggle and contributed to the demise of apartheid have one thing in common: they grew up in an environment that did not ensure even the most basic respect for human rights and dignity. Often they could not even trust those closest to them. They grew up without ever experiencing a childhood. Where could one go if even one's own parents could not offer protection? Where torture was commonplace, anyone could become a traitor – whatever the official slogans proclaimed.

After liberation from the terror of apartheid many former activists have suffered physical and psychological trauma, many have missed years of schooling, and very few have any realistic prospect of employment. In some, the idealism of the past has soured to bitter cynicism or anger. They feel marginalised and forgotten. On the one hand, they know very well that without them, without their sacrifices, there would not have been a new South Africa. On the other, many experience the idea of reconciliation as something reserved for those 'who can afford it' as one youth mentioned at a hearing. Graça Machel, who, after her marriage to Nelson Mandela, became South Africa's first 'democratic First Lady', observed during the youth hearing in Johannesburg: 'South Africa has found a peaceful transition, but the effects of what has happened to our children we are going to live with for more decades to come.'

The children have a voice and they have much to say. It is we who should learn to listen to them. It is our task to create opportunities where this will happen and where meaningful communication will ensue.

This book does not claim objectivity. Our selection of statements made by young people before the TRC cannot be objective or comprehensive. We have tried to create the space in which different young witnesses can be heard in a manner which gives some access to their thoughts and feelings. These pages feature youths from a broad spectrum – political and apolitical, rural and urban, township-dwellers and suburbanites, blacks, coloureds and whites (to use the crude classifications of apartheid for a last time), Christians, Moslems and Atheists.

We make no apology for the fact that our selection of voices does not mirror the reality of TRC hearings in terms of gender. In fact, many more young men than young women gave evidence and those women who did testify spoke most often about their husbands, brothers, fathers or friends and much less frequently about themselves. We have tried to achieve a balance in terms of gender.

From the vantage point of two and three years later we want to know: How has your life continued after the TRC hearing? Has it helped you or not, has it perhaps even been damaging to you? In some instances these meetings have led to new reflections which are contained in a separate chapter.

It remains to be noted that the way we listened was, of course, also influenced by our own biographies. Karin was born in Southern Africa and grew up there. Lutz spent most of his life in Western Europe.

In listening to the youth and writing about their life circumstances then and now, we aim to make a small contribution towards fulfilling the need expressed frequently by Sandra and Riefaat (who speak elsewhere in the book) and many others: that there should be people 'who are interested in who we were then and who we are now'. Above all, that we should not forget those who gave so much of themselves to ensure that a new generation had the chance to make something of their lives. It also seems to us to be one way of understanding better some of the 'effects' with which 'we will have to live for decades to come'.

Finally, we believe that the events in South Africa during the closing years of this century can be an inspiration to children, youths and adults in other parts of the world, where people seek ways out of violence, hatred and despair.

Karin Chubb, Cape Town
Lutz van Dijk, Amsterdam

I

TRUTH

No person's life is a waste.
Every person's life is too precious ...

Mrs Susan van der Merwe, witness before the TRC

EXCURSION
INTO
GERMAN HISTORY I

NUREMBERG, OCTOBER/NOVEMBER 1945

There they are, the first twenty-one accused before the International Military Tribunal in Nuremberg[1], Hitler's 'erstwhile citadel of the Movement'. Hard, stubborn faces, arms tightly crossed, they accept the headphones for translation with obvious reluctance. One of them is wearing dark glasses, a former general even still wears his uniform jacket – although all medals and ribbons have been removed. Their answers are pertinent, given matter-of-factly, completely without any emotion. One former minister commits suicide in his cell on the day before the executions are carried out.

All in all, from October 1945 to April 1949 the Tribunal heard cases against about 200 of the principal German war criminals. Of these, twenty-one were executed, five escaped the hangman through suicide, another five were declared unfit to stand trial. The rest were sentenced to long jail terms, in many cases to life imprisonment. From 1951 these sentences were significantly shortened, and some prisoners were even released.

The German people were represented in Nuremberg only as mass murderers and criminals of the worst kind. Even those Germans who had been most actively involved in resistance against the NS regime were excluded from the proceedings. The truly tragic aspect of the Nuremberg trials does not primarily lie in the much criticised 'justice of the victors', which did not deal with war crimes on the side of the Allies (such as the mass executions of Polish officers by the Red Army). It is to be found in the complete exclusion of the vast majority of Germans. Depending on their ideological orientation, most Germans could therefore either ignore or marginalise what was happening, in some cases even be indignant about it. But essentially, they could remain completely detached. From 1951 a number of those convicted at Nuremberg were pardoned, for reasons that all too obviously related to the Western Powers' Cold War strategy towards 'the Russians', their former allies. The fact that these pardons were given for reasons of economic and military expediency further served to undermine the status of the Nuremberg judgements.

None of these considerations in any way trivialises the ghastly crimes which were committed between 1933 and 1945 in the name of the German people. Uppermost in my mind is this urgent question: What lessons could have been learned already at that time? How could the great silence have been avoided, that 'inability to mourn' which for so long prevented a process of consensual re-orientation around basic human values in both German states?

It is winter, 1945/46, Germany is a landscape of ruins. Wrapped in a warm coat because there is no heating yet, Karl Jaspers, the Professor of Philosophy who was dismissed by the Nazis in 1937, holds a series of lectures on 'The Guilt Question'. While the lectures are generally ignored at the time, they will come to be known throughout the world. The beginning reads like an endeavour to communicate the basic ideas of truth and reconciliation – as well as the process of their realisation – to a German people who are still rigidly locked in their past:

> We want to learn to talk with each other. That is to say, we do not just want to reiterate our opinions but to hear what the other thinks. We do not just want to assert but to reflect connectedly, listen to reasons, remain prepared for a new insight. We want to accept the other, to try to see things from the other's point of view; in fact, we virtually want to seek out opposing views ... It is so easy to stand with emotional emphasis on decisive judgements; it is difficult calmly to visualise and to see truth in full knowledge of all objects ...We do not want to engage in melodramatic breast-beating, to

offend the other, nor to engage in self-satisfied praise of things
intended merely to hurt the other ...

But in common search for truth there must be no barriers
of charitable reserve, no gentle reticence, no comforting
deception. There can be no question that might not be raised,
nothing to be fondly taken for granted, no sentimental and
no practical lie that would have to be guarded or that would
be untouchable. But even less can it be permitted to brazenly
hit each other in the face with challenging, frivolous,
unfounded judgements ... All through these years we have
heard other people scorned. We do not want to continue that.

HAMBURG, OCTOBER / NOVEMBER 1967

It is more than twenty years later. Tensions begin to simmer on campuses
in the United States and in Western Europe. The first protest against the
Vietnam War in the US is like an initial flare which illuminates much more.
In West Germany young people begin their assault on the wall of silence
their parents' generation has erected.

By contrast, East Germany's younger generation has had to live with
a real and tangible wall since 1961. An ideology which provides handy
slogans that divide one's own 'anti-fascist past' neatly from the 'imperialistic
Western neighbours' furthermore serves to foil all attempts at critical
thinking.

Only in the late 50s and early 60s do preparations begin to bring former
high-ranking NS officials to trial in West German courts. Until then, this
has been the domain of the Allied Powers' judiciary. In Hamburg the first
trials begin only in 1967.

Now these perpetrators and officials are brought to justice. In the postwar years many of them have built up respectable new identities after
keeping a low profile for a while, and some have even managed to rise to
high positions. Frequently their downfall is brought about by a small detail,
something which finally compels the judiciary to take cognisance and

initiate steps to prosecute for crimes against humanity. More spectacular exposures are generally the result of much more active and determined investigations by organisations like the Israeli Secret Service. A prominent example is the arrest in the Argentine of Adolf Eichmann, the SS-Obersturmbannführer who was responsible for managing the logistics of the deportation of Jews to the concentration camps of Eastern Europe.

As the new German trials begin almost two decades after the Nuremberg Military Tribunals, it becomes increasingly obvious why the Nuremberg trials did not achieve a necessary re-orientation around humane and democratic values in the broader German society. These trials do not attract the glare of international publicity of their Nuremberg predecessors.

Gisela Wiese of Hamburg, whose family had opposed the Nazi regime and who is active in the Catholic peace movement Pax Christi, decides to organise support groups for witnesses who have come from Israel, the USA and Eastern Europe. 'Whatever for? They are quite well off, aren't they? With hotels and flights at taxpayer's expense!' was the reaction of the Hamburg judge to whom she submitted her proposal. She recruits thirty-five volunteers who form a support group which will last for the next seven years.

> The witnesses usually arrived in the morning and we visited them that evening. More often than not, they then carefully went through the testimony which would be required, in minute detail, in the following day's court proceedings. The next day we accompanied them to the court. Most of them had not spoken about their harrowing concentration camp experiences for many years. Their present families, with whom they had made a new start in the USA or Israel, had never been privy to these memories. Particularly men would often say things like: 'I don't want my children to know how I have been humiliated ...' The proceedings lasted for a day, a week, sometimes two weeks. Some people would break down completely, so that we had to accompany them to the doctor or the hospital.

I meet Gisela Wiese in the early 80s, in Hamburg. A young teacher at the time, my daily way to school leads me past the underground station where she is handing out flyers for the Peace Movement. I notice her, white-haired, well-dressed and middle-class so different from the other younger activists around her who conform to a more radical and alternative image. We strike up a conversation. In time to come her 'history lessons' will teach me much more about truth, reconciliation and the ability to overcome inhuman structures than all the history lectures I have enrolled for at the University.

'These trials should not have been conducted as though they were dealing with the theft of a bicycle,' she reminisces.

> The witness stands there and has to testify whether the Nazi, the murderer who shot her child, rode onto the scene from the right or from the left, whether he was wearing gloves or not. This appears to be vital in the leading of evidence, but for the witness it is a frontal assault. It's not her child who is the central focus of the enquiry, but the gloves of the accused. It was a matter of complete irrelevance to the court what these proceedings might do to the witness.
>
> The accused was treated as a respected citizen as he drove up in his Mercedes … If he defended his actions by stating that he had committed atrocities for the good of the German nation which he had to help keep free of Jews, then a judge who himself might have subscribed to such ideas in the past would not have thought such utterances either inhuman or deeply insulting. In this way the witness was turned into the victim for the second time. It was an atmosphere in which women could not speak about rape by SS men. These stories they told us afterwards.
>
> The atrocities which were recounted before the court seemed to emerge from a bygone era, a truly terrible time which had no connection with the present. It was merely a process of closing the book on the past. The potential for

enlightenment which might have been inherent in the trials was not recognised.

Much has happened and much has changed in Germany since then. This should not be read as mere rhetoric, it is a sincere observation. However, there are no guarantees ever, anywhere in the world, that human rights will be respected in the future. In South Africa at least, the TRC has been a powerful force for enlightenment in a conscious and public process to reach as many South Africans as possible. It has not always succeeded in effecting change. Apartheid's roots run deep.

I remembered the teaching of my childhood that the Holocaust must always be remembered so that it does not happen again. I asked myself: What is the IT? The IT cannot simply be the attempted extermination of Jews. The IT is the level of barbarity, the IT is happening in our own country ...

The IT is a level of barbarity where it does not matter who you are, what you think, what your values are – if they are gunning for your kind, you die. As a Jew in Nazi Germany, I die. Apartheid is based on the same logic: it does not matter what your other circumstances are, if you are black, you die.

Laurie Nathan,
Centre for Conflict Resolution

EXCURSION INTO GERMAN HISTORY II

In Amsterdam I am mesmerised by the news coverage from East Berlin as the Wall 'falls' in the city of my childhood (*de facto* it never did fall, it had gateways opened like so many valves; some time later, openings were hacked into it). Hordes of people running, laughing and crying, to the border checkpoints at which they once bid farewell to visitors from the West, and which are now ostensibly open to everyone.

For me and my friends in the West, 9 November had had a very different significance, as it had had for Gisela Wiese and some Auschwitz survivors in Hamburg. For us it had meant the attempt to remind the general public of that other 9 November, in 1938, when the pogrom was unleashed against the Jews of Germany, people were beaten up and synagogues and shops were destroyed. The sea of glass shards from broken windows the next morning gave rise to the Nazi's euphemistic description of the event as *Kristallnacht*. Later, in one's courses at school and also in human rights vigils one could use this pogrom night to illustrate the point that the NS evil did not suddenly overwhelm Germany but that a process of systematic deprivation in terms of human rights had preceded the holocaust. Some pupils understood the point that human rights have to be defended vigorously and timeously, before they are under threat, by which time it is too late. This pleased us as teachers.

During that evening in front of the television set in Amsterdam on 9 November two completely unrelated thoughts occupied my mind. The first was a humble memory from my childhood: of flying our kites in the fields

13

near the Wall, of the times when the string broke, the kite flew away over the Wall and we would simply say, 'Now it's gone'.

My other thought was an adult one: Now nobody will want to hear about that other time in 1938. Now they will all only talk about Germany today and about the pros and cons of reunification. They will argue that the GDR was apparently just as bad as Nazi Germany. And that, of course, the mistakes of 1945 will not be repeated ...

A lot of things were very different, that is true. The greatest triumph, and the image which first made me, too, feel hopeful was the storming of the State Security Centre (headquarters of the Security Police, the Staatssicherheitsdienst, colloquially known as 'Stasi') in East Berlin.

Truth and reconciliation? The truth about the extent of Stasi surveillance was revealed in a manner which shocked even those who knew: The Stasi folders, in which during a pre-computer age the reports of agents and spies were collected, would stretch for 180 kilometres if they were piled next to each other. During the height of Stasi surveillance about 90 000 men and women in the GDR were occupied in systematically spying on their fellow citizens. And that does not include those 'informal workers' who spied on a freelance basis and without regular payments. About 700 000 people have requested access to the files and many have found that not only were neighbours and trusted colleagues often revealed as spies, even spouses spied on each other.

The South African experience contrasts starkly with the situation in Germany, where Stasi files were preserved and made accessible to the public by the office of Joachim Gauck. In South Africa, when it became apparent that change was becoming inevitable, possibly incriminating documents were destroyed on a massive scale. In many cases this meant that successful criminal prosecutions would have been very difficult because the evidence would have been missing. In some cases documents were found almost by accident. In others, excellent and dedicated detective work by the Investigations Unit uncovered truths that had been carefully obscured by the regime. This happened in the case of the Guguletu Seven, when documents substantiating the culpability the police were found hidden in a police strong room.

Timothy Garton Ash argues that 'oppression spread broadly in Eastern Europe, while in Latin America it went deep down'. His simple diagram serves to illustrate that in Eastern Europe the system covered all aspects of life and an entire society became enmeshed in it; where an integral part of the system was the fudging of the borders between justice and injustice. In Latin America a small, brutal junta was in power and had no need to concern itself about deliberate and gross human rights violations, on the contrary, these seemed to be deliberate deterrents and as such part of a policy.

The two different systems present quite distinct challenges in terms of coming to terms with their past. It is no coincidence that military juntas in Latin America are wont to award themselves general amnesties as a macabre departure gift, whereas Eastern Europe chose 'cleansing actions' and 'audits' of varying thoroughness.

And South Africa? Both in the present and historically, the South African situation is characterised by a myriad ambiguities, by contradictions and conflicts, by ignorance and compromise – all of these in no way contradicting Ash's analogy. In South Africa, oppression was both deep and broad. There were atrocities committed by a small minority (these in the main being the focus of the TRC) and there was the broad oppression of the legalised inhumanity of apartheid, in which the majority were enmeshed, and which did not generally come within the ambit of the TRC. The idea of 'amnesty for the truth' was as much a compromise as was the fragility of 'recommendations in respect of reparations'. Both carry the seed of longer-term future conflicts in which solutions need to be sought with some urgency.

This is not a criticism of the TRC and certainly not of its commissioners and staff. They fulfilled their mission of 'restoring the dignity of the victims' in an historical and exemplary manner. Still, the warning of Professor Mahmood Mamdani during a public TRC discussion on reconciliation on 12 March 1998 should be heeded: 'not to declare a compromise to be a virtue' but to be critically aware of its limitations and to build on these insights.

One aspect of the TRC was tremendously successful. It gave a voice and a face to those who had for so long been silenced. The inhumanity of apartheid does not become comprehensible and tangible through statistics, however shocking these may be, of forced removals, detentions, even torture or mass graves. It can only become real through empathy. Just as reconciliation can only happen on the personal and individual level, so developing empathy, too, is an individual challenge which can lead to attitudes of political integrity and responsibility.

As the writer Judith Miller said about the Holocaust:

'We must remind ourselves
'That the Holocaust was not six million.
'It was one, by one, by one ...'

II

Graeme Williams/ South photographs

CHILDREN
AND YOUTH
BEFORE THE TRC

Let us speak for ourselves!

CAPE TOWN, MAY 1997

———— • ————

An official sightseeing programme has been planned: Waterfront and Table Mountain. A few readings in Cape Town at the invitation of the Goethe-Institute, after the award of a literary prize in Namibia. Karin and I have never met before. She, as head of the German Department of the University of the Western Cape (UWC)*, is hosting. Her interest in me is based solely on the fact that her students have read a few of my books.

As we drive into Cape Town from the airport, she puts out the first, tentative feeler: 'We could, of course, follow the programme as planned. But I don't know whether you are aware that there are Youth Hearings of the Truth Commission in Cape Town today. Bishop Tutu will be there ...'

Table Mountain will be there for a long time. Our smiles, relieved, acknowledge recognition of something in common. Karin changes course for Athlone.

Two people with individual and particular biographies and with German roots, of which the strongest shared legacy is love for the mother tongue. And there is, too, an unassuming but fundamental commitment to assisting in fighting against the humiliation and degradation of fellow human beings wherever and in whatever form it occurs. This, too is a heritage – one which, while it does not reflect present-day reality, still burdens the name of Germany in the international community after 1945: the marginalisation of and discrimination directed against Jews, the disabled, Roma and Sinti, homosexuals and other minority groups during the NS era and their more or less systematic murder. There is a search for causes, a question which will not rest: How could this have happened in an apparently highly civilised society? Were there not enough warning signs? Or were they simply not recognised? And the issue of responsibility which includes postwar generations: Never again to say 'we did not know!'

In Athlone we arrive just in time for the opening. It is a large hall, filled with hundreds of school children and their teachers. A few of the commissioners have already taken their seats on the platform underneath

19

the green and black banner with the distinctive logo of the Truth and Reconciliation Commission. At the entrance headphones are handed out for the simultaneous translations into English, Afrikaans and Xhosa. There are not enough. Two people will have to share one headphone – and that is fine.

Karin is greeted by Mary Burton, one of the seventeen Commissioners. She is a former President of the Black Sash*, an organisation consisting of mainly white women with a long and proud history in the struggle for human rights in South Africa. Karin was, for some years, Vice-President of the organisation. We are also introduced to Commissioner Glenda Wildschut who, on hearing that I live in Amsterdam, announces her forthcoming visit to that city.

Archbishop Tutu enters the hall. As he hurries through the long aisle to the stage, he greets to the left and right in his customary friendly way. Children nudge each other and strive to catch a glimpse of him. A few of them, lucky enough to be sitting on the aisle, dare to stretch out their hands in an effort to touch him. There is no doubt that he is known to every child in the hall, and that each one is aware of his stature. But today's proceedings are not about him – and in his own inimitable way he will shortly bring that home to all.

---

* Words marked with an asterisk are explained in the Glossary on page 243

SOUTH AFRICA'S YOUTH
– A (STILL) SILENT
MAJORITY

I t is estimated, in the year 2000, that 55 per cent of all South Africans are under sixteen. Of a total population of 38 million, the breakdown into racially defined groups is: 77 per cent black, 8,5 per cent coloured, 2,5 per cent Indian and 12 per cent white (fig. 1996).[1] Since the demise of apartheid, substantial efforts have been made to facilitate communication between these groups, which are still in many instances far removed from each other.

Apart from honouring the very significant and special role the youth have played in fighting apartheid, one of the motives for special youth hearings is surely a great and well-founded concern about the future: What will happen to a society which is confronted with a whole generation of young people who, though justifiably proud of their achievements in the resistance struggle, are also still deeply traumatised? Can ways be found to deal with the generation after that – the younger, new majority for whom the involvement of their older peers is already history, but whose everyday reality is characterised by pervasive social deprivation of the worst kind? Is it possible to find explanations, construct meaning, formulate and achieve meaningful goals in order to stem the rising tide of disillusionment and its escalation into blanket violence and crime?

The stories of children and youth, and of those young adults who were children during the era of apartheid may help to build bridges that are sorely needed. Bridges between the earlier values and goals of the struggle for freedom in a deeply and violently divided society, and the present emerging value system of nation striving for reconciliation and for the implementation of a just constitution. That is the theory. How, in God's name, will it be translated into practice?

WHO CAME – AND WHO WAS ASKED TO COME?

In principle every child and every youth was free to hand in a statement at one of the TRC offices throughout the country. A long and careful process of consultation was undertaken by the Truth Commission in months of preparation leading up to the Youth Hearings. The TRC sought advice from student organisations both at school and at tertiary level, from children and youth foundations, from trauma centres and other organisations dealing with the legacy of violence, from psychologists and medical doctors. The principles which guided the TRC in its approach and planning are laid down in the United Nations Convention on the Rights of the Child which the new South African government signed in 1995. Specifically they are contained in the clause that requires that children's voices should be heard and respected. Pre-hearing consultations with all concerned established whether their statements could and should be made available in public.

For a long time controversy reigned over the question of whether children younger than eighteen should testify in public hearings. After intensive consultation with a variety of experts in the field the adults decided unanimously that very young witnesses should be protected from public scrutiny and should give evidence only in closed hearings, under the guidance of experienced educators or psychologists. In the eyes of children and youth this decision has continued to be a controversial one.

PROTEST LETTER FROM AN 11-YEAR-OLD GIRL
The following letter was read out at the public Youth Hearing
in Athlone on 22 May 1997:

> To the Truth and Reconciliation Commission. My name is Rudie-
> Lee Reagan, I am an 11-year-old primary school pupil. I have heard
> about the Special Children's Hearing that will be held in Cape Town.
> I have also heard that children under the age of 18 cannot speak. I
> think this is very unfair and also stupid. Children over the age of
> 18 are not even children. I know that if a child was ten eight years
> ago they will be 18 now. The Truth Commission is violating the

rights of children under the age of 18 to speak. I do understand that the Truth Commission is trying to protect some children from having to go through all that pain and hurt again, but there are some children who would like to testify and see the perpetrators brought to justice. Children whose parents have been killed should be able to tell the Truth Commission how this has affected them. Speaking from a child's point of view, I think it would be very interesting to hear what children think should be done.

Last year was the first time I heard about a young boy. His name was Stompie Moketsi Sepei.[2] He was 13 years old. He had an opinion, he fought for it and in doing so lost his life. He was against racism and wanted to be equal. That really made me think. He was so young, but at such a young age he knew what was right and what was wrong and he fought for what was right and people listened to what he had to say. He made a difference in our country and by listening to children with similar experiences could help us to do the same. For instance, dealing with sexism. Apartheid is now gone because of children like Stompie, but I have been trying to get into a soccer team for two years, but I have not been able to, because I am a girl. That makes me mad. Listening to children will help deal with issues like this.

The main point is, children should be able to talk about things that hurt us like sexual abuse and violence. It will also be interesting, because it is about our country's history and we are not learning about this in schools. What I am trying to bring out is that it is necessary for children to speak, because children have opinions and feelings too. From a concerned 11 year old, Rudie Lee Reagan.

CHILDREN'S STATEMENTS

Children under the age of 18 were given the opportunity of having their statements incorporated in the evidence in the form of taped recordings. These recordings were preceded by individual and confidential consultations with staff who had received special training and who encouraged the children to give evidence in a form appropriate to their age, for example by drawing pictures. Examples of statements given on the basis of these drawings can be found in the chapter 'Voices of Children'.

STATEMENTS OF YOUNG ADULTS

As was the case in the adult hearings, the work of the TRC and its report could not feature the experiences of all of South Africa's children and youth. More specifically, the Report states in this regard (volume 4, chapter 9, p. 249):

> Given the Commission's focus on gross human rights violations, those who gave evidence at the hearings on children and youth spoke mainly of the suffering of young people. Few chose to speak of, or to report on, the heroic role of young people in the struggle against apartheid. Many saw themselves not as victims, but as soldiers or freedom fighters and, for this reason, chose not to appear before the Commission at all. Others, fearing reprisals from family or community, remained silent. Sometimes close family members were unaware of or strongly opposed to the political activities of young people ...

OPENING OF A PUBLIC HEARING

How is it possible in a hall filled with hundreds of interested schoolchildren and adults to achieve an atmosphere in which witnesses feel safe and listeners are attentive, without sacrificing any of the impact and gravity of the testimony? Beside the questioning techniques of the commissioners which were mainly very sensitive, and the clear rules of procedure, it was undoubtedly Archbishop Tutu who accomplished this by setting a very distinctive tone at the opening of the hearings. An example of this can be found in the following extracts from the opening of the Youth Hearing in East London on 18 June 1997:

> Thank you for your warm welcome!
> Twenty-one years ago we adults had, I think, spent a lot of time talking, talking, talking but on June 16th* young people said no, enough is enough. We have talked enough, now we must act.

We want to salute young people for the incredible courage that they showed then, for we are where we are today, very largely due to the contribution of young people and so I welcome you all very, very warmly to this special hearing. I welcome you very warmly in this gathering of the Commission today where we are going to listen to the youth. We welcome you all at this special public hearing of the Truth and Reconciliation Commission where the youth are going to give submissions about what they think happened and what their future is all about.

It's quite incredible actually. Have you noticed? You might not have noticed but it is not peculiar to South Africa that young people have made critical contributions. If you look for instance what happened in the United States at a time when the United States was fighting a war in Vietnam, it was largely young people through their agitation who forced the United States to get out of Vietnam. Some of us went overseas during that time to canvass support for sanctions. I, too, went to the USA, to schools and universities, and it was just before exam time when most students ought to be worrying about exams and grades and things of that sort, but they weren't. Many of them were demonstrating on behalf of us and it was very heartwarming to know that we had such tremendous support from young people. Not only young people but mainly young people.

Actually it's not a kind of aberration because if you look in the Bible, you see how God uses young people to accomplish God's purposes. When the children of Israel were in trouble … God didn't go around looking for old men like Archbishop Tutu, God got this young man David and David did his stuff and ended the boasting of Goliath.

God was saying something like, I mean I sometimes say nobody is an accident, we might look like accidents but nobody is an accident. When God wanted his son to be born he did not go to an old woman. Many forget that Mary was in fact a teenager and can you imagine if, when the archangel comes to her and says 'hi

Mary' and she says 'hi' then the archangel says 'God wants you to be the mother of his son.' Imagine if she had said 'What? Me? You expect me to be an unmarried mother? In this village if you scratch yourself, before you know it everybody in this village knows it and you are expecting me, me to be an unmarried mother!' If she had said 'Sorry, I'm a decent girl, try next door,' we would have been in real trouble. Mercifully she said 'Behold the hand maid of the Lord'.

Young people dream dreams. Young people dream of a different kind of world where we don't have these incredible disparities of the very rich and the very poor and so we come first of all to pay tribute to those who have helped us to be where we are today and hope that we will get inspiration to realise their dreams. Their dreams of a better kind of South Africa; their dreams of a South Africa without crime; their dreams of a South Africa where educational opportunities are available to all; where health care is accessible to all; where people can get clean water and where people can live in decent homes. We come saying we have a precious gift – our freedom. It was bought at a very great price, many died and may we cherish this gift, may we remember the price that was paid, may we never devalue it.

WHITE YOUTH

Young whites also gave evidence before the TRC. Two of them will be heard in more detail in Chapter 3. In a letter to radio-journalist and writer, Antjie Krog, 'Tim' describes the significance of appearing before the TRC as a young white man who refused to continue his service in the SADF*.[3]

In 1980 after matriculation I was called up to do my two years' national service. During my second year, I felt that I could no longer reconcile all that I believed in with the actions of the SADF in Namibia.

I had the fortune to attend very good schools during my teenage years, schools that tried to teach the old 'Mr Chips' values of 'being brave, and strong, and true, and to fill the world with love your whole life through ...'[4]

I deserted from the SADF and made my way to the Botswana border. I planned to go to Gaborone ... My long-term aim was to join MK* and do something against what I perceived to be an intrinsically evil system.

Being young, foolish, unprepared and on my own, I was caught as I was about to climb over the border fence at Ramatlhabama. It was then that the nightmare began. I was handed over to the Zeerust branch of the security police, who interrogated me for about a week. I was beaten, given electric shocks, suffocated, kept naked and repeatedly raped with a police baton. I remember very few details, except the screaming. I was nineteen years old at the time.

I was then handed over to the Walvis Bay security branch where everything continued ... It was a relief to be handed over into military custody after about two months – the military treated me far better than the police did ...

That brings me to the point of my story.

The TRC has deeply affected my life in the short space of time that has elapsed since I first went to their offices here in Cape Town and told my story to one of the investigators.

In my own life, I think that my parents found it most difficult of all to accept what I had done and what had happened to me. They have only this year begun to talk about it – before that, it was never mentioned. I think that the problem they had was that the regime criminalised the actions that I took – as law-abiding bourgeosie, they felt torn between their loyalty to me, as their son, and the fact that I had committed a crime.

Now, with me having gone to the TRC, with my story, it seems almost all right to talk about it. Slowly, things are changing. It's as if I have been freed from a prison that I've been in for eighteen years. At the same time, it's as if my family have also been freed – my brother is all of a sudden much softer, more human, more able to talk to me. The last time I saw him he told me that he should have done more, that he should have tried harder. After watching the television documentary on Eugene de Kock, my mother came up to me horrified: 'We didn't know,' she said to me. 'We just didn't know.'

Perhaps this is the most important role of the TRC. Not to extract confessions from FW and Magnus[5]. No. They must live with their own conscience. Fuck the perpetrators. The point of the TRC is to enable healing to happen. And let it be said that here in me there is at least one person they have helped to reconcile: myself to myself.

Yours sincerely

Tim

REQUESTS TO THE TRC

Usually young people were asked at the end of their testimony to say what they thought the TRC could or should do. As a rule, their demands were exceptionally modest – that someone should listen, again and again; that someone should take them seriously; that memorials should be created for those who gave their lives, or that schools should bear their names; that education which had been disrupted should be able to continue; sometimes also that bullets still remaining in their bodies should be removed, and that money should be made available for this.

Stories were told of places where tension still runs so deep that children and youth cannot return home to this day. People continue to live there, but communities are unstable and volatile. At a hearing in East London on 18 June a youth from the village of Potsdam spoke of such a situation and made the following requests:

> In 1985 at Potsdam there is a day which we will not forget because the police of the previous Government, this is the Ciskei Government killed our leaders as we were students. Two of the leaders were killed when they fell into a valley and when you are standing at the top you'll see a person at the bottom seeming very small.

In 1992 the police opened a police station in Potsdam where they were torturing the youth. The police would take you and sometimes ask you to slap a parent through the face. As the youth of Potsdam, we ask that the police that were deployed to Potsdam in 1985 and those who killed our leaders as the youth, come forward before the Truth and Reconciliation Commission.

Secondly, we also request that the Commission get back for us a hall because it belonged to the community so that the youth can entertain themselves in it. We just wanted our hall to hold meetings.

We would like the perpetrators under the previous regime to come forward and they mustn't be afraid, they must come and confess and tell us who gave them orders. We trust that the Commission will help us. Thank you Mr Chairperson, even though I'm nervous.

THE SELECTION FOR THIS BOOK

For chapter III, we chose ten statements by young people from youth hearings as well as from other hearings in which youth gave evidence. Also included is the story of a young woman who was murdered. In the scope of a book like this, it is impossible to achieve a representative selection from hundreds of cases and stories. We have tried to achieve some balance in terms of featuring youths from different ethnic, demographic, religious and socio-economic backgrounds. We have also endeavoured to feature different kinds of conflicts – intra- as well as inter-racial violence, and the stories of those who became victims quite by chance. Although fewer girls told their stories to the TRC we have tried to achieve equity in terms of gender.

Where possible, we have followed up the statements to find out how life has continued for the young people concerned. Two and three years after the hearings Karin Chubb conducted follow-up interviews with five of witnesses. These are contained in chapter IV. Also in that chapter are interviews with three women who are linked with the TRC in particular ways – the director of a Trauma Centre, a former TRC Commissioner, and a young woman who went out of her way to make contact with the young man who nearly killed her.

III

Graeme Williams / South photographs

SOMEONE
WHO LISTENS

'Children should not be targets…'

A STATEMENT MADE BY MRS GRAÇA MACHEL
AT THE YOUTH HEARING IN JOHANNESBURG ON 12 JUNE 1997

CHILDREN SHOULD NOT BE TARGETS

GRAÇA MACHEL

Graça Machel was born in 1945 and as a young woman took part in the liberation struggle of her country, Mozambique. From those early times she took an active interest in children and founded schools in the liberated areas controlled by Frelimo. When Frelimo came to power in 1975, she became Minister of Education in the first government of a liberated Mozambique. She married Samora Machel in September 1975. After the death of her husband in an aircraft crash over South African territory which still raises some unresolved questions, she continued to work for children in her country. As Chairperson of the National Organisation of Children in Mozambique she concentrated especially on the effects of war and violence on children. Through this work she gained recognition world wide and was appointed to several positions within UNICEF and UNESCO.

Today she is regarded as one of the world's experts on the influence of armed conflict on children and their development.

After her marriage to Nelson Mandela in 1998, Graça Machel became the first First Lady of a democratic South Africa.

Some sections of the speech have been paraphrased.

---•---

Thank you, I am very honoured today to be able to share with you some of the lessons and experiences and somehow the great pain I went through during about two and a half years, when the Secretary-General asked me to undertake what was known in the history of the UN as the Study of the Impact of Armed Conflict on Children.

The reasons why I was appointed are indeed very bad reasons. It is because I am Mozambican, so I come from a country which has gone through a very painful process for more than a decade. The Secretary-General knew that I had had the experience myself of dealing with children as victims of war. But I decided that we should perhaps transform this into a good reason – for the first time we had the opportunity to allow those who had been victims to outline what they had gone through and, more than that, to help the international community to shape a new framework of how to deal with these problems.

South Africa is probably among the first countries to implement one of the recommendations we made to the United Nations – to give a face to children; to give them visibility and to give them priority.

This is one of the few occasions in my experience on which children will be given a platform so that the nation, and even the international community will have to sit and listen. In other words, we have moved from the position where we adults try to speak on behalf of children and where we don't acknowledge their rights to participate in debate or in the shaping of their lives and their future.

You may know that at the beginning of this century when most of the conflicts were inter-state, only about 10 per cent of casualties were civilians – 90 per cent were soldiers. What we have learnt recently is that in the type of conflict which I call internal conflict – like that which took place in this country – we have witnessed a shift, a complete shift. Ninety per cent of casualties are civilians and only 10 per cent are soldiers. To put it another way, wars nowadays are against civilians, against defenceless people in villages, in streets, in schools. Half the refugees in the world are children.

In the past children might have been caught in the crossfire but that was accidental. Although many may have been killed, they were not the targets. But in the conflicts of recent decades, children have been deliberately targeted for killings. Why should this be?

The answer is that when you target the children of the other side, you eliminate the future enemy who would be able to attack you. So, in the process of a kind of ethnic cleansing, it is important to eliminate those who might challenge you tomorrow.

But it is more than that. If you want to break the morale of the community you are attacking, you have to attack what is most precious to them. As adults we know that it is children who are most precious. I can give examples. Here in South Africa schools were deliberately attacked and children were killed – this did not happen by chance. In Mozambique on countless occasions primary schools were deliberately attacked.

The same applied in all the places we went to. You have heard stories about Rwanda, but we found the same in Cambodia, we found it in Bosnia, we found it in Lebanon – children as a specific target ... not only for death but also sometimes for maiming. That is even more sadistic – not to kill the children, simply to disable them.

Such children become a problem for the family and the community for the rest of their lives so the suffering is constant, permanent, because that child will be a reminder of the conflict, even when that conflict is over.

Another dimension of targeting children is propaganda – taking a child who has lived with his colleagues, with his friends, with his neighbours, and introducing an element of suspicion, saying 'if you don't kill him, he will kill you'. Children know no boundaries. Children will kill their neighbours, their schoolmates, they are easily influenced. Their personalities are still developing and it is easy to motivate them to respect nothing in life.

But the worst way of targeting children is to make them participate in atrocities. The phenomenon of the so-called child soldiers is widespread all over the world ... It means to transfer the conflict of today to two or three generations to come. When you turn children of seven, six and even ten years old into instruments of violence, you can be sure that they will find it very difficult during the rest of their lives to live without violence. They will find it very difficult to be stable adults, to be parents.

And of course if they have difficulties in parenting, their children too will suffer the effects of conflicts which might have happened decades before. That is why today we are sitting here to discuss reconciliation and reparation.

South Africa has found a peaceful transition, but the effects of what has happened to our children we will live with for decades to come. It is no wonder that this country has high rates of criminality with people killing for a car or a cellular telephone. The meaning and value of human life have been destroyed and one of the most difficult problems we have to address is how to make our youngsters once more understand the value of human life, respect and cherish human life.

We have to develop a platform of common ground. We were so bombarded by divisions and discrimination that now we see people as 'Africans', as 'whites' as 'Indians', and within those as divisions, as Xhosa or Zulu. We don't consider that we belong to the same nation, we have the same origin, and we have the same destiny.

School is a major instrument of rebuilding from inside and developing a sense of belonging and acquiring skills to live in dignity. That is a challenge. People in South Africa have discussed whether it is possible to have reconciliation without justice. When I talk of justice, I am not talking of how to take the perpetrators to court, no, I am talking of how to build a just system in which people will feel that all of us together as a nation are building a society in which justice prevails.

Through what we will learn from the individual cases we will hear about and deal with, perhaps we will be able to respond to the needs of the thousands or millions of those who will not be able to come to light and to speak individually.

VOICES OF THE CHILDREN

Children under eighteen years of age testified before the TRC through personal interviews with especially trained staff members. During the Youth Hearings in Durban on 14 May 1997 and in Bloemfontein on 23 June 1997 these experts told the children's stories and showed their pictures to the public. We feature a few examples. In order to protect the identity of the children no further details are available about them.

BOY (8)
'And they were shooting ...'

Commissioner[1]
This drawing was drawn by an eight-year-old child. In it there's a man
who's pouring petrol in the house and setting the house alight. The child is
explaining that he still has bullets in his system, two of them. Doctors can't
remove them, and in his whole life he can't go away from this situation.
No matter how much he tries to forget it, he'll always have something to
remind him of what happened to him. ... Now we will play the tape of that
child.

Child
And my mother told my brother, Goli, not to sleep at home because she
was scared. And then the chief came late at night. We didn't see them
coming. What we heard was gunfire. They first set the house alight and
then they shot. They shot and killed my mother, my brother, Goli, my sister,
Mxane, who was also my twin sister. They were all killed.

Interviewer
And what happened to you and your brother?

Child
They also shot at me, but I survived because I escaped at the house. I went
outside, and it was me and my sister.They also shot my brother, Sanelo,
and he didn't die. He was eight years old. They shot at him. We left for the
clinic. When we arrived at the clinic my sister made a call to the police ...

Interviewer
What happened to your baby sister?

Child
They also shot her. They shot her at her head, and then my mother had
been burnt out at that time. Pilangezo, my brother, also died.

Interviewer
Explain now where are you staying.

Child
We are staying with my (older) sister. We don't know what happened to my father, and the house we're staying in it's very small.

GIRL(6)
'And then he raped me ...'

Commissioner
And there was also a six-year-old and a ten-year-old kid who were also violated. After the perpetrators came and killed everyone they didn't leave the house. Instead they continued to rape the child, a six-year-old, and now the child can't even relate the story. If she's relating this she is crying. Even in school she can't cope, and the teachers have sent her back by one class because they thought maybe she wasn't fit for the class she was in. She knows these perpetrators, she can still see them. I would like us to play her tape as well.

Child
They started throwing tear gas, and then they left – in February. And then he raped me ...
Now in school people came on Monday for me, and I wasn't there. My mother is not working. We don't have clothes to wear ... We don't have shoes.

Commissioner
As you have heard, the child can't even relate her story. Basically society hasn't paid much attention to children – when they talk about violence they talk about adults.

GIRL (13)
'We went to a slum area ...'

Commissioner
Yesterday one child made a drawing of a little boy who was killed, and that was her brother. And what is more sad is that in those drawings the child could reveal the person who actually killed the brother, and the child can still remember the name of the person who killed the brother, and the child had drawn everything. She has drawn the killer with a gun, and had painted this killer black because that's the vision the child has. And I would like the Commission to play the tape so that you hear what the child said yesterday.

Child
I was sleeping in the bed and my face was burnt, and my mother was burnt because she came to my rescue. Police van came, took us to hospital. When we arrived in hospital we were treated and then we came back.
We went to a slum area. That's where they killed my brother and my grandfather. My grandfather died. They wanted my uncle. I don't know why they were after my uncle, but they did all these killings because they were after my uncle.

Commissioner
When we asked youth in the townships around Durban what support they needed, they mentioned how important it was to be able to talk to experienced adults. They spoke about how important it is to have someone who is sensible to talk about your anger with, somebody who will not pour petrol on your anger, but will give you good advice and will really listen to you and help you find a solution ...

Many youths have reported experiencing amnesia, whereby they can't remember important things in their lives. Many others suffer psychosomatic problems – constant headaches, constant backache, stomach aches. Others develop eating and sleeping problems, and many, if not all, experience a constant sense of anger and betrayal, a sense of bitterness and resentfulness that the adults who were meant to have protected them, and the police, and the army and the teachers, and the school principals, and all the people in society who were supposed to protect children, let them down.

BOY (12)
'This bomb separated the family ...'

In 1993 I was eight years old. My father is a policeman. Now the members of the ANC were against the policemen. My father was harassed for something he did not do. They said he laughed at a dead body of an ANC member.

In April 1993, it was 9 o'clock, my parents were at work. I was left with my aunt at home. I was watching television. After a few hours I saw members of the ANC breaking the fence at home and they threw a petrol bomb at the roof of the house and into a bedroom. I ran to another bedroom and my aunt said to me 'Please call Mommy and Daddy!' because the house was already on fire.

My mother could not hear properly the message I wanted to convey and I had to go to our next-door neighbour to ask for help. The father next door called the police and we managed to inform our mother about this incident. At that time the neighbours tried to put out the fire. The water they were using actually strengthened the fire. The fire grew bigger. At some stage we were forced to call the fire brigade.

The elderly people where I was asking help did not allow me to go back to experience what was happening at home. They locked me inside the house and they went to put out the fire. Because it is not easy to stay calm when you know what is actually happening at home, I managed to escape, because I wanted to see what was happening.

When I arrived, our house was completely burnt. You could not even see a piece of cloth. I was very scared when I saw all these things happening ... Here on the right side [of my drawing] is a picture of our house while it was on fire. The house is empty. Everything is burnt down.

Look at me. I am crying for help so that people can come and help us. The feeling that was left with me after this incident, look at my heart, it shows clearly my feelings at that time. I was very sad and I also had a feeling of anger in me when I think of this great loss.

My father and my mother went to stay with my grandmother and I had to go and stay with one of our relatives. In other words, this petrol bomb separated the family. We were given clothes by people. It was terribly difficult.

After a few months my father tried his utmost best to get us a house. We came back together as a family, but the problem still outstanding was clothing, because my parents only managed to buy the beds and the blankets ...

BOY (16)

'My father was now a child ...'

In 1993 I was twelve years old. My father was a member of the ANC. He was transporting arms to different places. He was working with black and white people.

My father left for a few days and we did not know his whereabouts. When he came back he told me that he was in prison. His condition was terrible. His body was swollen because of the hittings [beatings]. His head had wounds, open wounds. He could not speak properly.

Grandmother took him to the doctor. His personality changed completely. He used to get angry without any reason and this continued and worsened. At one stage he developed epileptic fits. He was now forced to undergo treatment at the hospital. While under the good care of doctors his anger never subsided.

At times, when he was angry, he would fight my mother and he would kick her. He would break the dishes ... he had high blood pressure.

At that time I could not further my studies at school because my mother lost hope. She left me behind with my father and my grandmother. I had to carry the responsibility of taking care of my father. My father was now a child. We were doing everything to him that we would to a child. That is the reason I did not complete my studies.

When other children were preparing themselves to go to school I was left behind to take care of my father. This condition worsened and my father got a stroke. He was admitted a month at the hospital. This stroke took him from us. He died.

The death of my father affected me a lot. I was angry at all times. I was sitting alone, trying to make ends meet. I tried to go to school, but my mind would go to far away places. I would ask myself: 'How is Granny doing, because she is depending on me?' I so much wanted to have a grandmother and be close to her and help her at all times.

Now, this is a picture of my father that I drew. This is at the time when he was in prison, in the cell. Do you see him? That is the body of my father. His body is full of bruises. Look at his head. Wounds are shown clearly. The feeling that I had at that time – can you see it? That is my heart. I was sad at all times. This heart portrays the feeling of anger that I had within me. I want you to listen, and listen to my story carefully.

Interviewer
How were you affected by this?

Boy
I was deeply affected and in my heart I was full of revenge. But I realised that this was not good. I don't have to do it just because it was done to my father and I told myself that I have to grow up and get employed and work.

You see, my heart was full of anger and I had this feeling of revenge. I wanted to become a policeman to harass the people, to avenge the death of my father. Now, because a person is not supposed to do and practise an eye for an eye, I told myself that on completion of my studies I am going for another profession. This is, shortly, my story.

VOICES OF THE YOUTH

RIEFAAT HATTAS

'Sometimes I lie awake at night and hope … I could have been born again to live a normal life…'

Riefaat Hattas, born in Cape Town in 1968, was attending the Silverstream Senior Secondary School in the township of Manenberg and was fifteen years old when *fellow pupils spontaneously voted him their leader during a political demonstration. Riefaat comes from a Muslim family and his school is attended exclusively by 'coloured' children. Until he became a leader he had not been politically active and had had no experience or membership of any political organisation. His fellow pupils trusted him merely on the basis of his personal integrity. At the time, school pupils were organising strikes against the wishes of their parents but as yet had no particular programme to take the place of the lessons they did not attend. Riefaat developed a political consciousness by listening to and learning from his seniors. At the age of sixteen he was voted onto the ISCC* (Inter-Schools Co-ordinating Committee – a body on which several schools were represented). A year later he became a member of the executive of the ISCC. Soon afterwards he went into hiding because the police were looking for him. He was arrested, detained and tortured on several occasions.*

We have chosen Riefaat's testimony because in some ways it is a typical story – that of a young coloured Muslim from a volatile urban area who was humiliated at the hands of the police. The systematic torture and abuse he endured fractured his relationship with his comrades and brought deep inner conflicts which still determine his life.

TRC HEARING IN ATHLONE, CAPE TOWN, 22 MAY 1997

Commissioner
We recognise that you have thought long and hard about coming to the Commission today and we really do want to thank you for coming and publicly placing on record a statement which will focus on what you call your forgotten Comrades. We are aware of your request that we do not 'interrogate' you so we will not be interrogating you today. In fact, we try not to do that to any of the witnesses who come before us. What may happen at the end is that if there are things that we perhaps do not understand and we need some clarity on we will focus on that and perhaps ask you to restate it. Is that in order?

Riefaat
Yes.

Commissioner
Thank you very much. You may go ahead and read your statement.

Riefaat
Honourable Commissioners, I beg you not to put me through an interrogation all over again. I am attending the trauma centre every Thursday.

Commissioner
Riefaat, just take your time. If you feel it is too tough just take as much time as you need, okay, and Viola is next to you and she will be encouraging you, okay?

Riefaat
I am severely stressed, depressed, angry, frustrated.

Commissioner
Riefaat, would you prefer just to talk and not read and, perhaps, start at your second paragraph?

Riefaat
I have no confidence in myself. I am sometimes suicidal. I do not know whether I can carry myself alone. I am messed up because of what I went through during my high school years. I would not like to focus on myself, but I would like to focus on the story of my forgotten Comrades, those students who sacrificed their youth, their lives, for the sake of our freedom. Those Comrades who fought for liberation, who never knew what it was like to enjoy life as teenagers. They did not have time to develop their relationships or to participate in sport. Those students whose days were comprised of meetings, protest marches, facing rubber bullets and often live ammunition, but this was part of the daily struggle against an unjust enemy.

Our primary objective was to make the country ungovernable so that our leaders could return and lead us into a true democracy – a democracy where everybody would be equal; a culture where young people, especially children, do not have to be on the run from the security forces; where they do not have to jump out of windows in the middle of the night because they were sought for Section 51* and the Terrorism Act, Section 29*; where students could go to school and not have to fight a war; where they could enjoy their youth among their friends, going to parties, play sport and just be children ...

When we got instructions via MK structures to declare full-scale war, we took action 24 hours a day. The international press focused on the unrest of South Africa and this strategy was so successful that the business people of South Africa were forced to speak to the ANC leaders up in Lusaka. Through the pressure and sacrifices of all involved in the liberation struggle, we inevitably got our freedom we fought for so hard. We reached our objectives at a price.

However, many never realised the kind of psychological stress and trauma we have been subjected to. Many Comrades had to go into hiding, others were in exile away from their loved ones and friends, but the majority of us remained behind to continue the struggle for liberation. For those Comrades who were sought by security police it was the start of a nightmare, a nightmare that was going to be so horrendous, it was going to destroy our lives. Never could we have imagined that at the age of fifteen, sixteen, seventeen and eighteen, we would have been running away from police and going to safe houses only to find police coming to look for us there. We were going crazy with all the thoughts of being captured, tortured, maimed and even killed at the hands of the security police. We were never sure whether we would see our parents, brothers and sisters again. One thing was certain, we were not teenagers any longer. We aged ten to fifteen years in a matter of months and we had to be prepared to face whatever came our way whether we were prepared for it or not.

Many of us were caught by security police. In detention we were interrogated, tortured, maimed, violated and continuously harassed. After this horrid experience we suffered from nervous tension and were all nervous wrecks. We could not continue school like normal pupils. Our lives were destroyed. Some of us managed to complete matric under extremely difficult circumstances. Others could not take the pressure – they left school to later become drug addicts and gangsters. If only there had been people to help us through our trauma. We so much wanted the people to be there for us, because we could not carry on alone. Too many brilliant students never got the chance to reach their full potential as they were school drop-outs. They are still searching for themselves amongst all the turmoil in their lives. To tell you the truth, many of us ask whether the price that we had to pay for freedom was worth it in the end.

These are some of the recommendations that I myself and our Comrades thought I should list in front of the TRC. I first would like to say that many of our Comrades … are still unemployed today. The other thing I would like to urge the TRC, that they should urge employers to be sympathetic towards survivors by letting us go to support clinics, for example the Trauma Centre … Security police and police officers and army personnel who were promoted because of human rights violations should be demoted or should no longer serve in the South African Police Service, because they make it difficult for ordinary people to respect the police.

We should be financially compensated for all the emotional and psychological trauma we are still enduring. Memorials should be erected in all provinces to signify the significant role students and children, youth as well as others, played. The Government should take the responsibility to accommodate us in terms of all relevant support we would need. Special training courses as well as secondary and tertiary education should be made available to those Comrades whose lives have been messed up by the previous Government so that we can feel worthy of ourselves and not like a bunch of low-lives.

President Mandela should unveil a memorial in Parliament that will recognise the role the youth played as well as how our lives have been ruined by the previous Government. High schools and street names should be renamed in honour of those Comrades who paid the ultimate price for our freedom. Awareness programmes should be run at schools and other institutions where youth go to so that those students who are sitting here today, and those who will still go to school, will know how lucky they are not to go through what we went through. They should really know that you are very lucky to live in the normal South Africa and sometimes I lie awake at night and I hope … I could have been born again to live a normal life. The TRC should make sure that the National Party does not walk away unpunished for the crimes they committed against the people of South Africa …The National Party should take responsibility for destroying and ruining our lives. That is all.

Commissioner
Riefaat, do you want to read the names of some of the ones you want to remember? Would you like to do that?

Riefaat
This is the list of my forgotten Comrades. The first one, Celeste Naidoo, I have the greatest respect for her, because she was the one who trained me. She was my mentor and all things that I achieved in life was because of what she taught me and I want to tell the whole world that the principles that Celeste taught me, it is still with me and I will never forget those principles and one of those principles was that you stay loyal to your Comrades. …

The other Comrade, Katheem Neethling, his former name was Cecil. He was detained with me and he was part of our Action Committee at school. He was detained in Victor Verster (a prison about 40 km outside Cape Town). He is today a nervous wreck and a drug addict. Kevin is also a nervous wreck and a drug addict.

Deon Brink, he was detained with me, and whilst I was interrogated I managed not to name any names, but as I was beaten and as they did the things they did to me I do not want to name that, because I do not want it in the press, I told them I do not know. They were looking for Comrades Kevin Patel, Paul Doemat, Celeste Naidoo, I told them I do not know, because I was on the run and I was not in Manenberg or in Surrey Estate or wherever for a long period and I told them why do you not ask Deon, but I never knew Deon was also picked up, I never knew. I thought he was still on the run. They brought him in and they beat and they attacked and brutally beat Deon in front of me ... and I can never forgive myself for that. I never knew.

[*Pause. Riefaat is unable to speak further*]

Earl September, he was also in Victor Verster ... Karriem Adams and Medaat Adams ... Shahied Petersen ... Robert, today I do not even know where he went. ... Azie Zoedien, Jacky Hefele and Genevieve Zeeman, they are all traumatised.

These are only the Comrades that were, that worked close with me. There are thousands of other Comrades, I call them the forgotten Comrades, nobody took notice of us, nobody took notice of them. I would like the TRC to remember those people and I hope one day all the street children that must still attend school and those people who are sitting here who are coming from high schools, you have a responsibility towards us to try to reach your full potential and you must make the most of your normal lives that you have, because ... we are not able to do it. We have been messed up by the National Party. Please, I beg of you, to make the best of your lives. You owe it to us. Thank you.

[*Long, spontaneous applause. Some of the schoolchildren in the audience are crying*]

Commissioner

Ladies and gentlemen, I can understand why you are moved to applaud, but it really is not appropriate in these proceedings so can I ask you to refrain from doing so. Riefaat, you have touched us very deeply. Before I thank you for coming to us I just wonder whether the other panelists want to, perhaps, make a comment or ask you a question of clarity. We will not be interrogating you at all.

Riefaat, I just have one question. How old are you now and how old were you when you were detained?

Riefaat

I am twenty-nine now. I was fifteen when I started getting involved in the struggle and I was, I think I was about seventeen when I was detained.

Commissioner

Thank you, Riefaat. You are speaking on behalf of your Comrades ... the people you call forgotten heroes, but I think you are also speaking about yourself. I think it is important for us to understand that, that you are finding your voice through speaking about Comrades and that means, for us, that it is really difficult for you to recall what happened to you and to talk about it. Therefore, you find it easier to talk about your other Comrades than about yourself. That in itself shows us the intensity of what you have gone through and I think it is important for us to understand that.

It is hard to give you words that will strengthen you, because that is your reality, that is the reality you are going through, but thank you for sharing your experiences and our hearts go to you.

March 1999

Riefaat is now thirty-one years old. In Chapter IV he relates how his life continued after the TRC hearings.

FIKISWA M *

'After the rape I felt like vomiting when I saw a policeman ...'

Fikiswa M, born in 1978 in Matatiele, Natal, was eleven years old when she went home with her cousin one evening, after watching television at a neighbour's house. Her mother was at that time a known political activist. At their front door the children were stopped by two policemen and forced to accompany them. Shortly afterwards, Fikiswa was repeatedly raped by both policemen while her cousin was forced to watch helplessly.

After a long deliberation with her family, Fikiswa decided to testify before the TRC. After finishing Primary School, she attended the Tsoseleto High School in Bloemfontein. At the time of the hearing she was eighteen years old.

We have chosen her testimony because it highlights the special vulnerability of girls and also because, in spite of her youth Fikiswa has consciously made a very difficult and courageous choice. Her decision to go public

---

* We have withheld her name to protect the privacy of the family

about the rape was motivated by the desire to help other girls and to encourage others to expose such crimes.

TRC HEARING IN BLOEMFONTEIN, 23 JUNE 1997

Commissioner
We just want to say we really appreciate your courage and your willingness to be with us today to share your story. I will just check a few things. How old are you now, Fikiswa?

Fikiswa
I am eighteen years.

Commissioner
At the time the violation occurred, how old were you?

Fikiswa
I was eleven years old.

Commissioner
You were attending school. What standard?

Fikiswa
I was in Standard 5.[2]

Commissioner
Tell me more about your family, Fikiswa.

Fikiswa
I was staying with my mother and my grandmother. That is the sister to my mother. We didn't have a father. We were staying with the two of them and my cousin and my grandmother's last-born, and the sibling coming just after me.

It was a time of political turmoil. My grandmother and my mother were active in politics. My mother was a member of the Women's League of the ANC* together with the grandmother and they were at the same centre. The youth was arrested during that time. They were assaulted. Things were just happening and the schools were not going on as usual.

Commissioner
I know you were very young at that time, but did you understand politics or did you identify with any political activity or organisation?

Fikiswa
I was apolitical. I was just a person. I was just living a normal life.

Commissioner
Fikiswa, can you just tell us about what happened to you on the day you were violated, which was 19 ... what year was it?

Fikiswa
It was 1990.

Commissioner
Okay, can you briefly tell us ... do you remember the month?

Fikiswa
Yes. It was in February.

Commissioner
Can you tell us what happened?

Fikiswa
We were at home and in the afternoon my cousin Boikie and I decided to go to our next-door neighbour's to watch TV. If I remember we came back about 9 to 10 o'clock and we got into the yard when these two policemen approached. They were in police uniform and I went to the door to open it and get into the house.

They called my cousin and they talked to him. They said I should not first get into the house. As they were talking I got very impatient and I wanted to get into the house. They pulled out their guns and said: 'Should you make any noise, we are going to kill you. Let us go!' I did not shout. We just left.

They said we should go with them to point out Mr Modise's house. That is a comrade. They said I should take them there. I said to them: 'I do not know a Mr Modise who is a comrade. I am sorry, I won't take you there because I do not know him.' And they asked my cousin whether he knew a Mr Modise who was a comrade. He ended up saying yes, he knew him, because he wanted them to get out of our sight, but these people persisted.

They went along with us. They were pointing their gun at my neck, ordering me not to have a look at them. Somewhere along the line they communicated by two-way radio. They said: 'We've got suspects. What should we do about them?' I did not hear further what was said because I was afraid and scared. They told us that a van was going to be sent and we should wait. While we were waiting they said: 'We'll go.'

My cousin asked them 'Why can't we wait for the police van here? Where are we going to?' They did not provide an answer. They actually slapped him in the face. He had a big mark. I said to him: 'Keep quiet, because they will end up injuring you.' We walked with them up to a hill.

They asked me whether I was still refusing to tell them where Mr Modise was. I said: 'I do not know him. How can I take you to an unknown place?' They left me and went to my cousin. They asked him whether we were really refusing to take them to Mr Modise's house, because they wanted him. We kept quiet.

They said they were going to teach me a lesson because I didn't want to take them to Mr Modise's house. They were going to prove to us who they were. One of them got hold of me and the other one took my cousin away from us, slapped him and said: 'Lie down, don't look.' He left him there and the two of them came and one said I should undress. I refused.

[*Fikiswa cannot continue*]

Commissioner
Fikiswa, this is a very difficult time for you. Just take your time, please.
Just take your time. It must be very painful for the whole family ... Are
you ready? You can wait a little bit if you are not. Fikiswa, are you feeling
all right? Do you think you can go ahead?

Fikiswa
I am ready. This other man ordered me to undress and I did not want to,
and one of them, when my cousin was still trying to come to my rescue,
one of them went to him and said he will end up killing him. The other one
took me and made me lie on the ground and he undressed me and raped
me. They were taking turns. When one got tired he would get off and the
other one would come ...

I went back home in the morning. Before we got home my cousin
wanted to see where they were going. I could not walk and said to him: 'I
am not going to be in a position to.' Then he took me half way so that I first
got home and then he wanted to go around searching for them. I was so
scared to get into the house. I waited outside for him and when he came
back we woke up the people and it was then that they heard the story.

My mother was angry with me. She was telling me all sorts of stories.
She asked me what I was going to do with the child if I was pregnant,
because I was just a child. I couldn't cry any more, because I had cried
earlier on.

They called Dr Ziyane and I was taken to him. I didn't change. My
clothes were full of blood and I was just taken like that to the doctor. He
checked me up and said I should not wash. I should just take clean clothes.
I should go straight to the police station.

I went to the police station and was referred to a state doctor. I left
with the policemen who were handling my case and they took me to the
state surgery. They checked me and thereafter I went back to the police
station to submit my statement.

There were only men. No woman was among the males. They were
interrogating me. When I answered, one would come up with his question

and they ended up by asking me what kind of clothing I had on that day. I explained to them. They asked me, was I wearing a short dress. I said 'No'. They asked me how it was: 'Was it nice? Was it painful as they were doing it?' I didn't answer them because it was such a painful interrogation and I left. That day I did not feel well. I was just like an insane person. I spent a week with no movement. I could not walk. I would just wash myself and sit down.

A day after I went to submit my statement the police came back and they took my cousin. They said to him that he was a suspect. He might have raped me and not the police. We do not know what they said to him. They took a day with him. Nobody knows what they said to him and he didn't even tell us what they asked him. I was sick, I was sick ...

I went to doctors, trying all sorts of things, and doctors referred me to a psychiatric clinic, to Dr Masotho. I was undergoing treatment at Dr Masotho.

Commissioner
Fikiswa, it's one of the very tragic stories that you have told us here, a tragic story that happened when you were just an innocent child. I would like to say to you that more than ever before I would like to thank you for the courage you have, the courage you have shown today. I hope that most of the people are going to learn from you ... I will ask you a few questions, if that is all right for you now.

Fikiswa
You may proceed.

Commissioner
When that happened to you, to what extent did it affect your life, your school, your school performance, your relationship with friends, the family? Could you just share with us what you feel free to share?

Fikiswa
Because I was a child then, my life changed completely. I found myself in a

position of not speaking to people. I couldn't play with my peers because I was scared. The worst thing of all is that when I saw a policeman I felt like vomiting. I did not even want to see them.

The other thing that disturbed me most is that I was just about to write my final exams last year, when I was doing matric, I was sick and my mother advised me not to carry on with school. But I said to her: 'Mom, I'm not going to leave school, I am going to pass.' I tried my best, I studied, and you know what? I passed!

Commissioner
Fikiswa, I am very touched by the courage you have shown, the determination to go back to school, pass and have a future for yourself. I think the positive attitude you have will help you to go a very, very long way.

I would like to come back to you, Boikie. Can I refer to you by that name? I can see you are also in pain. Could you tell us some of the things that have not been mentioned by Fikiswa or some of the things you have experienced differently?

Boikie
I first refused to go where they wanted me to go with my cousin, but when the second person pulled out the shotgun ... Then I tried ... to save my cousin. I tried to tell them that they could just take me. I would take them wherever they wanted to, but they refused. So then ...

[*Boikie is at a loss for words*]

Commissioner
Take your time. Take your time, Boikie.

Boikie
Then we went behind the school. There is ... like a hill. Now it's occupied with some shelters there, but at that time there were no shelters. Then we went ... and I still pass that even today. Can I just say something?

Commissioner

Yes, say what you feel you need to, but we don't want to subject you to any further pain.

Boikie

If those guys are listening or hearing now ... I'd just like to say, I am a guy too but I never met people like that, you know, and I don't think they would have the courage to meet me even today. But I would love to meet them, really. Just to see them. Just ... I don't know, but I would love to meet them.

I'll never forget that day, especially when the guy who was with me was stepping on my back, not to look or do anything or stand up. I mean, I tried to save my cousin by all means, and it was like he was holding a pistol to my head, standing on my back. I couldn't do anything. I was like, you know ... like I was ... He was hitting me like anything, stepping on a person like that ...

Commissioner

What I would like to say now is that I take note of your request that you would still like to meet the perpetrators. Probably you can help us in a way by giving us some information, because it looks like they have not been identified.

Boikie

They were never like ... for a second time I was taken to the police station to make a statement. They said the first statement we made is unreadable. So I said, okay, and I gave them the statement again. They said they will call a parade from those guys who were on duty that day and we could come and make an identification. Then we told them we could not see anything. They were still putting in poles for electricity in our street. It was dark in our street and on the hill anyway. We could not see anything.

Commissioner

Which police station was that?

Boikie
It was the Bantu Police Station.

Commissioner
Do you know the name of the district surgeon where you went, Fikiswa?

Fikiswa
No. I forgot the name of the State doctor I went to, but I can identify him. I just forgot his name.

Commissioner
What are you doing now, Boikie?

Boikie
I am working at a restaurant, as a waiter.

Commissioner
Did what happened to you then change your life?

Boikie
Well, I don't know. I am kind of, like, ignoring a person, you know. As I said, I still pass by that place even today, but I just ignore that. I did finish my matric.

February 1999
More than a year and a half later, Fikiswa agrees to talk to us, on condition that her family is present. (See chapter IV)

YAZIR HENRY
'In my head ... all the time ... the same question: Who sold me to the police? Who sold me to the police?'

Yazir Henry, born in Cape Town in 1970, was educated at the Wynberg Senior Secondary School where he became a pupil activist from 1985. Soon after that he

became involved in working with the illegal ANC underground. After the wave of
detentions in 1986 he went into exile, first in Swaziland then in Angola. During
1987 he spent ten months in the Soviet Union undergoing political and military
training. In April 1989 he returned to South Africa illegally. After some conflicts
with others in the ANC underground he distanced himself and remained
independently active until his arrest by the South African Security Police.

He remained in detention from November 1989 to mid-1990, during which
time he was tortured repeatedly. His release came in June 1990. At the time of the
TRC hearings he was a postgraduate student in Sociology at the University of
Cape Town. He is co-founder of an initiative which introduces tourists to the
historical sites of the freedom struggle in the Cape (see also Chapter V, Western
Cape Action Tours).

We chose Yazir Henry's testimony because it shows that young people with
high ideals could become trapped in unresolvable conflicts which influence
their lives to the present day.

TRC HEARING IN CAPE TOWN
(UNIVERSITY OF THE WESTERN CAPE), 6 AUGUST 1996

Commissioner
Yazir, we've come to know each other the past day or so and if you don't
mind, I'll use your first name.

Yazir
That's fine.

Commissioner
The testimony you will give relates to an experience which happened at a
very young age and which has affected and fundamentally changed your
life. But before we get to that, perhaps, just by way of introduction, tell us
about yourself, what you do, who you are …

Yazir
Well, I am a committed member of the African National Congress and an

officer of its former military wing, *Umkhonto we Sizwe**. At the moment I am twenty-six years old and I am reading for an Honours degree in Sociology at the University of Cape Town. In my statement I call it Political Sociology, because for me everything is political.

Before I read my statement there are two things I would like to say: The statement is about my story. It does not relate to my family who themselves have suffered tremendously. I have been estranged from my family for a long time.

There are some friends in the audience who know me as Yazir and who know nothing about my history. Who have helped me to get this far. To them I want to say 'thank you'. I don't mention them in my statement, they know who they are.

And I also want to say that the process of coming here has been a long and hard one. A decision that I didn't take lightly, a decision I took after careful consideration and lots of traumatic experience and discussions with people who have helped me to stay sane, if you can call me that at this point in my life. I want to say a special thanks to you – for being with me.

Commissioner
Thank you for those words of introduction. ... perhaps it's a good stage to take us through the statement.

Yazir
Okay, with your permission I would like to read my statement.

Commissioner
Certainly. You can proceed.

Yazir
My former name was Mark Henry. In 1991 I changed it to Yazir Henry because Mark was a name that I could no longer live with. I said that this was on religious grounds, but it was much more than that. Mark was a name that brought me shame and great danger ...

My experience is very painful, especially since my existence and what happened to me continues to be ignored by the African National Congress, from which until now I have not formally relinquished my membership. … I hope that by telling my story I may be able to wake up from this nightmare that I have lived ever since 16 November 1989.

A brief history before going into exile: I was first introduced to active politics in 1985. At the time I was in Std 7 at Wynberg Senior Secondary School and I was fifteen years old. This was a time of large-scale political disruption and activity at schools, met with excessive state brutality. After the banning of the Congress of South African Students (COSAS)* and of Student Representative Councils (SRCs)*, I became active in Student Action Committees which grew in response to the brutality of the State.

I witnessed the impunity with which the state detained, maimed and killed our people. That strengthened my resolve to resist and to fight back. I became increasingly more politically active and soon afterwards was recruited into the underground structures aligned to the ANC.

At the beginning of 1986, following a spate of arrests, myself and two other members of our underground structures – Ashley Forbes and Peter Jacobs – went into exile in the strong belief that we would return stronger and better equipped to fight the injustices of the state and to protect our people against its brutality. Even though I was the youngest of the three, the level of trust I enjoyed was such that I was given the responsibility to receive the most training and military specialisation. The plan was that they would come back and set up new structures and I would follow with the necessary military knowledge and expertise.

We went to Swaziland. From there, with the assistance of the United Nations High Commissioner, we made contact with and formally joined the ANC in Maputo, Mozambique. After about two weeks we were flown to Lusaka, Zambia, where we were screened and where we subsequently discussed and concluded our political and military objectives with the military and political structures of the ANC. We were then sent to Luanda, Angola, where our group was split up in order to put into motion everything we had planned. From Luanda I went to a training camp in what was known in ANC circles as 'The East'. There I underwent my basic military training. About two months into my training I was recruited into the Security

Structures of the ANC with the responsibility to look out for and to report directly any situation which might compromise the security of the camp. I was subsequently also selected to specialise in military engineering.

At the beginning of 1987, at the age of seventeen, I was sent to the Soviet Union for a period of ten months. There I specialised in Special Intelligence and Military Combat Work. During that period I was also appointed from Luanda as the political commissar for a group of ten combatants. For me this was a very great honour and responsibility. On the one hand, the trust which was placed in me helped me to consolidate and crystallise my own political understanding of our struggle, whilst on the other hand this brought with it an awareness of the gravity of the task that was at hand. I was thrust from boyhood into a world that demanded maturity and constant vigilance.

This also demanded discipline and it demanded responsibility, none the less all this served to increase my commitment to our struggle for liberation.

On completion of this training course I returned to Luanda, whereupon I was assigned to work with the Soviet representative responsible for training cadres of the underground inside South Africa who had come to Angola for short periods of training. When he left, I was given full responsibility for continuing this work.

Towards the end of 1988 I was recalled to Lusaka. I was informed that I would be part of a technical working group, subordinated to Ronnie Kasrils who then headed the Political Military Council. I felt that this assignment would not fulfil the objective for which I had gone into exile, namely to receive extensive military training and specialisation and return to the country. Secondly, the comrades with whom I had originally left the country had been arrested.

For these reasons I requested to be reassigned to Military Headquarters, to put into practice what I had learned and to continue what I had orginally planned with the comrades who had been arrested. In about April 1989 I was smuggled back into South Africa with Anton Franz, who was known to me as Mohammed. We infiltrated with the help of an MK operative who took us across the border. Inside South Africa, we were instructed that upon arrival in Johannesburg we were to book into a particular hotel where we would be contacted. Our contact took us to his home which was in Bez Valley, Johannesburg. After several days he informed us where and how we were to meet our contact in Cape Town.

In Cape Town we met our contact who took us to a house where we met two others. Contrary to my expectations there was no clear briefing as to what we were to do. Instead we were told that we were to be debriefed and we had to inform them in detail of our training, our political and military experience gained in exile, and practically instruct them in areas of combat with which they were not familiar. For example, for me there seemed to be an expectation of writing training manuals. As no time period was specified, this task seemed impossible as it could go on for a very long time. As there had been no prior briefing in Lusaka, the process that was now unfolding was extremely confusing. This was exacerbated by the fact that we were charged with all household chores, were confined to certain areas of the house only and were, I think, openly viewed with suspicion.

As a result our interpersonal relationships became strained to the point that there was open mistrust and hostility. After living under these circumstances for about a month I decided to leave. My decision was prompted by the fact that a lot of the basic rules of conspiracy which I had learnt were being broken. I felt that I was being mistrusted and I no longer trusted them. I felt that my life was in danger … I left the place without their knowledge and contacted my sister who helped me to set up a place of my own. I lived in a separate entrance under the guise of being a student from Johannesburg.

One day, purely by chance, I met Mohammed in a shop. We spoke frankly with each other. I conveyed to him my concerns. I … expressed the willingness to meet with them on neutral ground. His opinion was that since I had left in that manner I did not have the right to meet them on neutral ground and that I should go back with him to his place. I literally begged him not to show me where he stayed, but he coerced me into going with him. And once there he refused to let me go unless I told him where I stayed. Once he had extracted that information from me he informed me that I would be contacted at my house.

Following this interaction and my exposure I felt compelled to relocate. I felt particularly vulnerable as the distrust between me and the other comrades had not been dispelled. However, I had run out of funds. After careful consideration I decided to relocate to my family home for a maximum of about three days, during which time I hoped to organise alternative accommodation.

My arrest occurred about the second day – I am not exactly sure about the days any more. At about 3.30 in the afternoon I heard a commotion at the front door. The door was banged open and several plainclothes Security Police forced their way in, holding my father as a human shield with a gun against his head. On seeing me they shouted for me to raise my hands above my head. They pushed my father out of the way and rushed towards me. I must have had at least seven or eight guns pushed into my body. They pushed me against the passage wall and started searching me roughly. Once it became clear that I was unarmed they handcuffed my hands behind my back and shouted questions at me about where my weapons were.

Meanwhile more uniformed and plainclothes policemen entered the house. They were tearing things apart, pulling things out of cupboards, searching the ceiling ... they were all over. They took me outside where there were even more police, constantly hurling abuse at me. Some of them were laughing, they were shaking hands, congratulating one another, hugging. The officer in charge sent radio messages saying repeatedly: 'Die skaap is in die kraal!' ('The sheep is in the pen'). In my mind I thought that this would be my end.

I was put into a car with three security policemen. In the car they continued questioning me about weapons and about Mohammed. I told them that I had no weapons and that I did not know what they were talking about. They took me first to Grassy Park police station and then to the security police headquarters in Culemborg. Once at Culemborg the questioning continued. They had identified Mohammed as Anton Franz. They showed me photographs of myself, photographs of Mohammed, computer printouts which contained information about our infiltration into the country. This went on for hours. Several of them questioned me, others interjected, hurling insults, while others observed.

At one point somebody just walked in and said 'Wat praat julle nog met die fokken donder?' ('Why do you bother to talk to the fucking arsehole?') and he hit me twice across the chest. Captain Liebenberg, who seemed to be in charge, was the most vociferous, the most abusive, and seemed to be asking the most questions. Throughout this I maintained that I had no weapons and that I had no knowledge of Mohammed's whereabouts. After several hours of unabated questioning Captain Liebenberg informed me that my father had been arrested as well and that they would ruin him since he had aided and abetted a terrorist. Even then I maintained my position. I told them that Mohammed and I had had disagreements and that we had broken contact.

At this point Captain Liebenberg told me that unless I cooperated and informed them of Mohammed's whereabouts, they would kill my mother and my nephew, who at the time was only four. At the time I did not see this as an empty threat. The brutality and the tenacity with which they questioned me and my knowledge of what they had done to others and were capable of doing, made their threats to kill my family very real. I was nineteen. I don't think that any nineteen year old should have been given such a choice.

I had no choice basically. On the one hand I knew that the disclosure of Mohammed's whereabouts would lead to his arrest. And on the other hand, if I did not tell them, my family would be killed. Faced with this threat I agreed to tell them where Mohammed was. But only on the condition that my father would be released and that they would leave my mother and my nephew alone. Even then I tried to stall for time by saying that I didn't know Mohammed's exact address but could point it out on a map.

Immediately thereafter I was taken handcuffed to Pinelands Police Station where I was shown a very big map of the Peninsula. I took a while and then I showed them … I showed them where he stayed. They then took me in the presence of a large contingent of security police to his house. Upon confirmation that this was his house, more police came. I was then forced onto the floor of the car with my head between my legs and my hands cuffed behind my back. I thought that they would arrest Mohammed.

To my knowledge they entered the premises without warning. I soon heard gunshots, I could hear that the police were afraid, they were running up and down, somebody was shouting that one of them had been shot. They started shouting at Mohammed to come out. Then followed a fierce exchange of gun fire, I heard grenades, several grenades exploding. I think it was then that I knew it was not going to be about arresting him. Somebody shouted that they could not get in and that he had grenades. I heard a very big explosion, it sounded like a rocket being launched ... and then there was silence.

Somebody shouted that it was all over. In my head I heard all the time, and I hear even now, the same question: Who sold me to the police? Who sold me to the police? Anton dies with that question in his mouth and I wake up night after night with the same question.

[*Yazir breaks down. He cannot continue.*]

After all of this they took me to Athlone Police Station where I was left for two or three hours under guard. Thereafter I was taken back to Culemborg ... they wanted to know about my weapons and contacts, but I was adamant that I was not going to give them more information that could result in death. Probably late the following afternoon, with no break in the interrogation, I was forced to sign a document making me liable under Section 29. For the first time since my arrest I was allowed to sleep ...

For the following two to three weeks they interrogated me for hours on a daily basis at Culemborg. I stuck to the legend that I had broken contact. The interrogations lasted the whole day, day after day. The questions would be repeated day after day. I would be so exhausted ... After witnessing what had happened to Mohammed I could no longer believe that my family was not harmed. I requested to see my parents – this request was refused. I embarked on a hunger strike. For about nine days I refused to eat or drink anything before they gave in to a visit from my mother and father.

For a while the questioning happened less frequently with long periods of silence in between. Then they started showing me thousands and thousands of photographs asking me to identify and place people who they alleged were members of the ANC, both internally and in exile. Normally they showed me the albums and did all the paging. One day they gave me an album and asked me to page through it. On about the fourth or fifth page I saw something that to this day I have nightmares about. The photograph was that of a severed head of someone whom I had personally trained in Luanda. His lips and kidneys were rolled up alongside his neck, his eyes were open and there was dried blood on his lips. The rest of the album contained photographs of his body parts spread across his street.

[*Yazir cannot continue*]

Some time after this I was transferred to Pollsmoor prison in solitary confinement in a very small cell where the lights were never turned off. In the cell there was also a loudspeaker which was continuously buzzing day in and day out. Day in and day out this thing buzzed, the buzzing noise had gotten to my head and it was driving me crazy. My head at times felt like it was going to explode …

I don't recall [a lot of details] and the exact sequence of a lot of these events, but some time afterwards I was taken to Culemborg where Roelofse asked me what I would do if they let me go right now. I laughed at him and said they should stop playing games with me. He then asked me to sign a form which authorised my release. I signed it. Coetzee told me I was not such a bad guy and said that the two of us could work well together. He then asked me if I would not join the Security Police. He even offered me a rank.

Just like I had done before, I refused his offer. And I swear that throughout this entire period I had not revealed any information that could have compromised the security of my contact in Johannesburg and those that I had contacted in Cape Town. My years of training and my insight into the operations of intelligence and security afforded me to provide only information which would give credence to my legend while protecting information which was crucial. To the best of my knowledge, at no stage did I reveal anything that could have led to more arrests or deaths.

On the very day of my release I had a foretaste of what was to come. Some activists in the area came to see me. I remember one of them questioning me about what had happened in prison and what I thought should be done to comrades who sold out in prison. I remember being extremely tired. I replied that I had just been released and that I was tired and I would give them a more detailed response at some other time. They left and none of them came back.

I had similar encounters with other comrades, some of them seriously questioning my integrity and some even openly accusing me of being a sell out. I was told by a comrade who was extremely close to me that there were some people who were very angry about Anton's death and they were blaming me for it. She said people were being told that I am an askari*. She mentioned a particular incident in which another person who was detained under Section 29 at the same time had been interrogated and constantly in his interrogation the police were using the code Mike's Hotel – which had the same initials as my name. They were interpreting it to be me who was giving this information.

I realised that I was being viewed as a sell out and an askari. In the weeks following my release from Section 29 I began to disintegrate. I lost weight and at one point I weighed less than 40 kilograms. My self-confidence, self-esteem and dignity were eroded even further. My ability to concentrate and remember was seriously impaired. It became impossible to sleep. I was and still am constantly haunted by nightmares. I remember looking into the mirror and seeing somebody whom I did not know. I could not accept that some of my comrades whom I had trusted could believe that I had become an askari and an enemy.

I felt that maybe the two people who could attest to my integrity would be the ones with whom I had left the country in 1986 – Ashley Forbes and Peter Jacobs. I went to see them on Robben Island, hoping that there was something that they could do to help clear my name. They said that although they believed me, there was nothing they could do to convince others and that even on the Island they had been told that I had sold out. I avoided all political activity and organisation. I could not access any benefits or grants which were open to other political prisoners. I could not handle the contempt and the mistrust with which I was regarded, but I also refused to leave home and hide. I still hoped that according to the law of the underground a senior member of the movement would contact me and find out what really happened. But this never happened.

At one stage I heard that an ANC Military Commission was to sit at the ANC offices in Athlone. I went, hoping that I would have an opportunity to relate what really happened. The Commission consisted of three Comrades who were unknown to me. To the best of my ability I tried to explain but it appeared as though they were more interested in proving a verdict (of guilt). We agreed that at a follow-up meeting I should submit a written report. I wrote this report but did not have the confidence that if I were to include all the detail it would be understood in its proper perspective. On submission of this report they started to interrogate me and accused me of lying. I then requested to meet with a senior officer who would be known to me and whom I could speak to in confidence. They were adamant that I should rewrite my report and that they had sufficient authority to deal with my case. They said that the report was not good enough and that they would only accept a report which contained the truth. They must have questioned me for several hours. It was really painful as it felt similar to the way in which the boers had interrogated me.

I left feeling very sick and angry, because it appeared that basically all they wanted me to do was to admit that I had killed Anton Franz. I decided not to go back to them but to try to make contact with Chris Hani or Ronnie Kasrils. In my possession is the original draft of the report I submitted to the ANC. I am willing to make that available to the TRC. Some time later I heard of a march that was to take place in Cape Town, amongst others to be led by Ronnie Kasrils. I hoped that he would be able to organise a fair hearing. At the first opportunity during the march I approached Ronnie Kasrils and very briefly explained to him what the issue was and that I could be contacted at my parents' home. He responded that he did not have much time as he was returning to Johannesburg. I left with the impression that I would be contacted later. For months I waited and nothing happened.

I gave up hope that my name would ever be cleared. It has been hard living and not existing. I am alive but my existence continues to be ignored.

In retrospect, I believe that our infiltration into South Africa was poorly planned. The lack of briefing inside the country greatly compromised our security. I am concerned by the lack of concern which the ANC displayed for the lives and the security of its combatants who had infiltrated into the country. Secondly, the untimely death of Anton Franz must be viewed in the political and psychological circumstances which prevailed at the time. I do not believe that I can be held solely responsible for his death. And I believe that the role which the Security Police played must be exposed.

I request from the TRC that they facilitate the following: That the circumstances around the death of Anton Franz be investigated and that I am publicly cleared of all rumours that I am an askari. I want to reiterate that I have remained faithful and committed to the struggle of oppressed South Africa for human rights and human dignity. I wish to be recognised for who and what I am ... That the truth about the circumstances leading to my arrest and the names of those individuals or that individual who informed on me be made known to me. Only then would I be able to reconcile myself with my own experiences and with the death of Anton. That the TRC grants me the possibility of waking up from this terrible nightmare that I have been living with for so many years, so that I too may benefit from and hopefully contribute to the process of healing that is taking place in our country.

Chairperson

Yazir, thank you very much ... all of us are deeply moved by your own readiness to expose yourself in the manner in which you have done. They say sometimes that it is easy to fast on a full stomach. And those of us who have not undergone experiences such as the ones that you have been recounting, might comment too easily. But what I think everyone of us realises is the incredible cost, the very heavy price that has been paid for getting us where we are. And especially by young people like yourself. The cost has been enormous. And we salute all – all of you young people, we salute people like yourselves who have paid that price. The fruit of your contribution is being enjoyed by all of us now. We hope that we in the Commission may be able to put some of the things to the bodies you referred to and try to ascertain what the various truths may have been.

February 1999
Almost three years later. Yazir Henry is twenty-eight years old. In Chapter IV he speaks about how he has carried on with his life.

SANDRA ADONIS

'How much can a person take?'

Sandra Adonis, born 1969 in Cape Town, experienced the shooting of fellow pupils by police at the age of fifteen. From then on, her dedication to the anti-apartheid struggle intensified radically. She was voted onto the SRC of her school, the Ned Damon Senior Secondary, as their youngest member. At seventeen she was excluded from her school on the grounds of political activism. She joined the militant youth group the Bonteheuwel Military Wing (BMW)* where she met her future husband, Jacques Adonis, who was also an activist. A short time afterwards she was arrested. After her release she experienced the detention of her husband, who was returned to her a long time later, completely broken. He became increasingly violent towards her. Sandra thought for a long time about making a submission to the TRC.

We chose her because she has grown and developed through her political activism. However, this could not protect her from the effects of apartheid oppression which reached into the most personal and private areas of her life. She, too, is representative of many young people who have received little or no recognition for their tireless dedication to the struggle.

TRC HEARING IN ATHLONE (CAPE TOWN), 22 MAY 1997

Commissioner
Are you all right, Sandra? Can you hear me all right? You are going to tell us about your own experience as a young teenager and about that of your husband. So please go ahead and tell us in your own words.

Sandra
It was in 1985 when I started being involved in politics. I was about fifteen years old and I did not have any background of politics. I always heard my grandfather talk about politics and Vorster and all these things he used to make them bad. But when I got to realise why he was going on about these people, seeing how our Government was handling our people, it hurt me and I decided to get involved.

At the age of fifteen when school started again they decided to have SRCs at these different schools. I was elected from my class to be a representative for them on the SRC. Then I was voted chairperson of the SRC. But my principal decided that I was too young, too immature, to be the chairperson. He decided that we should vote amongst each other and then people voted me as Assistant Treasurer. Anyway, I also served on the Action Committee in Athlone, for the Ned Damon Senior Secondary.

I remember quite vividly that there was one day that I had to leave school after one of the teachers told me that the police came looking for me. I left the school and I went to the lawyer's offices, because I knew I could not go home. There would be no home for me now. I mean, as much as I wanted to, my family could not protect me and I just had to get somewhere. By the time they started looking for us all the other people of the executive were missing and then a few weeks after that it was the Trojan Horse case.[3]

Shaun Magmoet then was at the same school as I was. I just managed to get to school sometimes, and that particular morning after the shooting one of our teachers told me that Shaun was shot. Being the only person left of the SRC I had to convey the message to the students. I felt like, you know, being fifteen and also feeling like a mother at the same time. I was also thinking what would it have been like if it was me, because I just left them a couple of hours before this whole happening. Also seeing people being shot like Jonathan Claasen standing opposite me on the opposite side of the road ... that was not an easy thing to just put at the back of your mind.

Then it was the whole thing of the exams that we could not write. We took a stand that we are not going to write exams. Basically, I just used to go and have a look at what is happening at school and what people were doing and who ... is writing exams. It was my duty, because I was on the Action Committee. After that my principal said: 'I do not want you on my school any more'.

I forced and I forced and I forced (persisted, stayed on) until he in '86 finally said, 'No, I do not want you on my school any more, because you are an instigator.'

I left school. I had no alternative because I do not know whether he informed the police. Whenever I seemed to just be away from school then the police would come looking for me there. Then I decided, bullshit, I am leaving, I cannot cope with this any more.

I just got a casual job where I worked for about a month. Well, I could not keep up with this, because certain things happened and I was also instructed to do things. In the same time I got involved with the people of Bonteheuwel, that is Bonteheuwel Military Wing. Although we have done things that we are not very proud of, but the reasons why we have done it we are proud of them, because today we can stand with our heads up high and say that we together with the nation, we have done it.

In any event, in 1987 I decided that I cannot live my life without education. I went to a school in Bonteheuwel. I practically begged the principal there to take me back and I promised him that I will never participate in politics again although in my heart I knew that I would not be able to withdraw myself from my activities. I went on trying to finish my schooling.

Later on I got involved again within the SRC and I was chosen again to be the Chairperson of the SRC which was quite difficult for me, because I promised the principal that I am not going to be involved. As much as I tried, I could not, because my beliefs were too strong.

Because of my own background as well, my father is a white and my mother is a black or rather a coloured, as they want to call it, 'so-called'.

I never had a family life with them. My mother was a domestic maid at the so-called whites. So I feel that I had a difficult childhood from the start. I hated white people and I hated the Government for doing things to me and to my people and because of that I could not deny my people my fight as well.

Then I met my husband, Jacques Adonis. He is deceased. At the time when I met him he just came from detention after nine months. For the time that we had a relationship before we got married things were okay. Although we were still not at home, still roaming around, still not sleeping at home, still not being able to really see our family and spend even a whole day with them. In the time I left home they searched my house in every corner possible. What they were looking for I do not know and these were Mostert from the Loop Street Security Police and then when I joined up with them in Bonteheuwel, it was a certain Captain Van Brackel who started harassing me.

There was a time when there was heavy conflict amongst the Comrades As these conflicts went on, one particular night I could not go back to where I was hiding and I had to sleep at another lady's place and the next morning Van Brackel was at her door knocking. He found me lying in the bed and he did not know it was me. He went downstairs and he came back up, like, in a matter of five to six seconds and he said to me: 'Wow, you are the person we have been looking for for five years and I am not going to let you go again. You have run away from Mostert, but you are not going to run away from me.' And he said to me: 'You are a terrorist and you should come with me.'

I was preparing myself all the time for this day. You know, it is like you prepare yourself for death, because you do not know what is going to happen and even if you want to prepare yourself how much, you will never be able to prepare yourself really. Then I decided to have a bath that specific morning and not just go ... because I thought to myself, well, Section 29 or what the hell, I do not know, for the next fourteen to fifteen days, or maybe three, four weeks I might not be able to see my family, I might not get clean clothes. So, well, I will take a bath. Whilst I was in the bath he started shouting from outside: 'If you do not finish up now, I will come in there and I will fetch you!' and then I realised that the door could not lock. I said to him: 'If you dare enter this bathroom I will certainly lay charges against you for attempted rape,' because I did not have any clothes on.

I finished off and I went with them. I tried to relax and I could not. I had a hell of a headache by the time I got into their car, because I was expecting the worst. A certain Mr Strydom – I do not know what his rank was, but he was always with this Captain Van Brackel – he asked me now, 'why do you hate policemen?'.

So I said, 'I do not hate policemen, in fact, I just hate what they are doing to my people' and then I, because I thought, well, I have to say something to these people to get them out of my hair and I said to him: 'In fact, I would also like to be a policeman, a policewoman one day.' I think I played right into their hands.

At the police station Van Brackel said: 'Well, I have got two big hands and I will just slap you, I will not ask questions.'

So I said to him: 'Well, I will charge you for assault then if you do anything to me.' I was trying to hit back at him all the time, but also in a very gentle way not to have him think that this is a stubborn woman, because once you show stubbornness, they would show no mercy.

Then we went to the police station where they questioned me and later on told me that they are going to give me a form to fill in ... to become a policewoman.

Then I would like to come to my husband, Jacques. He was also a member of Bonteheuwel Military Wing and he was even more involved than I was. There was then at the time when, just a few months after we were married and I was about nineteen or something like that, I cannot remember, when one morning Van Brackel and this, I think he was a Lieutenant, yes, Strydom walked into our place and they said to my husband: 'You are running away again you bastard!'.

They took him out of bed and they took him with them. The last time I have seen him he had clothes on, he was decently dressed and then the search started. They told me that I am going to find him at Bishop Lavis Police Station and then I went to Bishop Lavis Police Station and he was not there.

I went home and I phoned there and they said I should phone Bellville. I phoned Bellville, nobody there. Phoned Bellville South and I just went on and on and on. I think it was for about five days it went on like that and I do not know if any of you people can imagine what it is like looking for somebody and knowing that this person is in the hands of people who are very dangerous, who are capable of doing anything, even capable of killing. By the time I got hold of my husband he was at the Bellville South Police Station.

I had such a shock when I saw him, because he was full of blue and purple marks We could not really speak, it was one of the ordinary policemen that took him out of the cell and said to me that they are not able to let me speak long, because if the Security Branch people come and they find me standing there talking to him, they might lock me up as well.

Then he briefly told me what they did. He said to me that they have blindfolded him and they first, I think they beat him up and then they took him into a car where they drove for about five to six minutes and they took him out of the car and they took him into a building which sounded very empty with long passages and they took him into some kind of room, whether it was an office or, I do not know.

He was handcuffed from the police station and they took off the handcuffs and they handcuffed him on the chair on which he was sitting. The next thing he felt was the wires that they connected to his fingers and … to his toes as well … The next thing he felt was like his whole body was going to burst into pieces the way they gave him this shock treatment and I think they have done this repeatedly and he collapsed for a few minutes. By the time when he got to, they tried to shock him again, but as they did that he moved to the front and he pulled off his, whatever, scarf or whatever it was and he saw Captain Van Brackel, Strydom and, I am not sure, but I think Pikke was also with them.

Then after the seventh day he was released. Not even charged, just released, and I actually never heard of Van Brackel after that, but I am telling you he has not tortured me … but what he has done to my husband is, I think, the worst …

My life started being a mess. My husband was … he would sometimes go off his trolley. He would be like a mad person and he knows that his anger, his frustrations that he felt at that time were supposed to be directed at the state, but because I was the nearest person to him, he lashed out. Well, I understood to a certain extent, but, I mean, how much can a person take? And being involved since fifteen, not really having enjoyed a teenage life. In fact, I said the other day to one of my Comrades, you know, it is only now that I realise that I do not know what it is to go to a bioscope on a Saturday afternoon or even to a disco, like many young people do today or maybe that time as well. I mean I never had friends really. My friends, my *compadres* were my Comrades. Those were the only people that I could trust at that point in time and sometimes you were not even sure if you could trust them.

As I said, like, my husband got worse and worse and worse. I tried to get him to counsellors but he would not accept being counselled. He would not accept being told by other people, because what he used to say to me is: 'I had enough of people telling me, trying to rule my life for me, and I will do as I please!' ... He was never this kind of person before. I did not know him like that and always afterwards he would say he is sorry, but, I mean, as I said, how long can a person take somebody saying sorry to you.

Just like these very Boers who have been interrogating us and torturing us, trying to say to us today, we are sorry, we did not mean that. We do not need their apologies. Well, I do not need them, because I think my life is messed up as it is – directionless. I have lost my education and I have lost my childhood although we have in return received our freedom and our democracy in this country.

But to what extent did we, as the Comrades, members of BMW gain? I do not think we have gained anything, because we are still in the same position as we used to be – unemployed, homeless, abandoned. There is nobody that looks back and says, well, these are the people that have fought the struggle, that have been part and parcel of the struggle and have brought us to the point where we are now. Not any recognition, I mean, and I do not want recognition for myself, but I believe and I have never ever heard anybody say anything in recognition to the youth of that time. In fact, this is the first time that I have seen there are some people who are interested in who we were and who we are now. Thank you.

April 1999

Two years later Sandra reports how her life has continued after the hearing (Chapter IV).

MOLIFI ISHMAEL RANTSIENG

'Five bullets are still in my body!'

Molifi Ishmael Rantsieng, born in 1972, was a politically interested pupil at school without belonging to a specific organisation. At the age of nineteen he was taking part in a legal demonstration when police started to shoot without warning. He was hit by a total of thirteen pellets.

His story illustrates not only the brutality with which protests were met by the police, but also the long delays in effective medical treatment. Claims against the perpetrators seem even more difficult to achieve. This young man's future will largely be decided by the quality of intervention which the TRC is able to achieve for him.

TRC HEARING IN BLOEMFONTEIN, 23 JUNE 1997

Commissioner
Good morning, Mr Rantsieng. You are from the Koppies area and you have to tell us about a situation involving a school boycott and a march where you and others were shot. Is that correct?

Ishmael
That's correct.

Commissioner
Before you go on to the story of what happened, can you give us just a brief picture of your family? Are your parents still alive?

Ishmael
We are six children. I'm staying with my mother and my younger brother. My father has since died.

Commissioner
And the other four children, where are they?

Ishmael
They stay with their own mother.

Commissioner
So you have two different mothers?

Ishmael

I've got just one mother. The others are at their homes. They are married.

Commissioner

I beg your pardon, so they are old now, grown up?

Ishmael

That's correct.

Commissioner

Is your mother working?

Ishmael

No, she's on pension.

Commissioner

Thank you. Now, the situation you are going to be telling us about took place on 30 March 1990. Is that right?

Ishmael

That's true.

Commissioner

What was the situation in Koppies at that time?

Ishmael

Shortly. I was together with fellow students who were detained on 30 March. It was on Friday. We students decided to go to court to listen to the case. Before we left, the leader of the SRC requested permission for us to come to court to listen to that court case of our fellow students. The station commander agreed that we could go. We were thirty or thirty-four. We were singing freedom songs from the township. When we entered Koppies town we kept quiet and walked. Just when we were inside Koppies town the station commander, Mr Meiring, came with other police. He came out of the car. There was no notice or warning to us, they just started shooting.

We ran in different directions because we saw that we were in danger.
I ran away. Then I hid myself. At the place where I was hiding I saw my
younger brother lying down, being shot. When I saw that the police were
not there any more, I returned and my younger brother was lying on the
ground. I picked him up and we ran away.

Unfortunately, when we were running, when I was jumping the fence,
when I looked back to try to ... two white policemen were near me. They
started ... they shot me in the leg. I tried to lift myself from the fence. They
shot me in the back. Then I fell on the ground. Then shot me in the right leg
with seven bullets. I tried to stand up to run, but they shot me in the head
with five bullets and they shot me in the left hand with two bullets and in
the right hand they shot me with three bullets. I fell to the ground ...

My fellow comrades came to pick me up. I was not able to talk or do
anything. They took me to the doctor. On my arrival I found the police
waiting for me there. They took statements from us there. Because I was
not able to talk or do anything, the doctor explained to them that this person
could not do or say anything. The doctor put me on a drip and gave me
oxygen ...

Commissioner
Just a moment. Who were there to take statements?

Ishmael
The police.

Commissioner
And where was that? At a hospital or a clinic?

Ishmael
We were at the doctor's surgery when we were prepared to go to the
hospital ... After I got the drips and the oxygen so that I could inhale and
exhale again, they took me to hospital in Kroonstad. When we arrived at
Kroonstad Hospital we found policemen waiting there. We were admitted
to the hospital. Whilst we were still there one of the lawyers from

Johannesburg, Priscilla Jana, arrived and wanted to find out what happened. Some fellow comrades explained it to her.

I slept at the hospital guarded by police until Sunday. On Monday, when they were preparing me to be moved to Bloemfontein, we saw that the situation was tense. Then we decided that we should run away. I went home and stayed there from Monday until Thursday. Then the police arrived but my parents and siblings refused to let them see me. My mother phoned my father in Sebokeng to fetch me. Then I went to Sebokeng on Friday and they took me to Sebokeng Hospital.

Even there there were people who were shot and there was no accommodation. Then they took me to Johannesburg Hospital. At that time there was still segregation and I did not get any help. In Baragwanath Hospital (at that time reserved for blacks) I did not get any help either because of overcrowding. I found help in Natalspruit Hospital, but they told me to return on Monday. On Monday I went back. Then they said to me that they could not remove the bullets.

So I went back to my father in Sebokeng, where my grandmother managed to find a doctor. This doctor tried to remove the shrapnel in my body, but he was scared. He said if the police knew that he removed those pellets he would be detained himself. Because the police were looking for me I could not go home. I stayed in Sebokeng for a year and some months. I was not able to go to school.

When I returned home to Koppies, the police were waiting for me. They detained me and my younger brother in Koppies police station, where they tortured me ... They requested a statement from us, but we refused. But because we were both tortured and I was threatened with further detention, we were forced to make a statement. But somewhere in the statement they put their own ideas and when they said I should sign, I refused because it was not what I had said. But because of further pressure I eventually signed.

Then I was released and went to Sebokeng again, because I saw that my life was at risk in Koppies. After some time I went back home.

My mother met with with my fellow comrades and they talked with Priscilla Jana, who tried that we should be able to go back home and to school again.

After some time she tried to take the case to court. Because we didn't have enough money I could not promise her that I would be able to raise the legal fees. After we got the money we gave it to her, but even today I cannot tell what happened in the case.

They were only able to remove thirteen pellets and five are still in my body. After some time my left kidney was removed. My mother is struggling financially and she's not able to take me to doctors.

Commissioner
Thank you for that very graphic account of what happened to you. Did you ever lay a case or open a case at the police station, apart from the case that the lawyers brought?

Ishmael
Yes. We went to the police station to open a case against the police who shot us.

Commissioner
What happened about that case?

Ishmael
They said ... that the case would be heard in court, but until today it has not been heard.

Commissioner
Can you remember the name of the state doctor?

Ishmael
I do remember the name.

Commissioner
Please tell it to me. You say you do remember?

Ishmael
I still remember him.

Commissioner
Perhaps you are not sure of his name?

Ishmael
It's Dr Jan Bouwer.

Commissioner
Have you been able to continue your schooling since then?

Ishmael
Yes, I went back to school but it was after a long time.

Commissioner
And how far have you got?

Ishmael
I am doing Standard nine (grade 11) because of the time wasted.

Commissioner
Are you having any difficulties with your studies or are you coping quite okay?

Ishmael
I have problems. Just now when we were writing the June exams I didn't write. I was in hospital.

Commissioner
Thank you very much, Ishmael. It's quite clear that you suffered lots of physical violations, and I am amazed that you are still here today to tell your story. I would like to ask how all this has affected your life.

Ishmael
In short, I would say I was badly affected. Moreover, when I think back to the torture, even now … my mother was supposed to be here with me today. Because she is also badly affected she was not able to be here.

Commissioner
What is happening to her?

Ishmael
After I was shot she nearly had a stroke.

Commissioner
Why could you not write the exams?

Ishmael
It was because of a kidney operation – which they did four times. So I had
to go back again to hospital. They wanted to operate on me for the fifth
time, but my mother did not allow that.

Commissioner
Do you have to pay for the operations?

Ishmael
Yes. Every time I go into hospital I am supposed to pay … I have a private
doctor. I have to pay him and the transport and the hospital charges. That
is a problem I have because at times when I have to go for treatment my
mother hasn't got money I have to borrow money or get it somewhere.
Then I am able to go for treatment.

Commissioner
With regard to your studies do you have problems concentrating? Do you
often have to think about what happened to you?

Ishmael
It happens. It happens at times when I study that I think deeply about
what happened to me and then my nerves are affected. Then I leave my
books and sleep because I am not able to continue.

Commissioner
Thank you very much, Ishmael. I think we need to have your hospital

records. It looks as though you are in a poor state of health ... in the Commission we have a Reparations Committee that is working very hard to see how we can address problems like yours. We have listened to all you have said and we will try as much as possible to help where we can. Thank you.

Ishmael, just before we finish, it just struck me that you have not told anything about your brother who was shot. Can you quickly give us a picture of what happened to your brother?

Ishmael
Because I was able to make him stand, he was able to run. When I went to hospital I was partially unconscious. He then went to the District Surgeon. The pellets were not deep in his head. The District Surgeon was able to remove them.

Commisioner
Is he okay now?

Ishmael
I think he's all right.

Commissioner
Just one last question. It seems, from what you are saying, that there was a great deal of shooting on that day. How many other people were injured? Did anyone die in that particular incident? What else can you tell us about it?

Ishmael
No, no people died on that day. Many comrades were injured. I have one here who is now paralysed.

May 1999
Two years later. Eventually we succeed to find an address for Ishmael. After several weeks an answer comes back in which the now twenty-six-year-old writes: 'I want

to thank you for being interested in me … When I remove one pellet I had to pay R250. So I failed to remove all of them due to financial problems. The doctors told me that the pellets had damaged my kidney. My mother is paralysed. My plans were and are as follows: I planned to go back to school to further my studies. Because of my illness I can't … I hope that the government will listen to my cries …'

After initial difficulties in following up this case telephonically with the Reparations Committee of the TRC, a call comes from the Director, Tulani Grenville-Grey. He told us he had investigated the case and found that it was being processed, as Ishmael had filled in a claim form. Because of staff shortages there had been delays. But now more staff had been appointed to expedite reparations claims and payments. Once Ishmael is classified as a victim, he should receive compensation and be referred to medical treatment through the nearest welfare agency. The costs will be carried by the President's Reparation Fund. Relief all round. We will stay in touch with Ishmael.

Since Ishmael's story first became more widely known through the German edition of this book, there has been concern that he suffers poor health because of the delay in the payment of reparations to victims of violence. Ishmael has since been able to have his injuries fully investigated and has received additional medical treatment because of private donations and because some funding has at last become available from the Reparation Fund. During our communications with Ishmael over a period of some months we became acutely aware of the anger and frustration that has been generated by the Government's continued delays in the payment of reparations. There are many thousands of Ishmaels all over South Africa.

PRETTY MKALIPI
'I was too young to be burnt …'

Pretty Mkalipi, born in 1971, was a Standard 9 pupil at the High School in Bathurst near Port Alfred in the Eastern Cape when she and two other young women decided to become members of AZAPO*. She was fourteen years old at the time. They did not know much about the organisation they had joined save that it had been launched a few months before to 'free Blacks from oppression by *the state and to work for peace'. There was no other liberation movement in Bathurst at the time.*

A short while before her fifteenth birthday, on a Sunday in July, Pretty Mkalipi and her two friends travelled to Port Alfred to attend a regional AZAPO meeting. They had taken food to recently released Comrades and heard the story of their imprisonment. During the meeting a rumour did the rounds that the rival UDF* was planning an attack because it was alleged that police spies were attending the AZAPO meeting.

As there was no opportunity to return to Bathurst that night, the three friends and twenty others stayed over at a Comrade's house in Port Alfred. Late that night there was an attack by UDF supporters who forced their way into the house. Pretty Mkalipi tells the story of what happened after one of her friends managed to escape but she herself was seized.

Pretty Mkalipi's statement has been chosen because it illustrates the depth of mistrust and suspicion in the black community and how cruelly a young girl could be punished for a choice made in good faith. It also shows that a healing vision for the future could become a possibility if all victims of violence were to be honoured communally.

TRC HEARING IN GRAHAMSTOWN, 8 APRIL 1997

Pretty Mkalipi
I was taken by these Comrades. They said that they were going to burn me. Four people came and saved me, four young men came. They said that I was too young to be burnt. They pleaded for me and they said that I was a young girl. These people from Port Alfred, they did not want to listen, they wanted to burn me.

Commissioner
The people who wanted to burn you, did they say they were Comrades?

Pretty
Yes, they were Comrades belonging to UDF.

Commissioner
Did you know them?

Pretty
No, I did not know them. I did not notice them, because it was dark.

Commissioner
Why did they want to burn you?

Pretty
They said why am I a member of this organisation [meaning AZAPO].

Commissioner
Did they tell you which organisation they belonged to?

Pretty
No, but it was clear which organisation they belonged to.

Commissioner
Let us now talk about the injuries you sustained when you were attacked.

Pretty
I was axed in the head five times. I also have wounds in my leg. They also beat me with sjamboks. I have five wounds in my head and in my leg and they beat me all over the body with sticks and sjamboks. They were beating me while I was lying down.

Commissioner
Were you taken to the hospital or to a doctor?

Pretty
I was taken to Settlers Hospital here in Grahamstown. We were just operated, the people told us there that they did not have time for us, there were many people to be attended to.

Commissioner
Do you receive treatment now because of the injuries you sustained?

Pretty
I used to go to the clinic to be bandaged and I also consulted a traditional healer, because my eyes were swollen.

Commissioner
Is there a need for you to get treatment today?

Pretty
Yes, I would like to be checked properly in my head, because I get dizzy sometimes and sometimes I just get moody, I do not want to be with people.

Commissioner
Do you have requests to the Commission today?

Pretty
My request is that I would like the people who did this to us to come forward to the Commission.

Commissioner
If they would come forward to the Commission and apologise to you for what they did to you, what would you say to them?

Pretty
I would forgive them if they would come forward. I would be satisfied, because I do not know who did this to me. If I knew the people who did these things to me, I would be satisfied.

Commissioner
What are you doing now, are you working or are you a student?

Pretty
No, I am not a student, I am not working. I stopped school after I got injured.

Commissioner
When did you stop school?

Pretty
I was in standard seven. I went back to school when I was better, but I stopped, because when I am at school I get frequent headaches, I do not concentrate on what the teachers are saying at school.

Commissioner
Were you a member of AZAPO?

Pretty
Yes, but we had no membership card at the time because the organisation was just formed in Bathurst.

Commissioner
In this conflict between UDF and AZAPO were there victims on both sides or were the victims just on the AZAPO side? Were there any UDF members who died during that time?

Pretty
No, it was just on our side.

Commissioner
Because you wanted a place where the victims can be remembered. I just want to know whether the victims were supposed to be separated or are supposed to be put together.

Pretty
I request the victims to be placed together.

Commissioner
We thank you. We remember this time, the conflict between AZAPO and UDF. There are many statements we received concerning this era. There

are conflicting ideas in these different statements, but what we are looking at is that you are victims, you are women and you were harassed. This is what is important to us more than a conflict that was between UDF and AZAPO or who was working with who in collaborating with the police. We are not concentrating on that now. We have noted your request that the people who did this to you are amongst your community and you would like them to come forward so that they can apologise to you. If it is possible we would like peace to prevail amongst you.

May 1999

With the help of a Black Sash Advice Office worker in Grahamstown who established contact with Pretty, we managed to find out more about her present situation. She was now twenty-eight years old, happily married with two children, thirteen and three years old. She was unemployed and her husband Mpumelelo Samuel Viso was a farm worker who did not earn enough to support the family. There was no further financial support and the family had to rely on a relative who received a special grant and assisted with basic necessities. Her situation is a typical example of rural poverty. After the TRC hearing Pretty felt relieved that she had been able to talk about the way she had been humiliated. Her community accepted and welcomed her after the hearing and there were no repercussions about her political affiliations at that time.

She was, however, disappointed that she had not received specialist medical attention to date. She suffered from pains in her joints and limbs and foresaw future health problems. The perpetrators had not apologised to her. This had dismayed her for a while but she was determined to get on with her life and to put this experience behind her. Her suggestion of a memorial for all victims was considered by community leaders but the situation remains unresolved.

GEORGE NDLOZI
'If it were not for the Self Defence Units, many of us would not be sitting here today!'

George Ndlozi, born in 1973 in the Katorus, East Rand township of Katlehong, grew up amid the violence generated by the clashes between members of the ANC *and the IFP which dominated headlines in the 1980s and 1990s. He tells the story particularly of the youthful members of the ANC-linked SDUs*, but it is also his own story. Because of the high level of violence, he could not attend school regularly. He had to prepare for his matriculation examinations by moving his books from one hiding place to the next. At times they accompanied him on his various active duties in the SDU. In spite of these difficulties, he completed his matric in 1993, when the violence between the ANC and the IFP had reached its height.*

His story was chosen because his experiences show so clearly how youths are absorbed in the spiral of violence. The SDUs remain a controversial element even today, and George's account points to the complexities of a phenomenon which cannot simply be categorised as either good or evil.

TRC HEARING IN JOHANNESBURG, 12 JUNE 1997

Commissioner
George, thank you very much for coming here today and for being so patient. You have come to talk about the youth of Katorus, the East Rand.

George Ndlozi
I thank you. I think I will first start by reading the document that we have prepared.

The historical background of the conflict in the Katorus area from mid-1990 to 1994 has been well documented. Much has been said about the role of the Self Defence Units, but very little has come to light as to the effect this conflict had on the youth of the area.

Whether you were involved in defence or not, the violence affected you. It was not unknown for children attending nursery schools or crèches to find a body near their jungle gym or swings. Hostel* inmates and SDUs took potshots at each other across school yards.

Children were not spared the horror. Schooling in the area came to a complete standstill. Children barely in their teens left schools to defend life and property. Areas situated near hostels were particularly affected.

Hundreds of people were forced out of their houses, and in many instances parents left their sons to defend whatever was left of the family home. In some cases families were targeted because sons had joined the Self Defence Unit.

In Tokoza for example, one Macashu Mabaso's family was brutally murdered in their Kumalo Street home in August, 1993 because of his SDU activities.

Macashu joined a Self Defence Unit at sixteen. According to Mabaso, people were being killed at an alarming rate for refusing to join the IFP*. Along with a few friends, they formed a Self Defence Unit.

At first they had no weapons and relied on petrol bombs, pangas and knives. As the conflict intensified and the IFP became increasingly armed, the Self Defence Unit started recruiting known criminals. It was the criminals who supplied the first weapons to the Self Defence Unit.

Later the community got together and started donating money for guns. That is when the Section got its first AK47. At seventeen, Mabaso was elected Commander of the larger Thambo Section.

The vast majority of SDU members in Katorus were forced to leave school and most left at very critical times, either in standard 8 or 9.[4]

There are of course exceptions. Lucky Mtumkulu is just one. At thirteen he was shot in the head and stomach while watching television. He was true to his name, he survived and four youths with him were killed. Lucky was a member of the Thambo SDU. He was saved by his Commander Macashu, who carried him unconscious, from the house.

This wasn't the first person Macashu has saved but you will never hear him talking about those things. He doesn't talk about it, but the other boys do. Asked if he was scared to go into enemy territory to rescue friends, he said if they shoot one of our boys, I will always go there, even if they are dead, I will risk it to fetch them.

There is no denying that some of the SDUs have been involved in serious human rights abuses. In Katorus these are the exceptions, rather than the rule, given the evidence available to us.

Most SDUs were engaged in defending their families and homes from the IFP and its communities. With the recent revelation that members of South African Police were actively involved in supplying the IFP with arms, it is no surprise in retrospect that SDUs were particularly targeted by the Security Forces.

Organisations working in the East Rand at the time, particularly the Independent Board of Enquiry, noted that the Security Forces operated on a shoot-to-kill policy. It was far easier to shoot SDUs than to arrest them and go through a tiresome court procedure.

Tales of torture at the hands of policemen based at the Political and Violent Crime Unit at Vlakplaas* and Enoni*, are legendary. For example, at Enoni there was a dog called Stoffel which often bit detainees. Electric shocks and tubing were the order of the day.

Michael Marte was a sixteen-year-old member of the SDU in Ramakonope West in Katlehong. He was arrested by members of the ISU and the Political and Violent Crime Unit. Apart from being smothered with the inner tube of a tyre and sat upon by Stoffel, a rope was wound around his body and pulled tight like a spinning top. The police would then turn the rope and Michael would go spinning off and smash into the wall.

This was done several times. Amnesty International took up this case when Michael was denied bail and kept in police cells for six months.

Research shows that the South African Defence Force was involved in acts of torture in the area. In August 1993 at least eleven youths were arrested by the South African Defence Force. Black bags were placed over their heads and sharp needles were shoved under their nails.

Subsequent medical evidence proved that this had indeed taken place. Members of the Self Protection Unit and the IFP were also tortured by the SAP. They were often arrested and told that if they did not talk, they would be dumped in an ANC area. Conversely, ANC supporters would be told that they would be dumped in an IFP area.

A victim of one of the shootings in Tokoza tells a typical story of what happened.

'I heard a knock on the door, just after midnight. The person said, "I want to come in". I thought it was a friend and went to the door. Five men with AK47s and petrol bombs came in. They shot me. I fell down and another one with a pistol came to finish up. I thought this is the last time, I am going to die, but he missed me. My friends came to help me.'

This was the most striking theme of the Self Defence Units – friendship and comradeship. With that being a daily reality as Sydney Nkozi said, balancing on a crippled leg: 'I depend on the members of the SDUs. If they leave me, I have nothing, we help each other.'

Jimmy Nkondo was born on November 26, 1977. He joined the SDU at thirteen, in 1990. His house is about a stone's throw from the notorious Biofoto hostel. He was not recruited by any particular person, but joined the SDU to protect his family.

When the violence erupted, his parents ran away with his younger brother and sisters. He decided to stay to protect his home.

He gave up attending school and food was scarce. Very often they only ate cabbage, potatoes and carrots. Sometimes parents of the other boys who had not left would give him money for food. When Jimmy joined the SDU, he changed from a carefree young man who enjoyed school and sport, to a person with no mercy. Instead of being nurtured in the family home he was forced to become a killing machine.

There was no choice, it was kill or be killed. In 1993 he was given his first AK47 by his Commander. He used to patrol his area with his Unit, ensuring that there would be no attack. He became known as *abafana, abanikrag* which, roughly translated, means 'the ones who carry out missions bravely and perfectly with no mistakes'.

On November 6, 1993, Jimmy was on patrol when members of the East Rand Murder and Robbery Unit spotted him with his AK47.

He was shot and arrested. Jimmy was arrested at about five o'clock in the morning. He had tried to run, but was shot in the leg. He tried to crawl away to safety, but the police spotted him.

Once he was found, he was beaten and dragged into a police vehicle. Jimmy claims that the police took a pair of scissors and dug them into his left leg, trying to remove the bullet. He lay next to the vehicle for at least thirty minutes before an ambulance came.

He was then taken to hospital and placed under police guard. He was hospitalised for a week and then taken to Germiston police cells. This is when Jimmy's problems really began.

Nobody had informed the family as to where he was. The next three to four days were spent frantically searching for him. Numerous visits were made to the cells to no avail. Eventually attorneys intervened and found Jimmy chained to a wall in a cell in Germiston.

He was eventually granted bail and faced charges of attempted murder and possession of an AK47. Jimmy was found guilty and sentenced to twelve years. An appeal was launched and he is currently on bail, pending appeal.

Commissioner
George, if you don't mind, I am going to stop you at that stage. We've all got your submission. I wonder if you want to actually sum up and conclude your document?

George
It may be argued in conclusion that far from being a bunch of undisciplined comrades or the lost generation, SDUs were in many ways the backbone of defence in Katorus. If it were not for them, many of us would not be sitting here today. It is clear even from this brief submission that youth involved in SDU activities have suffered a loss that can never be replaced – their childhood.

Commissioner
I still think many things went wrong in the operation of the SDUs mainly because, though the aim was to protect communities, as you are saying, against the Security Forces, you failed to be impartial.

The group failed to be impartial and tended to be a danger to people who were not of the same political persuasion – that is just my naïve and maybe provocative interpretation of the whole thing.[5]

George
Yes, if I may answer on that. A lot of things happened in that area and for the community to decide at the end of the day that they have to carry up arms, it took them at least three years. As it is mentioned in the submission, the SDUs never had weapons, they had to depend on criminals and some of the people took advantage of the situation.

And they ended up operating out of their personal gain. That is why at the end of the day, the community decided that we needed money to get firearms over which we would have control.

Commissioner
Just one last question. Were so-called 'people's courts' somehow associated with the SDUs?

George
In most cases members of the Self Defence Unit were allowed to come to those meetings, but not to have a say. Parents would have to decide in the street committee meetings on how we operated. In certain other areas I know that there were people's courts in which certain decisions were taken and were given to the SDU members to accomplish. In short, I would say people's courts were not associated with SDUs.

Commissioner
Could I just follow up on this question? Did I understand your answer correctly? You say that in some cases SDUs had to carry out the finding of the people's court?

George
No, not really. The executions that came, it was not because it was discussed by the street committees that now you need to go and kill someone else, it was not in that fashion.

Commissioner
Would the understanding be incorrect that the SDUs also on occasion took initiative, in other words went out after individuals in the township, as a kind of reprisal or preemptive strike in the sense of defence?

George
I could say yes, in a sense that at some stage they never used to get an order to do something, because things happened whilst you were still at home. You would be sitting at home eating, and then you could hear fire, and then you would take your AK47 from under the table and go …

Commissioner
George, just basically a comment from my side. This is the confusion in total of the conflict of the past – in a sense many of the people you've described as heroes and victims were perpetrators and victims at the same time. Was there an age restriction in terms of being allowed to be an official member of the SDUs?

George
No. There was no age restriction. The war doesn't choose whether you are six years old or ten years old. So it was very difficult to convince young children not to be involved, but if they insisted, there was no choice. If you look at other people like Lucky Buthelezi, they were very young, but at the same time they said you cannot stop me from protecting the community and it was very difficult to argue that issue … He will tell you about families who have been killed, brutally murdered – like Macashu for instance. He will tell you about his family who has been brutally murdered and such a person cannot be stopped.

Commissioner
George were there girl SDUs?

George
Yes.

Commissioner
And what was their role?

George
There were some of them who used to say we also need to take part, I also need to carry an AK47 to defend, I should not be discriminated against because I am a female. And there were those who were very important, who played parts in cooking. Although it may look a bit sexist, but they decided that they better cook for people who will be going outside to actually defend the community.

Commissioner
But there were those who also carried AK47s?

George
Definitely, there were those.

Commissioner
George, just one more question. Katorus was chosen as a Presidential lead project soon after the 1994 elections. Is there any part of that project that lends itself towards assisting the hundreds of young people that you have been speaking about today and the problems that you have so eloquently talked about?

George
Yes. Some of the SDU and SPU* members were incorporated into the police service. One never believed that these two groups would work without problems with each other. But through the series of discussions that took

place amongst them, today the crime around that area is decreased, looking at the police statistics …

And there are a lot of youth groupings trying to formulate themselves into some kind of a club. For instance I can mention *Itembalethu*, which is existing in Katlehong, trying to bring all the youth who were affected by the violence together and think about things that they might do to try and develop the community, to try and restore a dignity of the youth, to try and restore a culture of living because the most problematic thing is going to school.

Commissioner
Thank you very much George for coming forward. I mean the way we have interacted with you, it is a situation where one has got a split between one's heart and one's mind … Having made that almost apology on our part, I really want to thank you. You are one of the survivors in this country who is a source of encouragement. The past was difficult, but young people, given an opportunity, are able to make sense of what they went through and to pursue positive goals and we thank you very much.

We hope you will be the agent even in your community to help other young people to think about these things and to plan for the better future for all. Thank you.

March 1999
George Ndlozi is now 26 years old. Even before the TRC started its work he had been using his experience and skills to work towards a peaceful democratic election in 1994. In May 1994, after the election, all SDUs and SPUs were dissolved, with some members being integrated into the Police Force and other choosing to continue their education. The above-mentioned President's Project formed the framework within which previously warring factions cooperated towards the upliftment of their communities and shared responsibility for building schools, clinics, playgrounds, radio stations and took responsibility for various other social and cultural programmes. Progress depended on groups co-operating with each other.

George contributed to the success of the pilot project. He took part in peace negotiations between the ANC and the IFP in his region. He was involved in

*security operations to protect the election process. As an employee of the TRC he
worked in the Investigative Unit and encouraged other youths to testify.*

*In January 1999 he became a student at the University of the Witwatersrand,
studying International Relations, Sociology and History. His aim is to represent
his country abroad as a diplomat.*

*In a telephone interview in March 1999 he told us: 'I think that I can
contribute to the future of my country, now that we are free. I am optimistic about
my future because I know people who believe in me and who support me. There is
something else I would like to do, but I do not know yet how: I want to help the
children of my former SDU comrades who were murdered. I knew many of their
fathers. Many look so much like their fathers that I always think of them when I
look at these children. I want to make sure that they will have a future.'*

NOSIPHO MARWEXU

'I was pregnant when they tortured me ...'

*Nosipho Blossom Marwexu[6], born in 1966, was in Standard 9 (Grade 11) of the
Qaqamba High School in Duncan Village near East London in the Eastern Cape
when she learnt that the police were looking for her. The then nineteen-year-old
student was not aware of any reason why she should be wanted by the police. She
had joined COSAS before the organisation was banned in 1985. Her only 'crime'
appeared to be that some members of the police force still knew her as a COSAS
activist. During the State of Emergency in 1985 she had to leave home and go into
hiding.*

We have chosen Nosipho Marwexu's testimony because it illustrates the
ruthlessness with which women, even young pregnant women, were
treated at the time, sometimes by policemen who were once neighbours in
their own communities.

TRC HEARING IN EAST LONDON, 12 JUNE 1997

Nosipho Marwexu
There were riots at Duncan Village. The police then would regularly come

to my home looking for me. I got a message that the police are looking for me. I left and stayed at Mdantsane, NU15[7], with my sister. My mother said that I must just go and surrender to the police because she could not sleep, the police were regularly there. They were going to arrest her if I did not give myself up. I then said I would go to the Cambridge Police Station.

But Heather, my sister, said that I should go to Cape Town to my eldest sister. I went to Cape Town. I stayed there in 1985. In 1986, May, I came back. I thought that perhaps everything had subsided. On 18 June I was at home sleeping. There was a knock at the door. It was the police. It was about one or two a.m. My mother opened the door. When they got in they did not say anything to my mother. They were with a policeman who knows me, Mandisi Mbewana. They could not see me, because I had covered myself. They said to my mother that they are going to arrest her if they cannot find me. They then took me. However, they took my two other brothers as well – Thembinkosi and Mbuyiseli.

I was in pyjamas. They did not even let me change. When I got outside I saw a Casspir*. They put me into that vehicle. It was packed with people. They were probably going around collecting people. They took us to a place called Strongpoint where the soldiers were in Duncan Village.

The next morning we were taken to Cambridge Police Station. The Captain asked what the charges were. This man then responded that he did not know. He was just given a list to arrest all the people. Mr Mandisi Mbewana, who knew me, came saying that he wanted all of us at Westbank. We were taken to Westbank.

We could not even get visitors for two months. They had arrested me, I was in pyjamas. I was using the clothes that they provided for me in prison. I was three months pregnant. Then the interrogation started.

They took us one by one to Cambridge. They asked me if I knew that COSAS had been banned. I said yes. So they asked me why I worked for COSAS even though it had been banned. I said I did no such. They then said that I was a member at, of COSAS at Qaqamba. They asked if I know that the riots at Duncan Village were all inspired by Qaqamba students. They asked who had burnt down a policeman's house. I said I did not know.

They took me back to the cell. They called me back. I did not know I was going to go there. I was going to Frere Hospital regularly at that time. They said that I am supposed to go to the Frere Hospital. I told them that I had no appointment there. Nomsa's attorney, a co-prisoner, gave me her headscarf to put on.

They took me to Cambridge to an office there. Mr Mpumelelo Madliwa was there and Mpumelelo Nkonzombi. They asked me who had burnt down his house. I said I do not know. They strangled me. They pulled down my headscarf, put it around my neck. The one pulled from the left and the other from the right. I lost all strength. I urinated on myself. I was pregnant at the time.

They said I must tell the truth, who burnt the house down. I said it was me. Who else? I said by myself. They told me that I was lying. They put down the headscarf and they strangled me with their own hands. They were not beating me up, just strangling me. What happened is that my eyes went red.

Commissioner
How long had you been in prison by then?

Nosipho
It was around September.

Commissioner
You had been arrested in June?

Nosipho
Yes.

Commissioner
You were on your own. What happened?

Nosipho
They would take me to the Frere Hospital at the clinic there regularly. From solitary confinement they took me to Cambridge again. On 6 December …

I started hurting – contractions. I was then taken to hospital. I gave birth to a premature child at seven months. There was a policeman at my side all the time. I got out, back to the prison with my child, Thinasonke[8]. In the morning they would come and count us and they would take my child and bring the baby back late.

Commissioner
Where would you sleep in the cell?

Nosipho
On the floor.

Commissioner
With the baby?

Nosipho
Yes.

Commissioner
Do you know who looked after the child, who fed the child?

Nosipho
No, when I would ask they would say that they would take the child to the crèche.

Commissioner
What happened eventually?

Nosipho
When they felt like releasing me they just released me.

Commissioner
What month was that?

Nosipho
It was in 1987. I cannot remember whether it was March or April.

Commissioner
How old was the child?

Nosipho
Three months.

Commissioner
Were you politically active at the time?

Nosipho
Yes, I was a COSAS member before COSAS was banned and then after that it was banned.

Commissioner
Thereafter, no charges were laid against you? That was the end of your harassment?

Nosipho
They put me into a car and took me to a taxi rank. They told me that the people that I had been arrested with were still in jail. I was the only one who had been released. I was free but I was not allowed to meet more than one person at a time. Otherwise it was a political meeting.

Commissioner
How did they treat you when you were actually pregnant, before you had your baby?

Nosipho
They swore at me, saying I am a bitch. They said they had wasted a lot of the Government's money looking for me ... they were strangling me and said I am going to tell the truth, whether I like it or not. I gave them the truth that was not really the truth ...

Commissioner
If you were a man they would not have said that to you. Is it all they said to you?

Nosipho
Well, they said much more, but I cannot repeat those swear words.

Commissioner
Okay, we respect that. Thank you very much ... Did you know Nkonzombi
or Mbewana before the arrest and the torture? Did you know them?

Nosipho
I knew him well. Mr Mbewana was my father's friend. He, we were
neighbours. My father called him uncle ... I was shocked in the way he
treated me.

Commissioner
Nosipho, thank you so much for sharing your painful story with us. Perhaps
some other people, especially people who are not women, do not know the
significance of giving birth to a child. I do not know how it would be to give
birth to a child and have to keep that child in the first few months in prison.
Your story is very painful especially because your baby would be taken
from you for the whole day ... Women have suffered in a way that men,
perhaps, can never understand, and I hope that the men in this hall are
listening so that this does not happen again in future. Thank you so much.

April 1999
*Nosipho Marwexu is now thirty-three years old. She is unemployed and suffers
from arthritis, which she believes is due to the conditions of her detention. Her
daughter Thinasonke is now twelve years old, very small for her age, and suffers
from chronic hoarseness. Nosipho has not yet received any compensation through
the TRC but is still hopeful because she knows of others who have received money.
She requests Karin to make enquiries through the Black Sash Advice Office.*

CHRIS VAN EEDEN, JANNIE DU PLESSIS, CHRISTO UYS
'The freedom struggle is not unknown to the Afrikaner!'

*Three young Afrikaners appear before the Truth Commission as representatives of
the Junior Rapportryers. According to its manifesto, this organisation is not directly*

linked to any political party. It is dedicated to promoting the Afrikaans language and is a forum for supporting the interests of Afrikaners in business and in the cultural domain. Membership is open to all male Afrikaans-speaking South Africans who identify with the aims of the organisation – 'orientation around the language, identity and religion of the Afrikaner'. The political campaigns of the movement fall within a conservative orientation, for example the campaign for reintroducing the death penalty (which has been abolished under the new Constitution). According to information from a member of the executive in June 1999, membership of the Junior Rapportryers is open to other population groups provided they share its aims.

In fact, the Junior Rapportryers were known to be a feeder organisation of the powerful Broederbond, the Afrikaner secret society which, for a long time, exercised a pervasive influence in South Africa and to which the majority of leading Afrikaner businessmen, civil servants, educationists and politicians belonged.

Chris van Eeden, born in 1962, was president of the Junior Rapportryers at the time of the TRC Hearings. Jannie du Plessis and Christo Uys were members of the executive. They chose to appear before the TRC as they felt that it had marginalised the voice of the Afrikaner and had discriminated against white South Africans, particularly Afrikaners. Two years later they reflected differently on the experience. Chris van Eeeden felt he had been treated fairly and found the process to be a liberating experience and the treatment evenhanded. The Commission had listened without prejudice, had asked appropriate clarifying questions, and had been approachable and open. Jannie du Plessis still voiced the reservation that, through the findings of the TRC, Afrikaners would be characterised as monsters in future history books. However, he, too, was pleased to have had the opportunity to speak before the TRC and to tell his story 'to say how it was for those of us who actually were in the army, on the border, and in the Police Force'. He still viewed the Commission as one-sided and out to 'conduct a witchhunt against Afrikaners'.

TRC HEARING IN JOHANNESBURG, 12 JUNE 1997

Commissioner
You come to us to discuss with us the perspective of the young Afrikaner, most possibly the young Afrikaner man as seen in the whole movement

and we are open to listen to that. As with other submissions, we also realise and we accept that it represents a specific perspective and not the whole truth, but your truth as you see it. And against that background can you please discuss it with us.

Chris van Eeden:
Mr Malan, thank you very much. I want to emphasise that we don't talk on behalf of the Afrikaner youth, but we do this submission so that we hope that it can in fact lead to reconciliation and that people will in fact have greater understanding of each other and all South Africans. Afrikaners aren't perhaps as happy with the objectivity of the Truth Commission, but perhaps today is a step to put it in a different light.

Your mandate is to establish reconciliation, but the ideal for that reconciliation does not only depend on the fact that we can put the history in perspective, but also how the Afrikaner youth experience things at present and perhaps part of the submission will fall outside of your mandate. We ask that you will be patient and listen to it so that you can get the whole picture. I will ask Christo Uys to continue with the first part of the submission.

Christo Uys
Mr Malan, today we listened to how the last twenty years affected the youth of South Africa. Young Afrikaners were also affected by the last twenty years and we are wholeheartedly part of South Africa and part of this past history.

If one listens to how Afrikaners are pictured, it is often quite difficult for us to make a contribution at forums such as this because we as Afrikaners are proud of the contribution that we have made.

It would perhaps help if we give you a short background. You know, the freedom struggle is not unknown to the Afrikaner. The Afrikaner was most probably one of the first groups on this continent who stood up against colonialism[9], and we young Afrikaners grew up in this tradition.

And today we could therefore sit here and we could understand this whole struggle of the SDUs. Our forefathers' struggle was against the colonial way of thinking and it was a struggle for the Afrikaner. As history shows us, they tried to establish freedom for us as youth and they had different strategies.

The history has changed and the Afrikaner is part of a changing process where this freedom is still very important for us. In the past twenty years – in the 1970s and 1980s – our generation could do nothing more to stop the growth of black nationalism or to try and change history. We were born in the struggle. The war on the border was in progress and within South Africa there was a freedom struggle.

Today it is seen as a very just struggle, but the effects thereof were not always as just and we took part in this. And this was the struggle that we fought in the police and in the army – we did our service. Those of us who weren't in the police or did our national service prepared ourselves at school and university to play an active role in the economy of South Africa.

Sometimes it is overlooked and forgotten that we also played a role in the struggle against communism. Today it is seen to be ludicrous, but we believed that we did play a positive role there.

And in essence our struggle was against anarchy. Today we listened to how anarchy was prevalent in black communities, how it affected people's lives. There were references made to kangaroo courts* and to necklacing. This also affected us.

As a national serviceman in the army I believed, and I was sure that I contributed to keeping people's lives safe. We also heard about a lot of different atrocities that took place. The moment that an Afrikaner says it, it is not believed, but you know that while I was in the army, I didn't receive commands or instructions that led to the violation of human rights.

At present we cannot deny the existence thereof, but the majority of young Afrikaners such as myself and my friends here, tried to fight a just cause and we won this cause, the struggle. Is this something that could be perhaps contested? No.

The fact that we today have the infrastructure in this country that is the best in Africa; the fact that we have the potential to grow economically, that to me is proof that we succeeded in making a great contribution towards a peaceful transition in South Africa.

You know democracy is a wonderful thing, but you cannot eat it and it doesn't keep you warm in winter. If in South Africa there had been a transfer to a new democracy very hastily, we could also have awakened today in Bosnia.

Reconciliation is in our opinion embedded in respect and therefore we respect the struggle that was referred to in front of the TRC today in evidence, but we also ask that our role should be respected. We also have victims, people who died in the struggle, and eventual reconciliation can only come about if these people are also honoured together ...

Jannie du Plessis

We don't deny in any way that people were prejudiced in the past, we don't have a problem with the essence of affirmative action[10], but it doesn't always work in this way. Now it has become a system where people are appointed not because of the fact that they are well suited for the post, but because of the colour of their skin ...

After how many years will this now be put right? Five, ten years?

The next thing is the fact that Afrikaans is not recognised. The government and its departments discriminate against Afrikaans. There are eleven official languages in South Africa, but the indigenous languages are in fact diminished in favour of English. All the official documents make use of English. Afrikaans, the third biggest language spoken in South Africa, is ignored ... Even the TRC's whole attitude towards Afrikaans is not acceptable ...

Today we listened to atrocities and violations against children. No right-minded person would ever arrest children without a reason. Any paedophile or criminal who does this must be arrested and pay for his deeds.

I support Graça Machel's view that children should not be used in war. Today only one side of the whole situation was looked at and the Junior Rapportryersbeweging also believes and trusts that the other side of the story will also be looked at. Who were the monsters who used children in this political struggle? It must be determined which groups of people used children to burn down schools, throw stones, and then also to do the necklace murders. And in the interest of reconciliation, the TRC must be unbiased, otherwise it will be a futile exercise that will not lead to reconciliation.

We worked hard at becoming free – it was already mentioned that we had two Anglo-Boer wars. We fought against Queen Elizabeth and oppression and Afrikaners are people from Africa. We are here and we are here to stay ...

I want to conclude – we would like to extend a hand of friendship to all young South Africans, people who live with us in this country. We believe through mutual respect for each other's needs, values, we can enter the future.

Commissioner

Thank you very much gentlemen. In the TRC we come from different parts of the country. In a certain sense I have come through the route that you have come through. I am also in your shoes – one of your predecessors. Twenty-three years earlier I was also President of this movement, so I listened with empathy to what you had to say.

My first reaction was to actually to interrupt, but then I decided to stand back. But there are a few questions that I would like to ask. Where you criticise, we have to handle the criticism and not debate this with you, that is not my plan.

You refer to evidence of things that you didn't know of. Is it possible perhaps to elaborate on that? The extent of evidence concerning murders, torturing people, how do you experience it, what is the reaction of the Afrikaner young men in your organisation?

Chris

In our organisation there are a couple of thousand young men and more than fifty percent of them were National Servicemen, the rest were too young, and with my work in the JRB, I see most of these people during the year and we talk to each other.

I don't want to blame the TRC, but we always use the same names, the same police and Defence Units, but there is no mention made of the majority of people who were in the police and the Defence Force, that they weren't involved in this.

They provided a service for the country, because they loved the country as is the case at present and they might do it again.

Commissioner

Could I just interrupt you here, because I think we've got the message. I refer to the other part – you hear the same names and things, but those are things that you didn't hear when you were in the army, that is my question.

Chris

I can honestly say to you that these kinds of acts no one can approve of. It makes you furious and angry because that is not what I myself and thousands of young Afrikaner men ...why we got involved in the struggle.

Commissioner

Can I take the question a bit further? How is it possible that we didn't know anything of it or did anything about it? Do you have a perspective on that?

Chris

War as such is a crime against humanity, there are no victors. I had personal knowledge because I saw it, of certain of these actions that took place. I saw the result of bodies being burnt, I had knowledge of that.

I didn't have knowledge of orchestrated efforts of forces that I served to incite such incidents.

Commissioner

You say that you saw bodies that were burnt – what did you think was the reason for that?

Chris

I didn't have to think of what the reason was, it was quite clear. I did my service in the Vaal Triangle and at that stage it was in the midst of the whole issue in the 1990s and it was black-on-black violence.

That it could have been incited from another force, well we have evidence for that now. But I have personal knowledge of violence between ethnic groups, black ethnic groups.

Commissioner
You never saw some kind of an orchestrated effort from Government?

Chris
No, I never experienced it as such and I think the evidence came as a shock.

Commissioner
I don't want to labour this point, but I think it is perhaps necessary to just press on this, when you refer to reconciliation that is based on respect. You said that everybody must be honoured, not just the one side.

Mr Du Plessis said that no person in his right mind would arrest children without reason. I think I am quoting you correctly, but he also referred to the monsters who used children and used them in the conflict, and pushed them ahead in this conflict.

... I don't want to challenge you, but I want to contrast it with the other statement that the children would have been incited by the other side. So the old order, were the only right-minded people, but those who stood up against the old order, those were the monsters – that is the contrast that came through in what you said, would you like to comment on that?

Jannie
I feel very strongly about that, that a child's place is not in the midst of a war. He is not there to carry weapons. Any action where children are abused in this process, must be condemned. If we look at the past we see that there were children that were arrested and there were children who were thrown in jails – we cannot justify that. You cannot also justify that children are abused in a struggle. Both sides of this perspective must be investigated in the same detail.

Commissioner
Could I just perhaps be a devil's advocate here in my last question. Today

you attended the proceedings and I thank you for that. If you look at the way that the Commissioners went about the testimony, the questions they asked, do you feel that there are questions that should have been asked, that they didn't ask? Did you experience bias, prejudice?

Chris
No, the day itself wasn't a problem, it wasn't difficult. I think prejudice and bias perhaps, yes, because the one side of the struggle is seen as more justified than the other side. It appears that if you plant a bomb against apartheid, it is not as bad as planting a bomb for apartheid. For our young people just out of school, a crime is a crime. A young Afrikaner coming from school, if he applies for a bursary or goes for a job, and people say 'but sorry you have got the wrong skin colour', those are people who have to work in the future', he doesn't really understand the past, because he wasn't there, but he is now paying for it.

And this is what we ask of you today, don't discriminate against people who weren't part of the struggle. This is a person who must build with others a new South Africa, so we cannot now allow a situation that in twenty years you have Afrikaners, a whole generation, who feel that they have been discriminated against. We must stop it now and the TRC is the instrument that can do it, and you must really do this out of your own conviction. And this is what we tried to do with our perspective.

Commissioner
We take note of what you say. I want to thank you for being here, but I would also like to thank you and your organisation for your cooperation in getting information in front of us, such as Organisations of Equality before the Rights. You are one of the few organisations from the old order who actively cooperated to present us with a perspective that we would not have had and we would like to thank you for that.

LAURIE NATHAN
'We never regarded ourselves as heroes ... and certainly not as victims ...'

Laurie Nathan, born in Cape Town in 1959, was educated at the South African College High School (SACS) before he enrolled as a student at the University of Cape Town. From the beginning of the 1980s he worked on the topic of war resistance and he became one of the founders of the End Conscription Campaign (ECC)*. After the arrests of several activists under the State of Emergency he went into hiding from June 1985 to December 1986. Today he is Director of the Centre for Conflict Resolution attached to the University of Cape Town.

Laurie Nathan's statement was chosen because it illustrates the engagement of whites against apartheid under the umbrella of the ECC. It shows that some whites, too, were prepared to face harassment, detention or exile in that cause. Even though this resistance was sustained by only a very small minority within the white community, it is important to acknowledge its source and to understand the significance of these courageous actions in the context of the time.

TRC HEARING IN CAPE TOWN, 23 JULY 1997

Laurie Nathan

Good afternoon Commissioners, ladies and gentlemen. I've been invited to do a presentation on the End Conscription Campaign. Since the ECC was disbanded some years ago I obviously don't speak on anybody's behalf but offer some personal reflections. I was involved in the founding of the End Conscription Campaign in the early 80s. I subsequently served as National Organiser of ECC in 1985 and '86 and after that for a short period was Chair of ECC in Cape Town. Currently I am Director of the Centre for Conflict Resolution at the University of Cape Town. The War Resistance Movement in South Africa began in earnest in the late 1970s, following South Africa's invasion of Angola in 1975 and the Soweto uprising the following year. It manifested itself in a number of different forms, one of which was a group of conscripts going into exile where they joined the ANC. Some of them formed COSAW, the Committee on South African War Resistance with the aim of raising international awareness about the role of the SADF and providing support to objectors in exile.

The Government's response was to increase the penalty for conscientious objection to a maximum of six years in prison. The draconian measures had the opposite effect.

At its annual conference in 1983 the Black Sash made the first call for an end to conscription and shortly thereafter the ECC was established. One of the particularly exciting things about the campaign at the time was that we were a broad coalition – we had within our ranks English and Afrikaans-speaking people, school pupils, students and parents. Some of us regarded ourselves as liberals, others as radicals, Marxists, pacifists, Christians, humanists, we had rock musicians, poets, artists and all of these different sectors were able, through the ECC, to campaign against conscription in a way they felt comfortable. So we had traditional political activities like mass meetings etc, but we [also had] rock concerts with the title 'Rock against the Ratel' [the Ratel being the name of a military or police vehicle]. We built sand castles on Clifton beach in the shape of the Castle [Military Headquarters in the Western Cape] in Cape Town. The police came onto the beach in uniform in the middle of summer, can you imagine: Clifton beach! Police came onto the beach in uniform with their boots, and broke down the castles!

In the streets of Pretoria early one morning we tied yellow ribbons to trees and street poles as an effort to make the point that we were calling for troops out of townships, out of Namibia and out of Angola. Before the ECC activists were arrested the police climbed up the trees, up the poles, to untie the yellow ribbons.

We were serious about what we did, but I simply make the point at this stage that we were engaged in a kind of political activity that was dynamic and creative. We had a sense of purpose but we pursued the purpose having fun in the process.

I want to read the ECC Declaration because it sums up the mission of the campaign.

'This Declaration is headed towards a just peace in our land, a Declaration to end conscription. We live in an unjust society where basic human rights are denied to the majority of the people. We live in an unequal society where the land and wealth are owned by the minority. We live in a society in a state of civil war, where brother is called on to fight brother. We call for an end to conscription.

'Young men are conscripted to maintain the illegal occupation of Namibia and to wage unjust war against foreign countries. Young men are conscripted to assist in the implementation and defence of apartheid policies. Young men who refuse to serve are faced with the choice of a life of exile or a possible six years in prison. We call for an end to conscription.

'We believe that the financial costs of the war increase the poverty of our country and that money should be used rather in the interests of peace. We believe that the extension of conscription to coloured and Indian youth will increase conflict and further divide our country. We believe that it is the moral right of South Africans to exercise freedom of conscience and to choose not to serve in the SADF. We call for an end to conscription! We call for a just peace in our land!'

That was our Declaration of Intent and it captures neatly the objectives of our organisation. We set up ECC and we pursued our campaigns for three principal reasons.

The first was a matter of conscience. In conscience we were not prepared to take up arms in defence of apartheid against fellow citizens.

Secondly, we sought to actively contribute to the struggle against apartheid by opposing conscription and the role of the military, and this obviously had particular political sensitivity. The system of legislated racialism and white rule was rejected by the majority of South Africans. It necessarily relied on the extensive use of force to maintain and perpetuate the system. The role of the defence force and conscription were therefore of critical political and strategic importance to the apartheid government, and by challenging that system we believed that we could contribute to the struggle against apartheid.

Our involvement was also significant precisely because we were white. We had students at Afrikaans-speaking campuses and members of the defence force who would say to us they regarded us as worse than the enemy because we were traitors.

And thirdly, we sought to contribute to non-racialism through our campaign. The ANC and its internal allies sought to make the point in the course of their campaigns that the struggle in South Africa was not a struggle between white and black, it was a struggle between justice and injustice, and that the end goal was not to replace white domination with black domination but to establish a just and non-racial society.

The point was made further that non-racialism could not simply be a goal, it also had to be part of the process. So through our involvement we sought to demonstrate to both the white and the black community that not all whites were racists and some of us at least were committed to a struggle for justice and peace.

The significance of these objectives and the high profile nature of our campaigns led to extensive state repression. We were subjected to merciless vilification, the thrust of which was that we were traitors, cowards, mommy's boys, as Magnus Malan once put it, that we were in bed with Communists and that we were part of the revolutionary onslaught against South Africa.

There were also numerous acts of physical harassment. ECC members were beaten up, we had petrol bombs thrown into our homes, the motor vehicles of ECC activists were on the hit list of the Civil Cooperation Bureau, the CCB*, and during the state of emergency in 1985 roughly seventy or eighty of our activists were detained. The youngest of them was seventeen years old and the oldest seventy-five. Some of the activists were interrogated by military intelligence, others by security police, some were not questioned at all and not one was tried.

In 1988, following the successful court action against the Defence Force, and following also the stand of 143 conscripts who collectively announced their refusal to serve, the ECC was formally banned. It was really only with the lifting of the ban on the ANC that we were once more operative.

Commissioner

Thank you very much, Laurie! I have a comment which is almost like a question as well – the issue of conscience. I think one of the struggles we've had in our society is the difficulty for people to exercise individual decisions and to allow conscience to rise above authority. How best can we teach people strategies of self criticism?

Laurie

I think there are two ways which are extremely important in this regard. The first is the way in which we educate young people and whether we are educating them to be critical or we are discouraging questions and criticisms. The second obvious area is the response of government to criticism. The more tolerant government is of criticism, the more free we citizens will feel to be critical. And I've often made the point in other African countries, when we debate the issue of democracy, to illustrate how free I regard our country, unlike most other African countries. Here someone could stand up in front of Parliament, on a soapbox, and say that he thinks President Mandela is a silly old fool. No one would pay that person any attention. This is not something one can do in authoritarian states, so the degree of tolerance on the part of authorities is obviously critical.

January 1999

A meeting is arranged with Laurie Nathan to pursue some of the issues in his statement and to learn more about the young student then and the respected academic of today. (See Chapter IV)

IV

Peter Chubb

GETTING ON WITH LIFE:
ENCOUNTERS IN
THE PRESENT

WOMEN REFLECTING ON THEN AND NOW

What were the effects on some of those who were closely involved with the process? How do they view that time now – and what do they hope for the future? Three women whose work and life are intimately connected with the ideals of truth and reconciliation speak in this section, and five of the young people who made statements have been tracked down and are interviewed by Karin Chubb.

NOMFUNDO WALAZA

'What gives us the right to speak on behalf of children?'

Cape Town, 3 February 1999

Nomfundo Walaza was born in 1962 in Queenstown, Eastern Cape. Throughout her childhood in Langa, Cape Town, she witnessed human tragedies caused by the implementation of the pass laws*. She attended Langa High School and later studied at the University of Cape Town, where she qualified as a psychologist. Today she is the director of the Trauma Centre in Cowley House, Cape Town, one of several organisations in the country doing important counselling work and struggling to secure funding.

Cowley House, for many years the receiving centre for prisoners released from Robben Island, and for their families visiting the Island, is now dedicated to healing the wounds of the past. Here I meet Nomfundo to ask her about the work of the Centre in relation to the Truth Commission, especially the children's hearings.

It is with a sense of strangeness that I enter the lovely old courtyard, as I remember Cowley House as a very different kind of place. Here, in the bad old days, organisations like the Black Sash tried to make frightened, angry and bewildered people feel a little bit more at home by providing some basic comforts like a hot meal and a lift to the Robben Island ferry which would take them across for that precious visit. It was little enough.

Now, it seems, the ghosts of the past have been exorcised – but have they really? In the past, Cowley House provided psychological counselling for released political prisoners. Nowadays the Centre still treats survivors of our violent political past, but also addresses various forms of community violence by providing counselling for victims of robberies, drive-by shootings and other forms of urban crime.

Nomfundo: One of the needs in Cape Town is to provide psychological services for refugees and asylum seekers. They come from contexts of war and violence. If we are to look at healing the nation, we also need to heal the people who come to the nation. South Africans have not been very welcoming ... in the old days we all hoped that we could connect with the brothers and sisters in the North, but it has become difficult to embrace those from the outside as part of the African continent and deserving to be here. 'African Renaissance'[1] means nothing if we do not welcome our own people.

Could you comment on how you view the TRC hearings?

Some of the people who did not appear in public to tell their stories were furious. They thought their stories were thought to be less important.

In terms of the people who did appear ... there was not enough preparation for what 'breaking the silence' could really mean. Many people had to relive trauma of the most intimate kind, like women telling how they were raped. Many variables affect how the truth is told, and what effect this has. Whether the audience is responsive or not can affect how much of the truth is remembered. Then there are other things, like the lights, the media, the interpreters ... there are many factors. It can be very traumatic.

In the light of what you are saying: was it a good decision not to have children under eighteen give evidence?

That is debatable. One never knows ... much hinges on preparation. There are kids who can cope with it and kids who can't. For me the question also is who is in the audience. It is not appropriate to have six-, seven- or eight-year-olds speak for themselves. But when we get to twelve and beyond, we are looking at another level of development. They could well testify directly, especially with a person whom they trust. They could then speak in their own voice.

One finds resilience and strength in young people. For me it is about giving space to the people who have to speak and not obscuring the truth through others. If I talk on behalf of a 14-year-old ... there is no way I can give meaning to that. We acknowledge that the process was traumatic for some individuals – but it is different when experts testify on behalf of children. If you want to capture the essence of what it is like to be a teenager, you can only find it in that generation.

We are talking on behalf of somebody about experiences which are still there, which will never go. We so often speak on behalf of others, as teachers, as academics. It is really shocking. ... In fact, speaking on behalf of others, unconscious of the things we do, we render their voices silent, perhaps for ever.

We are so much afraid of feeling and of hearing ... we fear that we might feel so much more when we allow people to speak on their own behalf. So we protect ourselves by speaking for them.

Even amongst those who spoke, the emphasis was very much on the male voice. In the TRC documentation there is a very high percentage of male testimony. The women who do speak do so about their husbands, sons and fathers – not really about themselves.

Yes. The first woman in the very first TRC hearing in East London spoke about her husband who was killed. I only learned later from the reports in the newspapers that she herself had been tortured. ... For me, it was the mission of the TRC to render those voices audible, to listen, to ask: What did you suffer? This did not really happen, although the TRC had a number of women in it. We live in a patriarchal world where men are the heroes.

The TRC has, for example, not documented the stories of women who were traumatised by the Pass Laws. I remember, when I was a child growing up in Langa, that I would wake up in the morning and, maybe three or four times a week, find women squatting underneath our hedge. They had run away from the police in the night. Many had jumped out of the windows in the hostels to avoid arrest.

As a young child, I started to become afraid of growing up. I looked at these women and thought, 'I don't want to grow up because maybe when I am older, that will be my fate.' You do not understand such things as a child, you do not know who is targeted by these laws and who is not. Whatever explanation you get, you still harbour fears. Even if you have the right dompas* you still think this could happen to you if you go into Cape Town, for instance. I feared that I would not be safe. So you start to question the way you are located in the world.

I used to visit a friend in Rondebosch. One day she could not pick me up at the station and I had to walk along the street to her house. I was a very tall teenager of fourteen. Suddenly I saw a police van in the street and I could not move an inch. I was afraid, because I did not have a dompas and I was terrified that they might think I was already sixteen, because I was so tall. So I just stood there, not knowing what to do, and wished I could just disappear.

The police van came and passed by, the policemen smiled at me. But my heart was pounding … for the first time I realised that I could not just walk anywhere. Even now – 22 years later – I remember exactly where I stood and how I felt. I remember that moment of near-paralysis and thinking, 'I can't move'. When they had gone it was such a relief to find that I could still walk to my friend's house without feeling … totally dead. This is just one little story that is still there. There are millions like this. …

I now hear the echoes of these stories from the young children of asylum seekers. There are echoes of the same kind of thing: a different child, a different mother – but the same fear, the fear of annihilation.

I used to hear the women who had been arrested under the pass laws in the Langa Police Station when I walked home from school as a child. There were tiny windows, high up and with bars. The women could not reach the windows, but they used to shout and scream at the tops of their voices: 'Please go to room number such-and-such and tell my husband that I am here!' These women and their stories are now lost, the trauma of having to carry a child through a pass raid and staying in the police station ... Those are the everyday stories of how people had to survive. These stories are still not being told – and there was no space within the TRC where they could be told.

But has that not opened the way for us to say that more stories must be told? Some more of those that are still hidden?

Yes, it's probably given an impetus to that. My sense is that women and youth must be listened to. Men will have more ways of getting their story heard, many of them, because of their position in society. But my sense is that women will not get to that point, not unless they do something for themselves. We need more story-telling initiatives, for two reasons.

Firstly, we need to acknowledge the people whose story it is by creating a space where they can tell their story – not us telling it. Secondly, things are moving at a rapid pace and the young children do not know the stories, they do not know about women jumping out of windows to escape arrest in a pass raid. They are born of the mothers who hold those stories, but often the mothers do not think that the stories are important. There has to be an appropriate space for telling the stories, and it must be contained, so that the stories are not misinterpreted. Sometimes mothers can manipulate children with tales of the hardships they had to endure. They make them feel guilty that way, and this should not happen.

Nomfundo, what is your sense of what should happen now, beyond story telling? What should be happening post-TRC? Many youths are so bitter and they feel that they have wasted their lives and that nothing has really changed for them.

I think it is so very important to acknowledge. Sometimes we think in terms of money, but acknowledging pain and suffering and sacrifice goes a long way.

And I suppose we do not do that enough. We tend to just get on with life.

Yes, we think people are going to sort themselves out. The government should acknowledge that the brunt of the struggle has been carried by the youth. People often look at what Madiba* and other high-profile people who are now in Parliament have suffered. We must acknowledge all the others, all the sacrifices, all the missed opportunities. And we must also do something. We should ask the youth what is important to them. Some might want to complete their education, some will want other things.

We need to talk about their stories and to make sure that coming generations know them.

This whole question of losing identity bothers me. Black children who went to private schools or Model C schools[2] ... they became abridged versions of human beings in society, who do not know their own language. They have distanced themselves from their culture and its rituals. In a way they have disconnected themselves from their ancestors. In terms of the soul and the spirit, there is no connection – because they do not know who they are.

I am not saying that the private school system is wrong ... but one should not have to pay that price for it. I saw a woman here at the Trauma Centre who told me: 'My mother is appalled by the creature she has created.' This woman spent most of her life in private schools. She speaks English fluently but little Xhosa. When her mother expected her to perform cultural rituals when she came of age, she refused: 'You can't expect me to have any connection with that, having grown up as I did. I am not going to any rural areas, I am not having a sheep slaughtered for me. As far as I am concerned, that is cruelty to animals.'

In a very interesting way, in the quest to better ourselves we have killed the essence of who we are. That is a tragedy. Look at the generations of the eighties and nineties ... that people do not do something about that!

I am not saying that we should move back in time. Culture is not static, culture moves on. But there are certain tenets by which we live, certain beliefs that we have about our world and who we are, that make us, in interaction with others, to be solidly grounded in our identity, so that we can interact on an equal footing. But if I have imbibed most of your culture and what you are ...

Because I have told you that your culture is worthless ...

... then what happens is that I can never be talking with you on an equal footing. What makes you and I talk as equals now is that you know who you are and I know who I am. If I don't know that, or if I am an abridged version of you, then there is a problem.

And a hierarchy, because I would be on top....

... and that would be what I am aspiring to be. That brings frustration, anxiety, alienation, anger – and that is what we are seeing around us now. This violence we are experiencing now, there are layers and layers of disconnectedness to ourselves and who we are. It is a misplaced search for identity which relaunches itself in violent outrage. Individuals are hijacking a community struggle because of their own sense of being deprived of who they are.

That would explain why it is happening now, why it has not happened before.

It is also because we as black people are no longer fighting a common enemy. Now the divisions start to appear and we have to face who we are.

We are a society in crisis. It is a crisis about how we redefine ourselves. We were defined as objects, as outcasts. Now that we are in control – how do we deal with that? We have forgotten about the notion of being blacks.

The divisions are becoming clearer – and the task for us as educators and psychologists is in seeing that certain work needs to be done. It is at least a comfort that one can do something ...

Yes, one can do, but we all have to pull together. And we have to understand the broader contexts within which we work. It is important also who does the work. Professionals have to be activists in their minds. A narrow, specialised focus which is typical of a Eurocentric model, would not be appropriate. You need people who are thinking much more broadly than within their own narrow disciplines. We need to be activists in our minds ...

GLENDA WILDSCHUT
'Being a Commissioner was intensely lonely.'

Cape Town, 4 February 1999
Glenda Wildschut, born in 1953 in District Six,* Cape Town, attended the Alexander Sinton High School before she qualified as a psychiatric nurse at the Tygerberg Nursing College. She also studied Psychology and Physiology at the University of the Western Cape. In 1995 she was appointed as Commissioner to the TRC. In 1998 she adopted a son, Grant Sipho.

The decision to interview Glenda was natural, as she was one of the Commissioners most involved with youth hearings. My memory of Glenda goes back to cooking sessions at Cowley House, where, on holidays when the regular kitchen staff were given leave, members of the Black Sash would help to prepare huge meals for returning prisoners and families visiting political prisoners on Robben Island. Glenda was also a member of the small group of psychologists, nurses and other health professionals who, in spite of the draconian security laws and the states of emergency, would address house meetings of the Black Sash to inform us of conditions in prisons and the trauma faced by detainees and families.

Our meeting at her home in Cape Town starts with some delay, as I am totally captivated by Grant Sipho, her beautiful, 11-month-old adopted son: 'He has kept me sane throughout this time,' she laughs, proudly.

Glenda has become wary of interviews and is frank in voicing her misgivings about 'the many academics now descending on the TRC material in order to gain degrees, but without being emotionally involved, without necessarily also having a passion for what they are doing'.

Glenda, what do you think of when you now reflect on your time as Commissioner of the TRC?

Glenda: We have been so very fortunate in this country. We have been given a chance, an enormous amount of grace as a people. This country could so easily have descended into total anarchy, especially after the assassination of Chris Hani in 1993. It has been very moving for me to experience how people have responded to the TRC in many different parts of the country and in the most remote rural areas. They kept saying, in diverse ways, how much it meant that they could, for the first time, tell their story in dignity. 'Nobody has listened before like you have now done,' is what we kept hearing.

Often they asked us, the TRC, to help them reach out to the people they had injured. The perpetrators had a deep need to be restored to the communities, often their own, which they had violated – but in which they nevertheless belonged.

An example was in Upington, after a hearing in which a policeman testified – he had killed a child. We returned, some time after the TRC hearing, to a meeting where the community had gathered to hear the perpetrator. He spoke from the heart, addressing all the people gathered there. He was shaking with anxiety when he told them, from his perspective, what had happened. You could feel the tension in the room when he explained that he had joined the police because there was no other way to put food on the table for his family. At the time, the community had felt that he was a sellout, there had been an angry confrontation and an attack. In panic and out of pure fear he had shot and killed the young boy. He then left to go and live in Namibia.

But he came to the TRC to ask the community's forgiveness and to be restored to his people. In front of all the people gathered in the hall, he talked to the murdered boy's aunt. Eventually she said: 'I am but one member of my family. You need to come with your family to our family. We need to have a meeting.' The upshot was that they had this meeting of families at which the conflict was laid to rest. Then the whole village had a church service and a feast afterwards, so that he was re-integrated into the community. No court case will ever achieve that, because court cases are about retributive justice. This, on the other hand, was about healing and bringing a person back to live among his people. There are several such stories in the TRC. This is by no means a unique story.

Yet we did not really do anything. We were simply part of that narrative after the hearings and the official record-taking had been concluded. We only asked the community what, arising from the TRC process, the issues were for them – and there it was.

But without the TRC that could not have happened.

No. There had to be the official acknowledgement, the public recognition of people's stories.

I use the term 'forgiveness' very hesitatingly, as I don't really know what it means outside a strictly religious context. Let's put it this way: It appears to me that the TRC has enabled people to restore each other as human beings in each other's eyes. Perhaps that is what people can do more freely now: acknowledge each other's humanity.

It is so humbling to experience that, as we are not talking about people who have a sophisticated understanding of what these concepts mean. People are just doing.

I experienced some of that in the '80s, when I often wondered where the women found the strength to just keep going, while they and their families were harassed by police, detained, killed … and they just somehow went on, often under the worst socio-economic conditions. I remember how Nomaindia Mfekheto[3] came out of a long period of detention to attend the funeral of her son.

Yes, those terrible years … That was the time when I, after I had started my training as a nurse, asked myself what I could bring to the struggle. I had read Don Foster's book[4] and I decided to react to it. That is when a few of us health workers founded the Detention Treatment Team (DTT). To provide support to detainees and their families.

I was then also involved in providing logistical and other support for young MK-operatives. For example, I worked with Colleen Williams and Robby Waterwitch.[5] Colleen was a very active organiser and brought me in to help prepare young operatives for what could lie ahead of them if they were captured. The idea was to target young people at risk of being detained and to inform them of what they could expect in detention. We explained how the interrogators worked and how their techniques could affect the body and the mind, like the effects of sleep deprivation or sensory deprivation.

Looking at the TRC process, how did you cope with that enormous stress?

I had to have major surgery while I served on the TRC, and it was then that I decided to adopt Grant Sipho. The Archbishop was very supportive of me – he christened Grant and he really is Grant's Tatamkhulu.[6] I often felt that having the baby kept me sane in all the horror of the hearings.

Being a Commissioner was intensely lonely. You could not share anything. Often when I returned home at night to my family I became angry at their normality because I could not enter into it. Normal daily life was like watching a video – it had nothing to do with me.

Sometimes, when I walked on the beach and saw mothers playing with their children, I burst into tears – because so many mothers are without their children.

Perhaps it was good that I cried then, as it helped me not to break down during the actual hearings. Then it was the victims' moment, with the focus being on their story. We had to be careful not to divert attention to the Commissioners. My private moments of depression were probably important because of that.

Especially during the youth hearings, it must have been extremely difficult to be a Commissioner.

As you know, I was one of the Commissioners who insisted that we should have youth hearings. It was clear that young people needed space to tell their own stories. But we hit on a snag, because we did not want to expose very young people to the glare of publicity.

The United Nations Children's Charter specifies that children should be able to tell their own story. We knew, however, that we were followed by the world's media and we simply could not guarantee that all journalists would treat such hearings sensitively and carefully.

That is why the Commission decided to let young people tell retrospective narratives, with those who were eighteen and older talking about their experiences as children. We were severely criticised for this, but we really tried to be as responsible as we could. Graça Machel, for example, was very critical of our decision not to let children under eighteen testify.

For children younger than eighteen we had in-camera sessions, with professionals present who helped children to tell their stories with the aid of drawings. Then we also had the paintings and drawings at the public hearings.

In the Western Cape the youth hearings were linked with the Ubuntu* project. There children who had had direct experience of oppression and political violence were encouraged to interact with privileged children who had been sheltered from such experiences. We brought children together from townships and from the suburbs of Cape Town, in different age groups. The oldest group did a beautiful mural on Ubuntu, where they incorporated their experiences in patchwork-style. This mural is now used in St George's Cathedral. I would like to see this project snowball and to develop. We need to do so much more of this kind of work with young people.

Would you care to comment on any hearing in particular?

The Trojan Horse Hearing was very close to my heart. I was educated at Alexander Sinton High. I happened to arrive on the scene a few minutes after the shooting. One of the commanders of that operation is an educationist, and he is still playing a role in education today. He was then a member of the citizen force and was on duty that day.

I also want to ask you about girls and women. You have already mentioned Colleen Williams, who was killed. So few girls took the step to come forward and testify. When I look at the TRC documentation as a whole it strikes me as very male-oriented. Yet I know that women were very much part of the resistance struggle. Why this contradiction? Is it that women do not think their stories important enough? Did the TRC not encourage women to come forward? Or did they have particularly traumatic personal experiences, such as rape, which they do not want to talk about? I just feel that there are such silences there.

You are not wrong. There are silences, for all the reasons you mentioned. It is very daunting to testify. Sandra Adonis [*see Chapters III and IV*] was very articulate, very special. Many girls did testify to us privately about things they did not wish to say in public. One therefore had to find window cases, such as Sandra's, which stood for many others that were not made public. In that sense, Sandra testified on behalf of all those women who had similar experiences. Then, in the mass demonstrations where there were clashes with police, there were just fewer girls. Many girls suffered injuries by chance, because they simply happened to walk past.

Because of the mandate of the Commission, which focused specifically on gross violations of human rights, we are missing those who supported the victims of such violations and whose stories we did capture.

But those girls and women who remained in the background, their lives were also destroyed.

People who sacrificed, people who missed out on so much, who lost their childhood ... the Commission's mandate was simply not broad enough to focus on them.

There are so many more stories to tell.

I do not leave immediately after the tape recorder is switched off. Glenda invites me to look at the photographs of Grant Sipho's first year. There is a lovely one of Grant Sipho looking intently at the Archbishop – the man who gave so much of himself, and who suffered so much to build a future life for children such as him. Tiny as he is, he seems to feel something of the warmth which always radiates from this man.

A week or two after this interview I am again at Glenda's house. This time it is to share in the joy of Grant's first birthday with Glenda's immediate family and with Cynthia, Grant's Xhosa nanny who is entrusted to teach him his language and the traditions of the Xhosa culture. As I drive home, I think again of Judith Miller's reference to the six million of the Holocaust: One person, then another, and another ... (see also Chapter I) Is it too much to hope for that here, in this child of a new beginning, there is perhaps the tiny seed of a more hopeful accounting? ✧

✧ Tragically, in December 1999 Grant Sipho died in a swimming pool accident. All who knew him in his short life will continue to cherish the memory of his joyfulness.

GILLIAN SCHERMBRUCKER
'Go out into your life and make something of it!'

Cape Town, 12 February 1999
Born in Zimbabwe in 1973, Gillian Schermbrucker was educated at the Our Lady of Fatima Convent in Durban. In 1999 she was a final year medical student at the University of Cape Town (UCT)*. She was badly injured in the St James Church massacre, when APLA attacked the congregation on 25 July 1993.

The massacre sent shock waves through Cape Town for a number of reasons: eleven people were killed, fifty-eight injured, many extremely seriously. The country was then nine months away from a democratic election. All political parties, including the PAC whose armed wing APLA* was responsible for the massacre, were co-operating to ensure a smooth political transition and were working on a new constitution. There was no conceivable basis for such an action at such a time. And never before had a church congregation at prayer, and a racially mixed one at that, been the target of such a devastating attack. Our newspapers and television screens were filled with the horror and its aftermath for many days. Of course the comment was made by some that so much attention was given because most of the victims were white. However much criticism like this may have been justified in other cases in the past, this time it strikes me as a cynical distancing from the real issue of urban terrorism in the name of political change.

Many stories of tremendous courage emerged as the survivors slowly pulled away from the brink of death and regained some form of life, even if it was with three artificial limbs or without eyesight. My immediate affinity was perhaps particularly with Gillian who, like my own daughter at the time, was a medical student at UCT and who miraculously survived her serious injuries in a long and painful journey of recovery.

I saw Gillian some time later in a television programme on the TRC: She and Liezel Ackermann, whose mother was killed in the attack on the church, visited one of the perpetrators, Gcinikhaya Makoma, in Pollsmoor Prison where he is serving his sentence. This meeting took place before the amnesty hearing and later Gillian told me why she wanted to meet the man who very nearly killed her: 'I wanted to meet the men who did this. It is absurd that something which results in so much pain and which forces significant changes in one's life could remain faceless

*and hidden. What was he thinking when he taped those long nails on to the small,
mean hand grenade, making it even more destructive before throwing it into a
faceless congregation? I struggle to feel anything concrete about people I do not
know. I cannot, and choose not to, imagine what these men are like, in case I am
wrong. At the same time, beyond the rationalisation and political excuses, I feel
confused that they could justify hurting me without even knowing my name, my
background or my beliefs.'*

*As I watched the programme showing the three young people in conversation,
there was one thought uppermost in my mind: 'If only we had lived in the kind of
society where they could all have met and talked before, then perhaps all this horror
would never have happened.'*

*It is this impression that motivates me to seek out Gillian and to interview
her for this book. She is friendly but guarded on the telephone, being perhaps too
familiar with requests like this from a plethora of journalists. When I explain that
I am a South African academic and former activist, and that the book is specifically
for young people and will contribute to the President's Reparation Fund, her attitude
changes.*

*We meet in her parents' home in Newlands, not far from where I live. Gillian
is warm and friendly, a lovely young woman whose long blond hair is blown about
her face by the Cape South Easter as she greets me with a handshake and a friendly,
open smile. But there is a wariness about the eyes which is painful to see in so
young and vibrant a person. I had expected her to be scarred, perhaps to limp – but
there is no immediately obvious sign of injury. She looks just like any other young
student: confident, outgoing and very much in control of her life. But she is wearing
a long skirt which covers her legs. Gillian is very interested in our book and the
motivation behind it, and I explain it to her.*

Gillian: My main motivation in meeting Gcinikhaya was to find out where
his hatred originated. A book like yours will help people to understand
each other.

When you were at school … were you interested in political issues at all?

My interests were always in people and I count it a blessing that I was at a multiracial school, first in Zimbabwe and then later in Durban. We all came from very different backgrounds but roughly the same socio-economic class, as the school was semi-private and therefore expensive. A family friend kindly paid my school fees and I am hugely grateful for an education obtained with pupils of different religions and cultures. It was only at university that I realised the value of this. We had an hour's discussion every week about our different belief systems and that was so important in the whole process of forming an identity and testing and exploring what I believe.

So in terms of the apartheid era, your schooling was very untypical?

At the time everything seemed so normal, one did not have black or Indian friends – just friends. There were times when it made me angry and confused that not everyone saw us this way, when the reality of apartheid would intrude and sting us with its absurdity. When organising end of term parties, we had to be careful to go somewhere where everyone would feel comfortable. Even which beach to go to for an ice cream needed to be thought about, but that had relaxed a lot by the time I reached high school. We just ignored people who stared when we went around in a racially mixed group. I suppose school was a protected environment. Our 'normality' was unusual beyond the school gates where apartheid was a harsh fact that was unpleasant to acknowledge.

Did you explore that kind of contradiction when you were at university?

It was an issue, certainly. But I was always more interested in people than in politics. That is why I chose medicine – which I love.

Were you very active in the St James Church?

No. I just happened to be there on that evening ...

Would it upset you if I ask about your injuries?

No, not at all. We were sitting in church, I was praying. Then I heard a loud bang, looked up and saw three men silhouetted in the door, with a gun going up and down. I realised what was happening and ducked down, as the others around me did too. Then I saw a hand grenade next to me – a grey thing with two-inch nails strapped to it. My immediate reaction was to push it or to throw it back to them. They were not far away. But it is amazing how clearly you think in such a situation. I thought: If I pick that up, my hands or my face may be blown off, and if I throw it, someone else may be killed. And I am going to have to live with myself for the rest of my life with this knowledge, that I killed someone. There are things which are better left in God's hands ... and I started to pray. Then the grenade went off and I had this intense burning in my body, the numbness that comes when you are badly injured. I could not feel my legs and I feared that they had been blown off. I did not want to look. I just remember saying to my friend next to me, who looked horrified: 'Don't worry, God is with me.' That is all I remember. The man next to me and the man in front of him both died, and Dimitri in front of me lost an arm and both legs.

I had shrapnel in my lungs and a piece of shrapnel had cut right into my heart. By the time I got to hospital, my heart had practically stopped beating. Both my legs were very badly injured, also my back and my breast. Grenades are powerful things. I had a lot of surgery and the doctors thought it a miracle that I was alive. In the five years following the attack, I had more than fifty hours of surgery on my legs. It was pretty bad, but on the other hand, look what happened to some others – Dimitri, for example.

My family were very supportive, and my experience was very different to what many people suffer all over South Africa. I never felt alone. I had my family and my faith. As a medical student in the hospital, I received very special attention. Because of the media coverage, I had cards from many people from all over South Africa and all walks of life. I was shown so much kindness from hundreds of people – I was really spoiled! Violence happens all the time in South Africa, but it mostly goes unreported. Do you agree?

Yes. If you take KwaZulu-Natal for example, where people get shot up every day

... it does not make your experience any less, but I agree with you that you had much more attention. Did you ask yourself where the hatred comes from that led to the attack on you?

That is my main question: Where is the deep-seated hurt that fuels this type of anger? I was actually disappointed when I met Makoma. But perhaps it was also traumatic for him to meet me.

I did not want to give evidence before the TRC, because of all the glare of publicity. I really just wanted to meet Gcinikhaya Makoma and find out who he really was. They came and decided what I stood for and what I believed, but they did not even know me. So how could I then make judgements on him without having met him? I asked him, when we met in Pollsmoor prison, whether anything personal had happened to him or his family to set off this hatred in him. He said there was nothing personal, he was a soldier who followed orders.

How did you feel when you met him?

I did not feel much at the time. Before I met him, I tried not to expect too much. I did not want to be disappointed.

What was your impression of him?

That he is so normal! He is not mean, not horrible, he could be someone with whom I would have a friendly conversation in the street. He is a short man, quite small, he smiled, we interacted ... we had a good conversation for about an hour and a half. My impression of him was that this guy would not hurt anyone.

Did it help you to meet him?

I think that by then I had come to terms with things emotionally. In terms of getting answers to questions, I was a bit frustrated. I also felt that I needed to see more of him, that one meeting was not enough. He also expressed the desire to talk more.

Have you talked since then?

I made several attempts, but did not succeed. Then they got amnesty shortly afterwards.

How do you feel about that amnesty?

To be honest … I thought a lot cognitively, but I do not feel anything very strongly. I think … I never really felt angry with them. I am also really more concerned about how justice is administered in the country and on what grounds they were given amnesty. That disturbs me a lot more.

Are you disturbed that they were given amnesty on political grounds ?

Yes. Basically, the election date had been set when the attack happened. We were heading towards a democratic election. The aims of the armed struggle were being accomplished. Makona said that he was underground and did not know what was going on. How can you belong to a political organisation and not know what is going on? … I kept on asking Makona: 'What were your aims in attacking St James Church, and were any of those aims achieved?' I asked this many times and he did not answer me. He kept saying: 'I was a soldier, I obeyed commands.' Those were the grounds on which he was granted amnesty, that he was not the one responsible. That is true, but then again … you can be a soldier but you still think for yourself, you still retain your humanity.

This again raises the question we asked in the beginning: What brings young people to this point? After all, they are not born killers. They are normal people. What has made them do it?

That is exactly the question I battle with. He said that he joined the PAC because of all the oppression and injustice he saw and had heard about. He was underground and said that he did not know, when the operation was launched, that they would be attacking a church. I asked if it would have made any difference if he had known. He said no, that he would have trusted his superiors. Then I asked him: 'If you had seen all the black people in church, would you still have shot?' He had said that he just wanted to kill whites. He answered that it would have been a tough problem, and he would have found it difficult, but that he still would have done it because he would have trusted his superiors. He was obeying commands.

You were able to ask him all that?

Yes, that is what I had wanted to ask him. And he answered me, but I don't think he really answered from inside himself. He gave these answers because he had not been granted amnesty yet. He answered as the PAC had told him to answer.

I feel … it was also tough for him. It was the first time he had come into contact with a victim. To face what you have done, to come to terms with that … it must have been very difficult. I did not expect him to be suddenly contrite and full of repentance. I really don't want to sound pious, but my desire for Makoma is that he can find peace with God.

The forgiveness I can offer him, which I do freely, is meaningless. I don't want him to suffer or to come to harm in any way because of what he has done … When I left him in prison I wished that I could have given him a key and that I could have said: 'Go. Go out into your life and make something of it. Do good things now' … and, you know, I really think he would.

He was only seventeen at the time of the attack.

Yes … but at the same time I also think about justice. Justice was not really done. Forgiveness and justice are completely different things.

There are different kinds of justice. There is retributive justice, which a lot of people want. That was what the Nuremberg trials were about.

That is dangerous.

... and then there is restorative justice, which the TRC has set in motion, however imperfectly. A lot of people feel that justice has not been done, and many people are angry. And they have a right to be that, and the TRC acknowledges that right. But if court cases are the only option, the truth will probably not become known. Look what happened in the court case around the St James massacre: when the perpetrators were in court, they lied in the hope of getting a lighter sentence. It was only in the TRC hearings that they told the truth. The reason was that they knew they had to tell the full truth to have any hope of amnesty. In a trial the best hope for the accused is often in lying and obscuring the truth. At least, in a lot of cases, the TRC brought out the truth.

Yes. But the truth does not justify what happened. I strongly feel that. Forgiveness is something else. You can forgive someone without approving of what they did. The opposite of forgiveness is vengeance and retribution. I do not want that, because it just destroys. I don't want the perpetrators to come to any harm. I have the scars and the pain ...

Do you still have pain?

Sometimes. My pain is physical ... but the wounds that they have ... only God can heal those.

To achieve healing in our society ... where do we begin? Makoma is only one of so many that need healing.

What do you say? What is your answer to that?

It is difficult ... I think that much, much more attention and many more resources need to be channelled to the youth. The majority of those who died during apartheid were young people. We are going to be a nation where most of the population is under twenty years old. I don't see a really serious shift of resources towards this. That has to happen at a macro-level, it has to come from government. On a personal level, a lot of us who are privileged have to take cognisance of how we go on living in this country. To me, the TRC has helped everyone to see more clearly those many terrible injustices that could be pushed aside before.

Yes. In my class at medical school it was the black African students who knew what was going on in the TRC. The white students did not, on the whole ...

Few whites attended the hearings. But maybe the real challenge now is how we go on working with all the truths and all the knowledge that has come out of the TRC. To take really seriously what young people say – that nobody wants to listen, that they sacrificed in the struggle and are worse off now.

That's exactly what Gcinikhaya said. He said that he fought for democracy and all the things we are reaping now ... but he was in jail and not enjoying any of it!

So I thought ... [*Gillian laughs*] ... well, you really fought a bit too hard!

A lot of insights obviously still have to happen. One hopes that the people who were granted amnesty were not just left alone.

I am concerned about that. Given the unemployment situation, and the links between that and crime, what happens to someone like Gcinikhaya when he gets out? He has no education ... is there support for people like him? I know that the Trauma Centre provides support for victims of violence [*see also the interview with Nomfundo Walaza in this Chapter*] and that is so very necessary now. I have been thinking that I would like to raise funds for that. I really enjoy running and I used to be reasonably fast. I am getting back into it again, although I am not as fast as before. I hope that in a year or two I shall be able to run in the Two Oceans[7] and use my race to get support for victims of violence. That might strike a chord with people.

I know that I have been very privileged and very blessed. All my medical expenses have been taken care of by family, friends and by the church. How many people are so fortunate? When I was in hospital, and also later, I had the support of so many people. There are many victims of violence who are in a far, far worse situation than I have been. I want to find a way to make a difference in their lives, in a practical way.

Although I am not for a moment minimising the horror and the pain of it, I can honestly say that this experience has been strengthening for me. I saw the good side of this country in the way people pulled together to support the victims of the St James attack. In the news media, the focus in cases like this is always on death, destruction and evil. I experienced the healing, the loving and the kindness which are also there. That impressed me far, far more than the few people who threw a grenade at me. The five young men who were bent on destruction stand against hundreds and thousands of people who want to build and heal. That, for me, gets things into perspective.

And as a medical doctor? What are your plans for the future?

I want to go into primary health care and work in rural Natal. The people there are so warm and friendly. I used to speak a bit of Zulu when I was a child and I am sure to pick it up again when I am among people who do not speak English.

Since we have had a change of government, more resources have gone into the rural areas and it is making a difference. I see positive changes there and that is where I want to work, among rural people.

Some weeks after this interview, on Easter Saturday, the Two Oceans marathon is being run. As I watch the first athletes cross the finish line, I pick up the phone to Gillian: 'I'll watch out for you next year!'

Her clear, joyful laugh peals over the telephone: 'I am training hard! I will be there!'

THE WITNESSES
TODAY

RIEFAAT HATTAS

'I am afraid to advance in life ...'

Cape Town, 26 March 1999

My first contact with Riefaat is established through a third person who is able to reassure him about my intentions. After a few telephone conversations Riefaat finally agrees to be interviewed and we meet in the garden of the University of Cape Town.

During the 1980s Riefaat, a boy from a devout Muslim home, was detained twice and tortured both times. In his testimony before the TRC two years before this interview he stated: 'I am messed up because of what I went through during my school years.' When describing his torture at the hands of the police he breaks off his testimony with the words: 'The things they did to me I do not want to name because I do not want to read them in the press' (see also his statement in Chapter III).

As I prepare for the interview, I think back to the early and mid-1980s – the time during which Riefaat was at school. Many schools throughout the country became sites of struggle against apartheid. The UDF, as an umbrella organisation, spearheaded and co-ordinated resistance to the apartheid state. Schoolchildren responded en masse to the UDF's campaign, in which the underground ANC concurred, to 'make the country ungovernable' and so wrest power from the apartheid state. In schools, this form of opposition took the form of school and class boycotts against 'gutter education'. It is here that the slogan 'Liberation before Education' was born. It became the rallying cry of a whole generation of school pupils. At this point, students demanded the transfer of state power in a heady and misguided belief that student resistance could bring down the apartheid government.

It must be remembered that the UDF was a broad front organisation within which several ideological positions contested with each other at times for ideological space. The 'Liberation before Education' slogan did not reflect a considered policy and was not, for example, supported by the ANC in exile. This was made clear at a conference at the University of the Witwatersrand in December 1985, which ended with a call for students to return to school in January 1986. It was at this conference that the National Education Crisis Committee (NECC) was founded with the aim of directing the struggle for a transformation in education. Students were to advance the struggle for democracy by continuing their education and transforming schools and educational structures.

Because of the depth of the educational crisis, there was soon broad support for the NECC, which had proved its legitimacy and educational leadership. The NECC was able to hold back demands for an indefinite education boycott. The government response to the growing influence and credibility of the NECC was to detain its leaders and drastically tighten emergency regulations.

Riefaat's arrest falls into that time.

I start by asking him how he became active politically and a student leader in his school.

Riefaat: It was because I had not done my homework ...

What?

Yes, it is funny! The matrics had called a boycott because of something or other and asked us to come to a meeting. I had not done my Afrikaans homework and because I knew I would get six of the best I skipped the next period and joined them.

My idea of a boycott was, it's lekker you are not in class, you can bunk!

Because the principal threatened the matrics that they would not get interviews for colleges if they continued to boycott, they all went back to class, leaving us there alone. We sat there, just looking at each other. Then, out of the blue and I don't know why I did it, I shouted, 'You are a bunch of traitors!'

So, the others turned round to me and said, 'You are our leader now!' I said, 'Huh??'

They asked my name and then they all chanted, 'Hattas! Hattas!'

I knew nothing about politics, nothing about the Struggle. My idea of boycotts was picking up stones and fighting in the Manenberg way, fighting, running with stones. That was lekker. That is what I understood of boycotts.

Then some of the pupils, some of the girls, came to me and said, 'Hattas, you should really have a programme.' I said, 'Huh? A programme?'

'Yes, you should have a programme to educate people about politics.' So I said, 'But I know nothing about politics!' So I went to SOYA* meetings and there I became politically minded.

The boycott extended to three weeks. We did not belong to any organisation or structure, not to the Inter-Schools Co-ordinating Committee (ISCC). There was no structure, we were just boycotting. The principal told us to go back to class, as all the other schools had gone back. I answered him, 'That's just your propaganda.' That was the only word I knew. We just sang all day long: 'United we stand, divided we fall.' And when we got bored with singing 'Unity!' from eight in the morning to one in the afternoon, we sang other words, like 'Koek and tea!'[8] We sang that for three weeks. That was our idea of a programme.

But I could see that the pupils wanted something more, and I went for political training. I did not know what it was that they wanted. I just told them to sing. But in the evening, I would go and learn.

Then we had a structure and we started to sing freedom songs. We also started an SRC and threw out the prefect system. That was in 1985, when I was in matric.

When the other schools asked us why we were still boycotting, we found out that they really were all back at school. Then I was voted on to the ISCC. I was then sixteen years old.

After a year I was elected on to the executive of the ISCC. We were only organising coloured schools at that stage, we had no members in the black areas as at that time we were not organising over the lines.[9] In my last year of school everything blew up.

By then it was highly political, wasn't it? I remember that school boycotts were called in response to both local problems and the oppression in the Eastern Cape. How did your schools respond?

We had a march and the police came. They told us we had three minutes to disperse. We had never experienced such a thing before and did not really know how to react. We told pupils just to sit down. Then the police started to shoot ...

I never believed in violence but the pupils demanded to know what I, their leader, would do, as people had been hurt. At that time I still believed in Gandhi-style passive resistance. We had learned about Gandhi in our history lessons.

But then, one day at a rally at Manenberg High School the casspirs came. The boere went into the school and hit people with sjamboks. So the students came to me, angry, and demanded that I take a decision. I told the head girl to say a prayer for us, which she did. But the students said, 'What will a prayer do? That won't stop the boere hitting us.' So I decided, if they attack again we must respond.

It happened on 29 August 1985. We had a march through Manenberg, to the police station. The police came and they killed two people, Brian Lucas (16) and Lance Phillips (18). I will never forget those names. That was the turning point. At their funeral, we decided: No more passive resistance.

We started an Action Committee. I had difficulties because I was accused of 'always pushing a line', but I did not really know what they meant. I did not know about lines, only about washing lines. I thought you could really shout anything, as long as it had a 'Viva!' behind it and a 'Viva!' in front of it. Then I began to see the reality of the Struggle. You could not just `Viva!' for anything and anybody. In the townships, you had to shout 'Viva UDF!' and 'Viva ANC!' I had difficulty with accepting that people forced their ideas on me.

Then Celeste Naidoo, a woman with great political experience, came and attended our rallies. She asked me whether I understood politics and whether I did a lot of reading, whether I understood about alliances. I said that I did not read and did not know about alliances. All I knew was that we were oppressed, that I was a leader and had to do something.

She started to give me books to read and that is how my political education happened.

Where is she now?

She is around, back from exile, but I am too afraid to go to her and to face her. She had such high expectations of me and I feel that I am a failure. I cannot now see what I have contributed through my years of struggle. People who never struggled are far better off than we are.

That does not mean you have not contributed. It only means you have not benefited.

Yes, we are the people who made it happen. It was because of the youth struggle that this came about ...

And remember the purple rain march?[10] It was just one young man who turned that demonstration around.

Riefaat and I both laugh at the memory of that day. But soon we are serious again:

We used to spray on walls: 'Liberation before Education!' I was one of the people who did that. When my parents told me to go to school I said no, I must first get my freedom. Because one day my children must be able to go to school without having to go through this. We all said to our parents: 'If you had stood up in your time, it would not be necessary for us to do this now.' So I decided that I could not take an education and one day let my children fight instead of me.

All of us believed that. That is why we took action, every day, to make the country ungovernable. I told my comrades that we had to act, there should not be one day when the boere could sit still. The BMW was our inspiration. When we did go to school sometimes, we often fell asleep at our desks.

How were you finally arrested?

I was on the run but had returned home. That is when they came for me, early one morning. Two policemen, Kotze and Viljoen, arrested me. They wanted names from me. I refused. They tortured me. They pulled my legs apart and kicked me in my penis, for a long time ...

They beat me up so terribly that I knew I was going to talk. I did not know that my friend Deon had been picked up before me, so I said, 'Why don't you ask Deon?' So they fetched Deon and beat him up in front of me.

I still cannot deal with that. I still cannot face him, because I am a traitor to my comrade. Although I have played a role in the Struggle and mobilised students, it is this betrayal that will stick with me forever. In the Struggle you are not supposed to be a traitor, and we were all so committed ...

But you had no training to withstand that or to prepare for such interrogation ... You are not a traitor in such a situation.

That is true, and that is what I said at the TRC. I hope that Deon heard through the TRC how sorry I am. I can't forgive myself. I will live with that until I die.

You don't think that you can perhaps learn to forgive yourself?

When I was arrested, things happened that I can't talk about. They kill me inside. I am dead inside and I am not capable of having any relationships. I don't care about any achievements.

I can't live with myself. I am no longer in the Struggle, but this is my struggle now, inside me.

I got instructions, but I do not blame Celeste for that. She had instructions from the top, from outside the country. I made very sure that I did not disappoint her and did whatever she asked me to do. When she was in exile we worked hard in order not to disappoint her, so that she would come back to a job well done. The problem is, I convinced my comrades and they gave their lives and their education.

Now I can't face them. One of them told me that his mother, when she was on her deathbed, said to him that he had wasted his life. This is the reality.

And then you look at the TV and see the Winnie Mandelas and all those people getting rewards. Why are they still being honoured? They are already in Parliament. Why don't they give my comrades something?

My comrades don't have work. I have nothing. I clean toilets for a living.

I do not have an education. Yes. I finished matric. But I am not applying for jobs because I am afraid to better myself. What do I do with a better position if my comrades do not have work? I was the one that told them: 'Liberation before Education!' They believed in what I said and did not ask any questions.

But I must tell you that I am doing a course of study, in human resource management. I am now in my second year. But I will never tell my comrades that, because I am afraid to advance in life. I was the guy who told them to give up their education.

What do you think could realistically be done now?

First, there should be therapy and counselling on a large scale. Very many young people need that. After assistance of that kind, they must get proper educational opportunities in colleges and other institutions where these severe problems are understood. Many teachers do not understand about our anger, our aggression and craziness.

Has the TRC helped to make people more aware of what the youth has suffered?

I think so, but unfortunately there was not enough emphasis on youth. There was quite a lot of attention in the media, also from overseas. But in the end it has to be solved here, inside the country.

What made you go to the TRC?

My concern about Deon, and I thought they would get the policemen who tortured me and that they would hand them over to me.

I paid my price, lots of people did. But these policemen never came to me to say that they were sorry for what they had done. I discovered that the TRC had nothing on them, although I had given my evidence and told the TRC what they had done to me. I expected that they would apply for amnesty, but they did not. Nothing has happened to them.

Now I think it is possible that perhaps we will have a blanket amnesty, also because those high-profile ANC people who could not get amnesty as a group. Then all the people will get off, scot-free. What about us? I humiliated myself in public – for what?

Could you not now lay a charge against those two policemen?

Then I must go through everything again. If I ever get these guys I will shoot them. I have paid and they must also pay. But then I think … I have lived with violence all my life. I have never had a youth, and I must come out of it now. But politicians should not play with us. Why did they start the TRC in the first place? They must not create this expectation so that ordinary people like us think there will be answers …

Do you feel that the TRC has not done justice in your case?

No, I would not say that. The TRC was necessary for the country. As far as I am concerned … maybe I went for the wrong reason. Maybe I don't understand the Act or the TRC. But the TRC was very necessary and it is good that we had it. Now more people know about what happened.

What do you think about amnesty?

Sometimes I feel it is necessary for the country. We can't live in the past. I am in the past still, every day, and I want to get out of it. But it is so difficult … I am caught. On the one hand, I say we must forgive … but then I see something or something happens, and I get angry all over again. But in the end – and maybe I am answering myself now – the country must go forward.

If you stay in the past you cannot go forward … and maybe now is the time … I want to improve myself, I want to get an education.

If only the two policemen who tortured me could come forward and admit that they drove me to the point of no return. If they would admit that they are the reason Deon was there … it would take a load off me.

I want to live. At the moment I am not living. I want to feel what life is, I want to feel enjoyment. I am now thirty-one years old. I want to start living …

Have you got a girlfriend?

No. I don't have confidence in myself. The only thing I can do well is 'struggle' and organise.

Without people like you a lot of things would not have happened …

That is why I am grateful to Celeste. She taught me a lot of things. But now I must carry myself and I do not feel good about myself.

You say that you cannot face your comrades. Is that a feeling you have or is that what they communicate to you?

No, it is in my mind. They have not been in any way bad to me. I cannot deal with what happened. It will take a long time. Sometimes I cry because I just don't know. It is no good to tell me, 'Hattas, you can't take responsibility for everything.' It is not so easy.

If those two policemen confessed what they have done, perhaps you would no longer feel that you want to shoot them?

Yes. That would take such a load off me. I could look my comrades in the face again. I could say to Deon: 'In different circumstances, I would not have done it.'

It hurts so much … At home I do not communicate with anyone, I only play with my brother's children. I don't communicate with adults. I want to change that, because it is not normal. I have been dead for so many years. I want to live now. Before I die, I must at least have lived some time of my life.

On the way back to the car after the interview we walk through the building of the Social Sciences Faculty at UCT. Riefaat stops at a notice board, studies a list and detaches it from the board. 'This is a list of textbooks someone is selling. They are good, I can use some of these books ...'

FIKISWA M
'I think the world must know that rape is serious!'

November 1998
Out of the many hundreds of pages of human rights violations hearings some strike into my very bones. One of those that surfaces in my nightmares: a young, fragile girl of eleven, gang-raped by policemen throughout the night, in retaliation for God knows what ... her childhood torn from her in a few brutal hours. The all too familiar horror at the police station afterwards, a second rape piled on top of the first: 'Was it nice? Were you wearing a short dress?' Dear God, she was a child of eleven ...

How does anyone survive that? How does a mother go on living with that experience? And how does this young woman find the strength to tell this story to the TRC hearing – and to the nation? Her determination to survive shines out of her testimony. She speaks in a quiet but firm voice for so many who remain silent. It is for that reason that I am determined to find her.

January 1999
It is not easy to track her down, and time and bureaucracy frustrate my efforts for a while. Then some tenuous links are made, the network yields her mother's telephone number. I feel intrusive and uncomfortable as I put my request: Is there a gentle way of saying that you want to interview her daughter because she has been violated? But something seems to come across, I am not turned down out of hand but told to wait for Fikiswa's response. This is relayed a few days later: 'Yes, she will talk to you, if I am present and also her cousin.' Wonderful. I send her an outline of the book. Then Fikiswa's voice on the telephone – it is a very young, soft

voice, but very clear: 'Hello Karin. I will talk to you. I think your book is important.'

February 1999

One Sunday morning soon after, my husband Peter and I wait in the centre of Bloemfontein, to be met by Fikiswa's mother. Our thousand-kilometre trip from Cape Town the previous day through the vastness and heat of the Karoo has left us drained and exhausted, and this in a strange way seems necessary to the task. We become aware, yet again and at a physical level, just how vast the distances are that must be bridged, and that the road is not necessarily easy or comfortable, that it requires effort ...

While we wait I think back to the 1980s, to the devastating near-isolation of the Free State in terms of human rights organisations. They were stretched thin everywhere then, but in parts the Free State seems to have come off worst. There was no Black Sash here then, and there were very few other representatives of human rights organisations. Later, even the Truth Commission did not deal really evenhandedly with the Free State.

The previous evening we enjoyed the relaxed atmosphere of a Bloemfontein steakhouse with a racially mixed clientele – an unthinkable scenario in the Bloemfontein of old.

Two women approach us on the windswept street. The older one in a flowing white kaftan as generous as she – a warm hug: Dolly. Next to her a slender, pretty young woman in a huge hat and sunglasses: Fikiswa – a friendly handshake, a shy smile.

On this Sunday morning, three generations of women crowd into the small sitting room of Fikiswa's grandmother's house. I am brought here to interview Fikiswa, rather than to her mother's house, because it is from here that Fikiswa and Boikie walked that evening, in the company of two policemen ...

No confidential interviewing here, but it feels entirely comfortable. This is a family affair, this is ubuntu – the framework within which we talk. Dolly puts it into words later: 'Rape does not only destroy one person, it destroys a whole family.' For as much as the family has enabled Fikiswa to survive her ordeal, so much has the family itself been damaged. No one stands aloof from her fate: not the elder relatives who are in the know, and not the young sister whose childhood is blighted by the terrifying secret ...

The hat and the sunglasses have gone, Fikiswa's eyes are direct, wary but unwavering as she answers my questions.

Fikiswa, can you tell me something about where you were born something about your childhood, how you grew up – not about the terrible story, about your family ...

Fikiswa: I was born in Matatiele. I lived with my grandparents. It was wonderful. Everything was fine. I enjoyed staying with them. Sometimes I visited my parents, they stayed somewhere else. They got divorced, I don't know why and I am not interested. I have to go on with my own life. I sometimes see my father but we don't talk much. Now I live with my mother, my grandmother, my cousins and my little sister. I went to high school here in Bloemfontein. I grew up speaking English, but I also speak Sotho.

Dolly: I am Dolly, Fikiswa's mother. I am often with my sister here in Rocklands. Fikiswa grew up well, but then at the age of eleven, that's when everything started ... [*she speaks against her tears*] Karin, imagine somebody wakes you up and says ... Boikie woke me up and said to me ... he carried Fikiswa on his back ...

Break. Both Fikiswa and her mother are in tears. It is some time before we can go on.

I started to have nightmares, it was horrible. My life changed and I had a nervous breakdown. I don't know if I was happy at school, I don't really remember anything.

My mother said to me that I should leave school, that I would not make it. I told my mother: 'Even if you do not have faith in me, I am a survivor. I am going to make it and I am going to pass. ' I don't really know what happened. I used to go to school, sometimes people would take me home because I was crying. There was a time when I wanted to commit suicide, several times.

For weeks after it [the rape] happened I could not walk. It felt as if someone had just taken part of me away. It hurts me very deeply and I ask myself: 'Oh God, am I ever going to have children?'

At that stage I do not know the true extent of Fikiswa's injuries. Her mother told me about that later. Fikiswa had suffered deep genital tears and also very serious injuries to the womb itself. Consequently, she had been plagued not only by psychological trauma but also by serious physiological ill health since then and had been told that she might never be able to have children as a result of the rape.

I had to have an operation last year [1998] because back then I did not receive proper medical attention. So now the doctor says to me: 'I don't know if you will ever have children.'

For those who do not know the cultural traditions and customs of Africa, it must be pointed out that in African tradition a woman who cannot bear a child is worthless and not worth marrying. She is not worthy of lobola (the bride price) or of the respect of her husband's family.

When I go to sleep I dream of having a baby … but I don't know if I will ever have a baby of my own one day. It's just horrible, because I see myself doing whatever I am doing, just to get through the day. As to being healthy and happy, I don't know how to do that.

What made you go to the TRC? What made you take that step to expose yourself? What were you hoping for when you went?

Truly, I must tell you, I did not really want to go.

I said, why should I go to the TRC? I wanted to forget everything. Now, here is the TRC and they want to know, they want me to start all over again, to tell them what happened … But then, one day I said to myself: I think the world must know that rape is serious.

Some people say that when a woman is raped it is something you wanted.

Can I tell you a story from my own experience? When I was active in the Women's Movement in the eighties, when we built up FEDSAW,* which was really the ANC Women's League underground, there were many of us who felt the organisation

should address issues like rape and violence against women as well as all the political
liberation work. And there was a lot of tension among the women about that.
Many black women in particular said this is middle-class, white stuff, this is not
for the liberation. And there were many of us who felt it is for the liberation of
women, we must talk about rape, we must talk about sexual violence. So, I can
only underline what you have said. Rape is serious.

Yes, and nowadays it is even happening to young children. And people
don't take it seriously.

So one day I just said to myself: I need to do this, because I need to get
through to the President so that he must see that rape is serious. It hurts. It
destroys you, whether you like it or not. Whether you say, 'No, I am strong'
– it still destroys you.

One time when I was in Durban I said to the people there I wish I
could speak to the President personally, and say to him, 'Please Mr
President, I really wish that you could see that these people who do such
horrible things they must not get bail. They must stay in prison. They are
animals, how can somebody do this to a person? And afterwards they say,
"I am so sorry". Sorry is not going to make you feel okay or bring back
your life again.' Because, really, I am always angry. I am not myself. I don't
socialise much. I am always at home, staying inside the house, not going
anywhere.

I hear you ... And when you went to the Truth Commission, what were you hoping
for? That the world would hear and take it seriously?

Yes, that is what I wanted.

What were you hoping for in terms of the people that did it to you? May I ask
whether they were black policemen or white policemen? Not that it really matters,
they were men in power ...

Boikie
They were black policemen.

Were you hoping that something would happen to the perpetrators as a result of the Truth Commission?

At first I hoped that they would be caught, but now I just don't care whether they are caught or not. I don't want to see them, it's better if I don't.

How did you find giving evidence before the Truth Commission? How did you find the process? Did it do anything good for you?

Let me say this: People believe that when you say something, it's healing. But to me, I don't think it's healing, but I just think it's worth it to let other people know what you feel inside.

Yes, to share it to let people see that as a woman … we must have a say and they must respect us. A lot of people don't respect women and I feel very sad because I think women are people too. They have the right, they have the power to say no whenever they feel that they don't want or don't need something in their lives …

Let me tell you something. I don't want to sit back and feel sorry for myself and not let other people know what this thing of sitting back may do to you. By coming out you make other women see that rape is not the woman's fault. You did not say: 'Come and rape me!' It's somebody else's fault, not yours. So it is important not to sit back and do nothing. That's what I wanted to say to women: Go out there, fight for your rights, be strong. I know women are weak, the majority of people think that women are weak, but I think that women have strong personalities. It's all in their minds, in their hearts, they must let go their fears and stand up for themselves.

That's what I want to say.

At the TRC hearing you said that you were not politically minded. But what you have done is in the end also very political.

I am not involved in politics. But it's there, it's real: women are treated worse than any other people on this earth. I just hope that people will realise that we are people and we have a say in this world, and respect our wishes, and respect us as women. Not that a person who has power can come to me and do whatever he or she likes. I am a human being, I deserve anything I want in this world. People have to respect one another as well.

Do you feel that the Truth Commission is a way of helping to get to that goal, that we all respect each other more?

I think it is helping. I think all the people who went to the Truth Commission are brave. In black communities we are so secretive, it's 'We must not say this ... Do not say that'. So I think those people were strong, to go and tell those horrible things like 'My husband was killed for political reasons' ... but they are still here, they are still going on with their lives. They are strong, and I think the Truth Commission has played an important role because they have made them speak out, not to repress things and hold back something so horrible in their hearts. When you let something which is hurting you out, you feel better every day. Even though it's difficult, you are going to feel better. The more you talk about it, the more you accept it. Unlike keeping quiet, when you keep quiet about something, you will not accept it, you will not. Every day you'll deny it. When you speak about it, you learn to live with it and accept it.

It is our story.

Yes. And I think when you go to the Truth Commission and you speak about all the things that happened, you teach other people how to deal with those hurting things when they happen to them. Because they are going to know, if you stand up and say 'People, hear me, listen to what happened to me!', then people are going to listen. And it's up to them what they are going to do with the information you have given to them, whether they take it to be useful or to be useless. It's up to them. But I think if they are wise they will use it profitably.

Can I ask you ... you have talked earlier about your nightmares. You have had very many very bad dreams. But can I ask you to do me a favour? If you close your eyes and you think of a really good dream, how you would want the future to be ... close your eyes and tell me a really good dream.

I won't even close my eyes. I can tell what I would like, what would make me happy: If I could know that one day I could wake up and go to a doctor and he would tell me 'You are pregnant'. I would be happiest, the happiest to know that I can have a child of my own and could raise a child of my own.

That would make me happy, to know that I could have a baby and hold her in my arms ...

Boikie, can I ask you: You were also at the Truth Commission, how did you experience that?

Boikie: The thing is, after the incident ... I was not really thinking of it. I was raised by my grandfather. He taught me that if something happens, or if somebody does a bad thing to you, just take it like a man.

So when Fikiswa went to a psychologist, I did not go. I went on with my life.

By the time the TRC was coming up Fikiswa came to me and asked: Should we go? I told her I'll think about it. And then I said, if she does not have a problem with it we can go.

It hurts me to see her crying about this, because when it happened, it was in front of my eyes. So, if I think about it is really hurting.

Did it help you to go to the Truth Commission? Did it help you to tell the story?

Yes, I can say it helped me. I was keeping it ... at the back of my mind. It was still there.

And what are you hoping will come out of this?

That it can change our lives.

How? You know, the TRC were seventeen Commissioners, they could do a lot to write down the stories, publish the stories ... but after that they can do nothing ... The TRC was really very few people and they worked for only two years ... I am wondering if you have any ideas for your own future? What you dream of, that you would be able to do perhaps?

If they could just increase the sentences for those people who go to jail ... in cases like this.

And for your own future?

I just wish to live a normal life. I don't wish to have money – or to be poor. Just to be normal.

Fikiswa, do you have any plans for what you want to do, in terms of studying?

Fikiswa: I want to become a psychologist, because really I think I need to help people. So, I think if I study psychology, I am going to make it and I will help other people.

Fikiswa's mother Dolly takes over:

I am Fikiswa's mother. I have two daughters. Fikiswa is twenty, Palesa is ten. So, during our interview with Karin I had to chase Palesa away because she does not know yet what happened [*she speaks through her tears*]. I am still battling with myself, how to start telling what happened with her sister. I am afraid because I don't know how she is going to take it. Will she accept that I am telling the truth or will she take me for a liar ... One other thing is at the moment I am living in fear because Palesa is at the same age as Fikiswa when she was raped. So I am afraid it is going to happen to her. I am constantly checking, 'Where is Palesa?' because I think what happened to her sister is going to happen to her.

Fikiswa [*interrupts*]: I want to tell you something. My little sister was playing one day, She drew something ... She drew houses and families and little girls. Then she told me a story about her drawing, and how one little girl was raped in one of the houses … I did not want to hear her story, but she wanted me to listen … I think my mother should have told her then.

It happened again, because one day Palesa was talking with her friend who told her that she was raped when she was six. You know what my little sister said? 'You have to kill that man, because he did horrible things to you.' I said to her, 'No, you don't have to wait until he sleeps and then burn him or whatever.' She was only a little girl. So I said to her, 'You know what, I have a similar problem. It does not mean if a person has done something wrong we have to go and kill him. It won't help. You just have to deal with it, inside you. Whether you hit the person or kill the person, it is not going to solve anything. You must start with yourself first. You must search within yourself what you feel in your heart … because beating and killing won't help. It won't solve anything, believe me.' And she said: 'OK. I won't do it.'

Dolly: You know, it is difficult to tell the child what happened to her sister, it is very difficult. I don't know what to say, how to start.

Fikiswa: I told my mother, as I was attending my sessions at the Medical Centre, and the doctor said to me, 'I don't think you are going to have babies', I said to my mother, 'I really think I owe it to myself to have a child of my own. Then I will know why am I living on this earth.'

Because from that day … I just had to stay inside. I did not go out. I am afraid to go out with my boyfriend sometimes. I can't come home at night, I can't make it, I am afraid of the dark. My boyfriend helps me and I am trying my best, but I just can't.

If the whole thing had never happened, my life would be better now. I have lost a lot. I don't know what childhood is, really.

Dolly: My dream is to see Fikiswa happy. If I could see that somebody has cured her … because I am losing a lot. Fikiswa cannot go to university because I have to take her to this doctor and to that one … Because I am a single mother I can't pay her medical costs and her university fees. Every day when I go to work she is at home and not at university. It eats me inside, I want her to be happy and I want her to go to university.

You know, my younger daughter is now asking, 'What is happening here?' I tell her people are visiting Fikiswa. She asks, 'Why are you crying? What is happening?' I say to her, 'I'll tell you.' I don't know how I will start telling her, because she does not know.

Fikiswa: I sleep in a room with her. I often wake up screaming and crying in the night, and she will ask why, and I don't have an answer for her. I wish it would not happen, but it happens a lot.

Would it help you if either you or your mother told your sister?

Fikiswa: I think so.

Dolly: It is hurting, Karin. Because sometimes I also have bad dreams. Sometimes I dream that I have been raped. It is in me as though it had happened to me. I wake up screaming but I don't tell Palesa why, because I don't want to worry her. Then I have to think of a bad story, a scary story, for her to believe me.

Would it not help all of you if you tell her? Because she seems to know quite a lot already, she seems to feel quite a lot already of what actually happened.

Dolly: I think somebody should be there who'll help us to comfort her. Because I know that she'll go through the denial stage, anger and whatever stage, so somebody should be there for her.

Have you got such a person?

Not yet. But I'm scared. Scared to tell her ... You know, even if she is at school I feel scared.

As I thank the family and move to switch off the recorder, Fikiswa's grandmother demands a chance to speak.

My name is Puleng. I am Boikie's mother, Fikiswa's grandmother, and I just want to say thank you a lot to you, Karin and Peter, for your visit at this home … I think everybody will be healed. I can see that … I can see that some people are with us. We are happy about your visit here … I hope you won't leave us, you will always be with us.

After the end of the interview I asked Dolly whether her family and particularly her daughter might have been targeted by the police because she herself had been a political activist at the time in the underground ANC Women's League. She was hiding MK people who were coming into the country illegally and in other ways furthering the ANC underground structures. And it appears to me from what she says that there was an awareness of that somewhere. She was not detained, but she was clearly marked. Although she shared nothing of this with her daughter, in order not to endanger her and other children, she feels that what happened to Fakiswa was a case of the children being made to suffer for what the parents are doing.

After Fikiswa had been raped, Dolly completely withdrew from all her work and focused only on her child. Being a single parent, she has to bring up her daughters on her own and face problems and troubles on her own. Although she has very good support from her mother and her sister, there was still a lot she had to face completely alone.

She said to me then: 'This rape has destroyed our family. Fikiswa had no childhood and I had no life.'

YAZIR HENRY
'The healing is up to each one of us!'

Cape Town, 13 February 1999
Almost three months after our first conversation about an interview for this book, I drive out to meet Yazir. It is a stormy Cape morning as I turn away from the mountain towards the suburb of Grassy Park to meet this young ex-MK guerilla. The young man who faced the public in the TRC hearing at UWC on 6 August 1996 (see Chapter III) was deeply wounded, haunted by the nightmarish death of his comrade for which he believed himself responsible. Haunted also by a deeply

conflictual relationship with the ANC, to which he had entrusted his life. This life which had since become untenable to him, bleak and without hope.

When I first met him, just over two years later, Yazir's face and manner spoke of these deep scars. As he listened carefully to my explanations of why I wanted to interview him, his eyes and his body language spoke only of flight, of escape, above all of being haunted by nightmarish memories. These are not made easier to bear by the hounding of journalists and others who only want his story. He looks at both Lutz and me with deep distrust: Don't we, too, simply want to prey off him in this way? For what conceivable reason should he trust either a middle-class white South African woman or yet another European writer? The ability to trust is almost impossible to restore when it has been so deeply betrayed. Yazir clearly has no reason to trust anyone outside his small group of ex-cadres with whom he is struggling to rebuild a life.

But his obvious intelligence makes him a careful listener. Though the very thought of further exposure is painful to him, he does not reject our request out of hand. Then eventually a friendly, if guarded, phone call: 'Let's meet …'

Even before the meeting actually takes place, the ice between us is broken on a level that is almost farcical: I lose my way and have to phone him for directions from my car. A very amused Yazir guides me by cellphone (his and mine) to our meeting point: No, not high up on Victoria Road, much lower down than I expect, in territory with which I am not familiar and in which my orientation falters not only because I have a reputation for misreading maps … The space in which Yazir lives and in which he risked his life until a short few years ago is unfamiliar terrain to me. Without my being conscious of it, my urban geography is limited and marked by the fault lines of apartheid's divisions which have circumscribed my spaces and determined my movements in my home city. It is a galling realisation: had I not thought myself unaffected, able to transcend these imposed boundaries in my daily existence? How would my failure to negotiate his streets in my (albeit elderly) Mercedes look to this young man whose hardships are structurally linked to my privileges? But we do not meet as categories, we meet as people. A friendly hug, a relieved laugh from me and a teasing grin from him: having found my Achilles' heel, he is amused. He agrees with me that I would have been a hopeless failure in any underground guerilla army, liable to land up in enemy territory as easily as with a friendly force …

On the False Bay coast we find a coffee shop. I notice that Yazir is uncomfortable in this space, finds himself a seat against the wall from which he can survey the room. The waitress brings our snacks with a knife and fork rolled in a napkin, the cutlery pointing towards Yazir's face in the small space. She takes his reprimand not to point things at him with equanimity. Yazir explains to me, 'I can't take it when things are pointed at me …' Later, we are able to talk about post traumatic stress disorder; for now, we settle in as best we can. We talk about the necessity for changes to happen, and discuss how far the TRC has initiated a move towards that.

Yazir: I think that in many ways the TRC has already failed. For many who testified, there was an expectation of compensation, of immediate material relief. By and large, that has not happened. Individual reparations are inadequate and disappointing.

There are some positive aspects to the TRC, but on the material level it seems to have made promises that it could not deliver.

But what about the importance of acknowledgement of pain, of the restoration of dignity and identity?

That worked for some, but it made little difference for communities.

Was it positive for you to have gone through the TRC process?

In some respects, yes. It provided a space for me in what was a desperate attempt to survive. I did not really want to go to the TRC and only went quite late. But for me it was either that – go to the TRC and express myself or die. And now, a couple of years later, I am sitting here and talking to you. So in that sense, some positive things came out of the TRC for me, just in being able to occupy that space and express myself. I was physically breaking down, to the point that I would black out. Things had become too much and I recognised that I was dying. It was a personal decision to make an intervention. Before that I believed that I needed to die. I hated myself so much that I wanted to die. There was this tension between wanting and not wanting to die.

How are people enabled to go on living with pain rather than to die from it?

That is why I have a problem with people who say, 'Just put it behind you, let it go away.' And it is not only white people who say, 'Let's forget it all.' At the moment, 'Let's forget the past' is a popular discourse. And you cannot do that. Last night, I woke up at two o'clock and reached across my pillow, expecting there to be a gun.

How many years of your life did you spend with a gun on your pillow?

Since I was nearly fifteen.

In the Bonteheuwel Military Wing?

No, I was not in the BMW. I had contact with them in MK but I was not part of them. In the Western Cape, particularly in the flash points, Mitchell's Plain, Manenberg, Bonteheuwel and Wynberg, there were many different cells operating. They were later drawn together into MK.

We talk about the importance of writing the history of that time, and that it should be done by the people who were involved. Yazir is worried about histories written by those who do not own the stories. He feels that there is a lot of appropriation going on, at various levels.

In this connection, he feels that the public hearings of the TRC have started a process over which there is ultimately no control, and that this is very alienating for many of those who testified. This, he feels is a limitation, even a failure of the TRC which should be acknowledged.

Someone I know broke down crying because of a newspaper article. He saw that some of the people who had tortured him had been given amnesty. Why did he have to find that out from a newspaper? I spent a whole morning with that man, comforting him.

Knowing some of the things that have gone wrong, how can we go forward? How do we go on with what is good in the TRC?

For me there is a history lesson for humanity not only in the successes of the TRC but also in its failures. The most important thing is to learn from the failures. Those should be addressed together with all the positive experiences.

On a personal level, do you have support?

Yes, and it can even be problematic if people care too much. The reality is that life goes on and that people's lives don't stop and wait for you to recover. Inasmuch as they can help you, their attitude is often, 'Let go of the past. Get on with your life'. My experience is foreign to most people. I must recognise that people can't get into my skin and cannot feel what I feel.

And then you live in an apparently normal way and yet inside yourself you are in two different places at once ...

Sometimes five places. But that was partly positive in my experience of the TRC. Up until that point, I had told no one what I was feeling. Not even my mother or my family knew. They knew that I was completely messed up, but they did not know why. I had turned away from them ... I hated myself and I expected to die. And I wanted to die on my own ...

I invited my mother to the hearing ... and the hearing opened up a space. It was the first time my mother heard what had happened to me. They had gone through trauma because of what had happened to me, because of the age at which I left and because of what the police did to them. My mother died six months after the TRC process. For a few months she went through all these experiences, I believe that is why she died, that it all was too much.

I had broken down psychologically and the Commission process did not help them much at that time. If it was not for her, I would not be able to be here now. But I am, and it is because of her that I survived. I am here now – and she is not. And for that I feel partly responsible. She should be here.

Is it not that, because of the things which are coming to the surface in your life, you make yourself responsible for what is ultimately someone else's doing? That you take responsibility for the crime of a whole system?

A lot of people who have been involved in the hearings have died. The Commission has completed its work and handed in its report, but what about the people who paid the price, and who had to pay the price for the whole country?

I don't want to be too negative, and there is much that one has to acknowledge in a positive way. I've come from a war. I've been really, really scarred – and I don't want to go back to a war now. I want to look at things differently.

So how do we do that? You personally seem to be on a good track with the project that you are doing.

Yes. I ask myself that question, and others ask me. For me, there are certain NOs.

And those are?

War. That is a NO. And the second NO is that we don't want to exploit. The principle 'Let the victim not become the victimiser' is important.

Yes. And there are horrible examples of that.

Just look at Palestine and Israel.

Would it be right to say that because people have suffered oppression, even annihilation, they should be better than others? Your history of oppression does not necessarily make you a better person. People are the same wherever they are.

This is becoming an argument about the history of 'otherness', of setting people up and taking them down, whether they are gays, socialists or whatever. People ask me how I can be involved in business when I call myself a socialist. This is typical of a very aggressive liberal discourse.

Sure. I was trying to say that it is not fair to set groups up and expect them to be different – gays to be more sensitive, Jews more liberal, and so on. It cannot happen that way.

I agree. This is really about starting to listen to each other. We must do that so that we do not become victimisers.

That is what I am trying to do in my project. Whether I am right or wrong, time will show. Our project is about more than job creation. That is what moves me. The collective within which I work aims to enable people to move themselves. It is something I did not have before: that I can now say to myself, I appreciate myself. I am proud of who I am. I have achieved certain things and I can achieve much more. I recognise that.

And you – and others – are role models in your community. It is important that young people see that. What makes me more furious than almost anything else in this country is when people talk about a 'lost generation'. I don't think that anybody is ever lost, unless you choose to lose them.

That angers me also, because the person they talk about is me. I am that person.

And the person who says it is me. And does that mean that I as an educator have failed in my most important responsibility: to make sure that there is a future for the next generation?

Yes, exactly. And the people who say it – that's not us. They are academics who know nothing about us and what we are doing and what has happened to us. I won't be treated as an object any more. We will not be silenced any more.

Good! Because it is your voice that is important for your generation.

I also realised at university how academics dominate and appropriate, and also so often trivialise what is ultimately not their own experience. I am now determined to resist that, regardless of the consequences. I will not be silent any more. The police set me up against me. I was destroying myself. They left me alone and I completed the job they had started. I don't know why they did not kill me. But I won't kill myself any more. And I won't see other people like me kill themselves. Regardless of the consequences, I am going to stand up and be counted. If I can get more people to stand out with me and say enough! We can move somewhere. And that is what wakes me up in the morning. I have a very clear vision. I can see where I want to go, why and with whom. I have been abused and used. With all these things that have been done to me ... I will not get demoralised and depressed any more.

You have great strength. I admire that.

I appreciate you saying that. But you know, comments like that would have harmed me in the past. I did not think I deserved to be complimented. I used to think that I only deserved bad things happening to me. But I don't think that any more.

I was always haunted by dead faces, many of them. There are so many in my head and I could never get beyond the experience of death. Then, one day as I was driving, I saw the face of a comrade who had died, and I saw his face transform into a living face, as he had been before he died. And that process has continued.

More and more I see comrades come alive again. I still remember that they are dead, but I see them alive, running, doing things they used to do. And it fuels me, it is like a flame inside me. I can feel that flame. It wakes me up in the morning. I see what I want to do. It is all there in the future, it is there.

[*We leave the coffee shop and take a walk along the beach front, watch the waves crash over the breakwater. It seems a good place to explore the issues of healing and facing the future.*]

Twenty thousand people who testified before the TRC cannot be responsible for carrying healing to forty-five million people. We all have to do that. The TRC has opened up space for people to express their anguish. The healing is up to each one of us.

Apartheid has affected everybody in some way. If we want to avoid another war, a Bosnia, we must all take responsibility. The problem is that whites on the whole do not see the need for this. For them everything is fine. They complain the most and they come off best in the reconciliation process. They have everything – economically, socially, politically. And they don't see it. They have power and skills – but they still subscribe to a culture of entitlement. And they blame us for it. My message is: If we do not change this, and if we do not accept each other as human beings on an equal level, we will go into another war. White people, along with everybody else, must begin to take responsibility for what happened.

All my experience has been that as long as I change, there is no friction. There needs to be an equal reaching out. If we don't do that, we will have another war.

We conclude our conversation and arrange to meet again, so that I can see his project at work and take a few photographs.

SANDRA ADONIS
'Nothing will get better until we speak about it!'

Cape Town, 13 April 1999
I ring the doorbell to one of the UCT student flats in an old block on Rosebank Main Road. The door is opened by Sandra's friend Mary, who has been specially summoned to receive me, as Sandra will be late. I am shown into her room, which speaks of an organised and disciplined mind with three main areas of interest: intense and serious study, political and resistance history with posters of Chris Hani and Winnie Mandela, and children – photographs of her smiling children and toys in one corner.

Sandra enters in an apologetic flurry, a small, vivacious human dynamo: an assignment was due today, and there have been last-minute hold-ups. Her eyes

assess me in a frank but friendly way as she greets me with an open smile. My way
to her has been prepared by her friend and comrade Yazir Henry. I am clearly not
altogether a stranger to her. Her reaction to my request for a photograph, 'What?
When I look like this?' is endearing in a woman so clearly devoid of vanity and
pretence.

Sandra: I can't believe I am actually at university, with all the difficulties I had! I am so fortunate to be able to study ... it was Yazir who encouraged me. He was a student at UCT when he said to me: 'Why don't you make an effort to go to university?'

I had no idea how to go about it and I only had Standard 7 [Grade 9] because I left school at fifteen. So I first had to do my matric, which was very difficult as I had to teach myself from a few books and did not really know what was expected. I had no teacher, and I still had to look after my children as well. I sat for the examination in 1997 but achieved poor results.

At first, UCT rejected my application on the basis of my poor matric. But then I became really angry! When I think what I had to go through to come that far, and what I had achieved in the years of the struggle ... People who had all the benefits of apartheid are still better off now. They have all the educational advantages and have no trouble in getting into the best universities. I wrote a letter to the university in which I expressed all that anger ... and they accepted me! On the day I received the news, I started to cry ... I just could not believe that it was really true.

So here I am, studying sociology and politics, thinking even of postgraduate study overseas, when two years ago I seemed to have no chance at all.

[But that was only the beginning of another struggle for Sandra, as finding the
funds to keep herself and her children is an ongoing battle.]

Food is sometimes very scarce. But my life has improved. I have a good apartment here and my children can have a hot bath in the evenings. When I don't have food, I can ask friends. I can manage.

I also have a small research job at Groote Schuur Hospital, where I interview Aids patients to find out how they cope economically. Many people know so little about Aids that they think my job is dangerous! But really, we come into contact with so many people every day – and any one of them could have Aids and you wouldn't even know it.[11] People who are scared of mere contact with Aids patients really have not been taught about the disease.

Yes, my life is basically on track, but it took such a long time before I had the strength and the confidence to improve my situation. My suffering began after my husband was released. He became very violent and I was under great stress, I struggled with memory loss and could not concentrate on anything ...

[*Sandra explains how feelings of inferiority and uncertainty, which often translated into guilt, had made it very difficult for her to stand up for her rights. We discuss whether this is something women are prone to in view of their socialisation.*]

You are brought up to believe that lots of things are somehow your fault ... although women are actually so very strong, I believe stronger than men.

Racism works in a similar way. I have just studied some aspects of slavery where it is clear that blacks are always shown to be inherently inferior. That is how it still works in South Africa: whites still think they are superior and better than other people ...

It is interesting that you are now academically researching the influences and forces that have moulded you. That must be very motivating.

It is. When I think of where I came from and what I am studying now, it gives me much more insight into the experiences of others. I also realise now that many others have been oppressed much more than I was, to such an extent that they were quite unable to resist ... It is passed down through the generations.

Tell me more about those generations in your own family. You hinted at something in your submission to the TRC ...

My father was white. He was a German and he never acknowledged me. My mother was a black domestic worker. I used to know my father and I knew where he lived. I can count on the fingers of one hand the number of times I saw him and spoke to him. He will never be part of my life, and not just because he is white.

When I was younger I assumed that I just could not see him because of the laws of the country, the Immorality Act* and so on. Later, when I was older, I realised that he could have found ways of seeing me had he wanted to.

I used to hate all white people for those laws and I never associated with whites. At the beginning, it was a real problem for me to be in a racially mixed institution like UCT. Previous to this I only knew the few whites that worked in resistance organisations. Now I am always in contact with whites and I even have a white friend! I now laugh with my black friends about the way we compare notes on our social contact with whites. We used to be completely anti-white and would refuse ever to be seen with whites. Now some of us are even sharing houses or flats with whites! Our cultures are different and our ways of being socialised are different, but we can now all sit and chat normally together. I now accept that there are blacks and whites in this country.

I always felt that the struggle was really against apartheid and not against whites as such.

Yes, that is true, and it is terrible that the Amy Biehl murder happened. The struggle was against white domination, never against individuals. It was against the state and its structures, the public service, the police, the security system and so on. They all made race an issue. Nobody with any dignity could accept the way we were treated. I remember when I was five years old that I could not sit downstairs in a bus. Or later, when I was shouted at by some white schoolgirls when I sat in a third class coach on a train, where they had chosen to sit.

To me it is also insulting to be called 'coloured'. People who look at me do not call me 'black', but I hate to use the classifications that were forced on me by apartheid. I think our Constitution should have said that there are two races in this country, white and black.

I am glad that our Constitution rightly states that we are all South Africans. But the problem is that we have still to address issues like restitution and therefore some divisions still have to be made.

I think a lot about restitution. Now there is talk of blanket reparation rather than redress on an individual basis. But look at the way the people who tortured us are still in official positions, protected by the law and the Constitution, and they get golden handshakes when they leave. Whereas those who suffered at their hands are still where they were, or are even worse off. All of us were looking forward to liberation in this country ... but some are worse off than before, with no help for the injuries they suffered.

What do you think needs to be done about that?

I feel very strongly that provision must be made for all the young people who lost their education in the struggle. We left school to fight the system, the police and the boers. We took the slogan 'Liberation before Education' quite seriously. Now there needs to be a way of making up for those lost opportunities.

Would that be your first priority?

Yes. I have realised that without education you have nothing. Everything relies on that. But it is very difficult to get funding.

What actually motivated you to go to the TRC?

That took a long time. When the hearings started, I wanted to have nothing to do with politics, the TRC, the ANC or anything else. I thought then that the TRC was just a scam to get the boers out of the shit they were in. I felt it was just another way of using us, the youth, yet again. I feel that the youth have been completely used. Nobody now thinks of us, nobody wonders what has happened to all the young people who had been involved. We were all used ... But I am also proud that I participated in the Struggle, that I worked for democracy in this country. I am very proud of that, even if people used me. At least we have achieved what we fought for.

I felt very anti-TRC, but I also did not know how to reach them. Then I heard one of my comrades, Donovan Ferhelst, speak in a hearing which was broadcast on the radio. I started to cry when I remembered what we had all been through. Then I went to see Donovan and he urged me to approach the TRC. It still took me a while to go, even then.

You particularly drew attention to the plight of the youth. Were you hoping something would happen as a result?

Well, I still don't expect them to say thank you, because they will never do it. What I did was not for thanks. I was thinking then of my own children, and of making life better for them.

To whom do you refer when you say 'they'?

To the ANC's hierarchy. They never looked back and said: 'Wow, it's actually the youth that has caused us to come this far.'

So you feel that there is not sufficient acknowledgement by those now in power?

Yes. If they would set up education facilities for people to empower themselves – that would be a way of showing appreciation and an acknowledgement for what the youth achieved.

I understand that not everyone can get what he or she hoped for, but I would be satisfied if there could at least be such opportunities. I am not concerned about any other form of recognition from the ANC. Perhaps a monument to youth would be an acknowledgement of some sort.

If you reflect now on your TRC experience: do you think it was worth it?

Yes, even if there are no reparations it was worthwhile. There was a weight on me and the TRC has lifted that weight through the mere fact that I could share my story with others. It is especially important because for the youth today apartheid has never existed. As far as they are concerned, we never struggled or had bad times ...

You mean people who are now fourteen or fifteen?

Even those of eighteen or twenty. Even at university now, students don't want to know and are not interested in apartheid. People at university are really very selfish and I don't want to become like that. I want to stay humble and remain a community person. Education should not change you as a person.

I am glad that through the TRC I made a contribution to our story. It won't be lost now. The record is there.

What about the story of women? It seems that, because of the mandate of the Commission, women were marginalised in the hearings.

Our society is structured in patriarchal ways. I could have spoken on behalf of myself and what I suffered at the hands of my husband when he was released from detention. I tried to get him to speak about what happened, but he would not. He became very violent.

That must have happened many thousands of times ...

[The telephone rings and Sandra speaks to a friend in Afrikaans. When we continue, we switch to Afrikaans and focus briefly on the language issue.]

I think it is stupid when people refuse to speak Afrikaans. After all, English is really the primary colonial language worldwide, isn't it?

Precisely. And Afrikaans is the mother tongue of more black people than whites. It is a wonderful and colourful language with a vibrant literature ...

Especially in the Cape. You can express yourself in so many ways!

Getting back to women: You have provided, through your evidence before the TRC, an access to an experience which has been almost completely silenced. In spite of having women's hearings, the TRC did not look at oppression from a gender perspective. That is one criticism one can make. Proportionally, it also did not give enough space to the youth. But on the other hand, the TRC is only the beginning of a process and a discussion which must continue.

I am very interested in gender issues. I want to help other women. It is time that we as women uplift each other. We should speak out about violence. In our society we are brought up to be very private and we are discouraged from speaking about things like domestic violence. I came out of that, and I am speaking out now. It was very difficult to do that, to speak about my marriage and the violence in it – which I believe was indirectly caused by apartheid. I could have been killed, it was so bad. Now I will no longer perpetuate a situation by keeping quiet, and I want to encourage other women to speak out. We are planning to start a gender forum here at which women in abusive relationships can speak out. Because nothing will get better until we speak about it.

We conclude our interview in the knowledge that there is still much to discuss and that we will surely meet again. Now Sandra has to rush back to campus in order not to miss a lecture. I drive her up to her class. She is obviously determined to make the most of all her hard-won opportunities, in spite of money worries, three children, a part-time job ... There seems to be no obstacle that cannot be overcome by sheer determination and tremendous courage.

LAURIE NATHAN
'As a Jew I would have died in Nazi Germany'

Cape Town, 20 January 1999
Then he was just in his early twenties: a charismatic young man with dark, curly hair who, in spite of his youth, already chaired the Cape Town branch of the End

Conscription Campaign. Archbishop Tutu made a memorable comment about the organisation during that time: 'The ECC's rapid growth and popularity are signs of hope in this crazy, crazy but beautiful country.'

While I anticipate the interview with Laurie in his office at the Centre for Conflict Resolution on the beautiful old Hiddingh campus of the University, in the historic heart of Cape Town, the past suddenly comes back into sharp focus.

The Regional Council meetings of the Black Sash with an ECC representative reporting; helping to organise campaigns and meetings; painting banners and holding placards with banned slogans like TROOPS OUT OF TOWNSHIPS; hiding ECC activists in our homes; wearing banned T-shirts under plain blouses, with only just enough of the ECC designs showing to signal solidarity …

There was our nervousness at taking on the powerful state security system, knowing that we were being watched … and our near-hysterical laughter at the sight of uniformed cops demolishing sand castles on the beach at Clifton or scaling trees and lamp posts to remove yellow ribbons! Our anger at the smear campaigns directed at the young homosexual doctor Ivan Thoms, whose personal integrity and courageous and effective opposition to conscription were vilified in the most disgusting way, using his sexual orientation as pretext. Our going out in the early dawn to tear down those insulting posters; our admiration for those like David Bruce who went to jail for six years; our gnawing worry about activists like Janet Cherry, detained without trial and in solitary confinement in Port Elizabeth for ECC activities …

But also the laughter and fun at ECC gatherings and events, the sheer enjoyment of irreverence and play as subversive tools. Nowhere was the lunacy of apartheid's military mind more starkly evident than in its war against songs, T-shirts, buttons and bumper stickers, sand castles, yellow ribbons and children's balloons. But always, always the very personal and private worry about your own sons, faced with the choices of prison, exile or SADF … Military Police appearing at your home to check whether your eldest son had finished his studies, just to intimidate, just to let you know that they were watching …

My own anger at the cowardly headmaster who would not allow the ECC equal opportunity to speak at my son's school, where the SADF could spread their propaganda each year unchecked … All this goes through my mind as I make my way to Laurie. But on seeing him again after all these years I start with a different question. It is one I did not ask then, but which now seems more important than ever if one wants to understand those times and prevent such things from happening again: What is it that turns a privileged middle class Jewish boy from a caring but apolitical home into a fiery young activist prepared to take on the apartheid state and to suffer the consequences? What makes a highly gifted young intellectual forgo the privileges of study at a top-rate, prestigious institution like the University of Cape Town and choose to complete his thesis in hiding, always on the run, always waiting for that knock on the door?

Laurie explains: I was oblivious to the impact of apartheid and never questioned it while I was growing up.

Perhaps occasionally, when as a child around the Pesach table I would listen to the story of the Jews' liberation from slavery, it would strike me as contradictory that there were black servants hovering around. But I was unaware and uninvolved until I got to university.

It was there that I first heard black trade unionists speak, blacks who were not submissive but who stood up and argued their case. I was also, for the first time, confronted with information on the true devastation wrought by apartheid through statistics in NUSAS* pamphlets on infant mortality, differential spending on education – figures that were chilling and shocking. I could not believe that it was that bad.

However, all this was in a sense only the preparation for what Laurie himself terms the key experience that changed his life: a visit to the concentration camp Dachau after his first year at university. His overriding impression is one of complete unreality and alienation. How could this starkly beautiful and quiet place in its blanket of snow have been a site of organised extermination of human beings? Some Austrian businessmen walk through, ahead of him, eating and chatting; young Americans play the fool at the fence, pretending to escape, to be shot ... Where in all this is there a connection to the life of a young South African Jew?

I left, feeling completely alienated. But then I remembered the teaching of my childhood that the Holocaust must always be remembered so that it does not happen again. I asked myself: what is the IT? The IT cannot simply be the attempted extermination of Jews. The IT is the level of barbarity, the IT is happening in our own country ...

The IT is a level of barbarity where it does not matter who you are, what you think, what your values are – if they are gunning for your kind, you die. As a Jew in Nazi Germany, I die. Apartheid is based on the same logic: it does not matter what your other circumstances are, if you are black, you die.

It is a profound problem in the Jewish community that we are more concerned about ourselves than about others. I, as a Jew, am in a good position to challenge my own community on that. If you are concerned only about injustice done to yourself, and not about injustice done to others, the position has no integrity. And this does not detract from the fact that the Holocaust was unique, as the genocide in Rwanda or in Bosnia was unique – specific comparisons as to which was worse would be extremely facile and anti-humanitarian. But to draw other kinds of comparisons does not deny the significance or uniqueness of each event.

Dachau was my deciding experience. Travelling back from the former concentration camp I remember conversations around the dinner table at home: 'Why did the German people not do anything? How can they say they did not know what was happening?' And I thought: This question is going to be asked of us one day, as the white community in South Africa. And from that point on my commitment to involvement in anti-apartheid politics was clear and absolute.

For me there was no doubt whatsoever that this is what I would do with my life, in whatever form, until the ending of apartheid.

From there, the decision not to go into the army was obvious. You do not go and carry a gun for apartheid, whatever the consequences. I was deeply entrenched in NUSAS and the UDF and then in 1983, at the age of twenty-four, I became involved in the founding of the ECC. I had various leadership roles in the ECC. During the 1986/87 State of Emergency I was forced to go into hiding. During that time, I completed a Master's dissertation on war resistance in South Africa.

Looking back today, the ECC made an enormously valuable contribution, perhaps more so than we even knew at the time. The contributions to the liberation struggle from the white community were very few. The ECC did enormous damage to the system by undermining the legitimacy of the state in the eyes of the white community. We were seen not as enemies but as traitors. We targeted the institution that maintained apartheid, the military. It was that which stood between white rule and majority rule. In questioning the duty to serve, you are questioning the legitimacy of the state. That is why we incurred the full wrath of the state. The ECC took a Just War position, it was not pacifist *per se*, but clear in its rejection of service in this army to uphold this state. Thus the ECC attracted a much higher level of repression than other white organisations.[12]

We also provided a home for those who, both as citizens and as parents, rejected military service in an apartheid army. The ECC, as an inclusive umbrella organisation devoted to this single campaign, was an important rallying force for people from a variety of ideological backgrounds.

The other very significant contribution that the ECC made was that we sent a powerful statement of non-racialism to the black community.

Many whites who consider themselves liberal have missed one of the most fundamental points about freedom. For them freedom is a primary value, but it is about liberal rights: the right to free association, to property, to free expression and freedom from censorship. All are core values in a democracy, but given our history and our context, the freedom from poverty is the prime one, and so many seem oblivious of that.

Look at it this way: I steal your bicycle. After five years I come to you and say, 'I am very sorry, I stole your bicycle.' You may, if you are Archbishop Tutu, say, 'I forgive you'. The more normal response would be, 'Yes, okay – where is my bicycle?' If what I stole was not your bicycle but your land, your dreams, your hope? What then? How much does my apology count?

I have done interviews with people in rural areas on their views on reconciliation, without reference to the TRC. The whites, virtually without exception, say, 'Enough of the TRC, let bygones be bygones'. The coloured and African people, virtually without exception, never refer to the TRC, never refer to the past. The common response is, 'What are you talking about, reconciliation? Look at how we live, look at our shacks, and look at how the whites live, look at the cars, the swimming pools'. So the concern is material, for good reason, and to have the current inequities addressed.

I would like to repeat something I said before the TRC, regarding the attitudes within the white community. There tend to be three distinct positions among whites.

The first one is that they say they are shocked by the revelations of the TRC, had they only known about the atrocities at the time they would surely have objected. This is a self-serving myth. It is patently dishonest to claim today that any of us were unaware of apartheid, unaware of forced removals and pass laws, unaware of deaths in detention or unaware of the killing of children in our streets.

The second response from the white community is that, yes, we knew what was happening and we did everything in our power to object. This is also a myth. The truth of the matter is that only a tiny minority of whites voiced any opposition and then in conditions of relative safety and comfort. An even smaller minority of whites participated directly in the campaigns, in the daily struggle of black people.

The third position comes from whites who say let bygones be bygones, rehashing the past will only perpetuate divisions and inhibit reconciliation. Let us concentrate instead, they say, on building a new future. In my view this position adds insult to injury. It's a monumental deceit. Whatever the individual talents and efforts of whites, our lives of privilege today are the product of a grand historical act of theft. We stole the land, the labour, the dignity and, in countless instances, the lives of the black people of our country. The majority of the black people still live with the consequences and the majority of whites still enjoy the fruits of our acts of violence.

The past is present. White racism is alive and kicking. It no longer takes the form of legislated supremacy but it continues to manifest itself in crude and subtle ways. The most offensive is the endless complaining about corruption, inefficiency and falling standards. This is one of the bad jokes of the new South Africa. The previous government set unsurpassed standards for corruption, incompetence and neglect.

There is a fourth position which is seldom heard and which I believe is the appropriate response. The white community should confront its pervasive racism and stare our ugly history and its long shelf life in the face. We should acknowledge collective responsibility for our efforts and our acquiescence in constructing and maintaining a wretched system of discrimination, exclusion and repression. The challenge is to become self-critical, not uncritical, to acquire some humility, not to be submissive, to become empathetic, not paternalistic. The challenge has nothing to do with self-flagellation or wallowing in guilt, it has everything to do with accepting responsibility for our actions or lack of actions.

If the End Conscription Campaign existed today, I would propose that we issue stickers for distribution in the white community which say: Stop complaining, start building!

Focusing on youth, this is the area where most restorative justice is needed. Poverty and the violent gang culture bred by poverty stifle hope and development. You don't have to be a sociologist to understand that if you grow up in Manenberg[13] you have no future. You only have to walk along the streets of Manenberg to understand that, or to sit in a classroom. Children are hungry, and children are scared – scared to walk to school, and scared to walk home. I challenge those who say to these children that they should not join gangs, I challenge them with questions that are asked every day by those same kids, some of them as young as ten: 'What do you offer me, what are you offering by way of hope? Why should I not join a gang if that means that I do not get beaten up on my way to and from school, and if it also means that my unemployed parents get some food?'

Looking at Laurie I still see evidence of the charismatic student leader whose conviction and energy helped to drive the ECC. It is a mature face now, but the idealism, the commitment, the ability to see clearly what needs to be done – all that is still there in his eyes. Especially so when he talks about his Institute's Conflict Resolution and Peace Education project in schools in the Cape Flats, in the self-same schools where the gangs reign. As I leave, he gives me a documentary on one of the projects which I view as soon as I get home (see Chapter V: Centre for Conflict Resolution). I am deeply moved by what is being achieved with humble means and against great odds. Simply through dedication, through a determination not to give up, to prove those wrong who speak of the 'lost generation'. The movie is aptly titled Hope in Hell *... The story of the film is told in the next chapter.*

V

REMEMBRANCE
AND
THE FUTURE

THE ROBBEN ISLAND
MUSEUM

'YOUTH PROJECTS FACING OUR HISTORY'

Visitors to Robben Island may not always realise that the Museum is an important site of pedagogical initiatives. Schoolchildren from all over the country enjoy island holidays of a particular kind – for a day, for a weekend or even for longer. A recurring theme before the Truth Commission has been the importance of narrative and storytelling. The South African poet Njabulo Ndebele writes:

> The narrative of apartheid, which can now be told, has reached the part of the plot where vital facts leading to the emergence of understanding are now being revealed ... In few countries in the contemporary world do we have a living example of people reinventing themselves through narrative. ... the real challenge is ... in the capacity for our society to stimulate the imaginations of its peoples through voices that can go beyond the giving of testimony, towards creating new thoughts and new worlds.[1]

But before stories can be told and heard there has to be contact and communication. Only then can experiences of some young people become an accessible reality for others. In this regard, the educational initiatives on Robben Island open up an important space for pupils and teachers alike by holding seminars and encouraging creative exploration of stories and history. Much more than facts and statistics, these creative experiences open up the other worlds that Ndebele talks about.

One example is a workshop linked with the remembrance of the Soweto Uprising, on 16 June 1976*, when young students rebelled against the imposition of Afrikaans as a medium of instruction. A group of about 100 Afrikaans and English-speaking school pupils were recently brought to the Island. Most of them, familiar with the broad outlines of the history of the Soweto Uprising, did not expect to learn anything new and were simply looking forward to an enjoyable outing. Nobody expected to be confronted with an entirely different reality when, to their utter consternation, they did not hear a familiar language either during embarkation or throughout the crossing: all group leaders and facilitators spoke only Xhosa. The pupils' reaction ranged from insecurity and alienation to anger, fear and aggression. These emotions were discussed when, to their great relief, the facilitators finally spoke English and Afrikaans, in which they could all communicate. In this way, a change of perspective was achieved and a learning process initiated which encouraged real understanding of the issues that drove the pupils of Soweto into conflict with the apartheid state.

Robben Island is a living museum, not a static memorial site. It is a place where young people from very different backgrounds can meet and experiment with different media in order to communicate their stories and share their histories in mime and dance, in drama and poetry. Everything possible is done to enable previously marginalised history to be given space and form. It is much more than the sum total of history lessons – it is an opportunity to experience a site connected with memories of inhumanity and brutality, but also with the triumph of the human spirit. 'Pupils learn that the spirit can triumph over evil', as an ex-detainee has put it.

I had the opportunity to observe how much creativity is released when young people can appropriate their own history, and how human rights become concrete experiences during this process. I watched a young boy named Themba, from Khayelitsha.[2]

Themba did not really notice me, because all his attention was absorbed by an apple box. I did not ask his name, not because I do not speak Xhosa, but because that would not have helped: Themba is deaf and dumb, and I do not 'speak' sign language. I could not guess his age, as he was growth-retarded and severely disabled, so that he could not move very well. He was sitting on the floor, absorbed in his own world, with this ordinary apple box. No, that is not right: In South Africa, particularly in Cape Town and on Robben Island, apple boxes are not ordinary things. When a prisoner was released from the Island, after having served his sentence, he was given his belongings in an apple box. When you saw someone in a receiving centre like Cowley House looking a bit lost and disoriented, clutching an apple box, you knew without needing to be told that this person had just spent a number of years in one of the most inhuman of prisons, and that he was disoriented because all rudiments of normal life and social interchange had been denied him. People with apple boxes populated our collective memory in those years, the ordinary household object a symbol of the callous disregard for human dignity and human rights which formed the basis of apartheid policy.

Why, then, was this child Themba so absorbed in an apple box, he who must have been little more than a toddler when Mandela was finally released in 1990? He was one of a group of about 25 young people from all over the Cape who were spending their week of spring holiday on Robben Island, attending a workshop in which they learnt about its history. During that week they themselves planned and put together an exhibition which would travel to all their different schools, and which they would introduce to their own school, to other schools in the vicinity and to the community in which they lived. Apple boxes formed the basic structure of this exhibition. With apple boxes, a huge prison wall was constructed, each box forming a block in this wall. On to these blocks, the children pasted stories and drawings to illustrate various aspects of the history of the Island: accounts of the early history, of famous prisoners in the previous century, the leper colony, of daring escape attempts and, most of all, of the political prisoners housed there since the Rivonia trial. Some of the boxes were carefully cut with a very sharp knife, to resemble barred windows: a painstaking task that required concentration if injury was to be avoided. This is how I came across Themba: he was completely and happily absorbed in this very important task. I could tell from the way his eyes shone just how much he was enjoying his work. Every now and then one of his schoolmates would come up to him and communicate something in sign language. He would wave them away and continue slowly and carefully. Only when he had finished all the bars to his satisfaction did he get up, awkwardly and slowly, to retrieve a papier mâché-covered balloon from outside, where it had been drying in the hot spring sun. He carefully pasted a face that he had drawn on white paper on to the papier mâché head. Then he placed the head into the apple box, behind the

bars. He smiled, satisfied, the other children came to look and all voiced or signed
their approval (by now most of the others had acquired some sign language): Themba
had done well, he had made an image of Nelson Mandela in his cell. This most
important of the apple boxes was slotted in amongst the others and all approved.
Yes, this was an exhibition they would be proud to take to their schools, an exhibition
they all owned with pride and accomplishment, a history they could tell with
authority, even with passion.

Within this little story are pointers to the successes as well as to some of
the problems of the Robben Island Museum. The initiatives undertaken
with schoolchildren are, as far as I have observed, highly creative and
successful. They are limited on the Museum side by budget constraints, by
staff shortages and at times by a struggle to manage resources and people
skilfully. However, there is tremendous commitment on the part of the
staff, most of whom were either prisoners or activists in the time of the
Struggle. There is an immediacy and authenticity in the way they are able
to inform others about the history of resistance generally and of the Island
in particular. The tour of the prison with commentary and explanation by
a former political prisoner is, again and again, the highlight of an island
tour. It is also the point at which children's imagination is kindled, their
interest suddenly sparking many questions, all of which are answered,
fully and patiently.

The question arises that must be a problem for all such initiatives,
worldwide: What happens when the last of the witnesses is gone? The
testimony of *Zeitzeugen* (witnesses who were part of the events) is without
any doubt the backbone of Robben Island teaching at the moment. It is a
source of authenticity and inspiration – and it is also the key to what is
uniquely transformative and healing in the present South African context.
It is amazing and humbling that a former prisoner who was treated in an
abominably inhuman fashion, in a system of mindless cruelty designed to
break the human spirit, can communicate freely his own gentleness of spirit
and his own generosity towards the many bystanders (and even some
perpetrators) who pass daily through the big prison gates. This without
ever becoming impatient or angry with the lack of imagination, the

defensiveness, hostility and indifference – or the banal and ignorant curiosity – that he encounters daily.

When I asked this man how he could possibly cope with this invasion of his own most private and painful memories, he admitted that it was at times very difficult, but added: 'We must make our young people understand and see.' This he most definitely achieves, but who will do it after him?

At the moment we all, as South Africans, live in a period of grace, where the nation is still offered healing by many who have suffered. Nelson Mandela is not the only such person by far – he is only the most famous of them.

As soon as museums are constituted to enshrine history, there are two dangers: Firstly, that the past is enshrined and encoded selectively, and secondly, that it is eventually cast in stone. It is inevitable that history is written or rewritten by the victors. To some extent, this is the case in Robben Island too. The focus is very strongly, though not exclusively, on the heroes of the ANC who now constitute the government of the country. This is where most of the limelight falls, not entirely to the satisfaction of people who stand elsewhere, mostly further left, in the political spectrum.

Robben Island as a memorial and an educational site is driven by the sense that it constitutes a symbol of transformation to modernity after apartheid. However, this is a transformation which has barely begun, which draws legitimation from hope, rhetoric and symbolism as much as from reality. At the same time, this vision is powerful and necessary to drive the process of transformation. A part of the cost of such a symbolic mission is that history is mainstreamed, and contradictions, countercurrents and personal histories may be sacrificed to the common good, to ensure the unifying force of the visionary goal, in this case a 'rainbow nation'.

There is a further problematic form of selectivity embedded deeply within the history and fabric of the Robben Island story: that of gender. There were no female political prisoners on the Island. No woman ever carried an apple box off Robben Island. In that sense, women are entirely excluded from the gallery of political heroes and the celebration of victory.

It is ironical that on the one hand, the personal stories of the men imprisoned there show that they survived emotionally and psychologically largely because they jettisoned much of their gendered conditioning and developed qualities of gentleness, caring and nurturing not generally regarded as typically male. There were no King Rats on the Island. Yet, as the prime symbol of victory over apartheid the Island necessarily enshrines a purely male hierarchy and honours the struggle and suffering of men. This has quite serious implications for the way the history of women and resistance is written and celebrated.

Perhaps one of the most important things one can say about Robben Island today is that it is open, flexible, not (yet) cast in stone. It is a site where the interpretation of South African history is still being formed and it projects a vision of a harmony that is not yet reality in South Africa, as much a reminder of what has not yet been achieved as it is a proud memorial and symbol – as one ex-prisoner puts it – of the victory of the human spirit, the proof that this spirit cannot be broken. It is this sense of creation that drives the project on Robben Island and that gives such vitality to the educational work being done there. It is vital that such openness should be retained, that Robben Island should not in time turn into a shrine for heroes. As time goes by there will be more and more tension between those who want to preserve the past in its unique and pure form and those who want to make it work for the future, whatever the demands of that future may be.

It is a great challenge to maintain the balance between these different forces at a memorial site and it is a struggle made more difficult by the increasing demands of tourism. The management of Robben Island has resisted demands to commercialise the memorial site, but there are other perceptual constraints imposed by tourism. In a sense, tourists do not come to learn but to recognise and find what they already know or believe they know. To be successful, any memorial site has to adapt to these forces to some extent. It is not possible to convey the complexities of South African history in a three-hour tour, simplifications and omissions are inevitable, and thus become reinforced.

Perhaps the downside of tourism shows us something else: the difficulty of having to offer up to the expectations of others a ready-made, complete and ultimately consumable package of the past when this is actually still being explored and being constituted.

Co-ordinator Education
Robben Island Museum
Robben Island 7400
South Africa
e-mail: educate@robben-island.org.za

THE WESTERN CAPE
ACTION TOURS

This is a project conceived by a group of ex-*Umkhonto we Sizwe* soldiers around Yazir Henry (see also Chapters III and IV). Their aim is fourfold:

- To provide an alternative form of tourism by facilitating access to Cape townships and educating South Africans and foreigners about the history of oppression and resistance in South Africa;
- To commemorate those who have fought for liberation;
- To enable people to meet and interact across racial and spatial boundaries that were rigidly upheld in the past;
- To create jobs and income for ex-cadres and other people in the townships of Cape Town.

IN THE NEW SOUTH AFRICA

It is a sunny Saturday morning and we are leaving central Cape Town for a tour of the townships. We are a racially mixed group of twelve former UWC students, their teachers and a couple of American visitors, in a slightly battered VW Kombi-Taxi, of the kind that usually causes havoc on Cape roads. But this time we feel quite safe – because a jovial, burly former *Umkhonto we Sizwe* soldier is at the wheel, with two comrades next to him. They are softly singing Umkhonto songs which I had last heard sung in loud defiance, by angry Young Lions at banned meetings in the eighties. Now these songs form a melodious backdrop to the soft-spoken but authoritative leader of the tour, Yazir Henry, who prepares us not only to see, but also to understand what we are about to experience. And it is all a matter of seeing, of removing the blindfolds with which we have all lived for so long. As we drive towards the suburb of Athlone, Yazir points out the visible separations of roads and railway lines which enforced the invisible boundaries of rigidly engineered racial ghettos.

192

Our first stop is the bustling central business area of Athlone, where Yazir talks to our group about the politics of racial separation and the way this created invisible walls in minds and perceptions. So much so that a fifth-generation South African woman living in Athlone still calls herself Indian according to apartheid classification. Yazir also speaks about student activism of the eighties and about resistance struggles which emanated from a support base in this area. We then visit the site, a toilet block, where the murdered young Umkhonto cadres Colleen Williams and Robert Waterwitch were found, their deaths a clumsily faked 'grenade accident'. There is no commemorative plaque yet. There is no visible remembrance.

Yazir and his comrades Nkhululeko, Thabo and Otto systematically build a picture of the resistance struggle in the stops and walkabouts that follow. We visit the site where police ambushed young demonstrators and shot them from wooden crates on the back of a truck, an event which became known as the Trojan Horse killings. Someone has sprayed the names of the murdered children on a garden wall, a gesture which conveys not only mourning but also anger at the way this spot is unmarked in any officially recognised way: there is no commemorative sign on this ordinary street corner, no tree, no memorial, not even a bed of flowers.

I feel a mixture of shame and anger throughout the stops that follow: the Pass Office in Langa, now derelict, then one of the sites where, through rigorous application of the draconian pass laws,* the lives of thousands of families were destroyed over many years (see also the story of Nomfundo Walaza in Chapter IV). The legacy of broken families and fragmented communities is with us still – and will be for many years to come.

We stop on the busy road in Gugulethu where the 'Gugulethu Seven' were murdered in cold blood – one of the worst of the atrocities in the Western Cape. I think – and speak – of Cynthia Ngewu at this spot, of her extraordinary, well-nigh incomprehensible generosity towards the perpetrators:

'What we are hoping for when we embrace the notion of reconciliation is that we restore the humanity to those who were perpetrators ... We do not want to see people suffer in the same way that we did suffer ... all South Africans should be committed to the idea of re-accepting these people into the community. We want to demonstrate humaneness towards them, so that they in turn may restore their own humanity' (spoken at the forum on Reconciliation, 19 March 1997).

Would she not at least deserve some form of commemoration, of communal acknowledgement for the son she lost in this brutal way?

But the map of that history, the construction of memory against forgetting, is still almost entirely confined to the minds and energies of those who suffered through these years. Yazir and his comrades have determined to pit their efforts against the general amnesia, against the tendency 'to just get on with our lives'. It is clear to me from the reactions of my former students (all in their early twenties) that even they hear much of this for the first time, and they certainly have not visited these sites before – although they, too, have grown up in townships.

Five years into the new South Africa, we are about to have our second general election, and there are still no visible signposts that encourage reflection on recent history and remembrance of those who suffered anywhere in the townships – or almost anywhere else in Cape Town for that matter. At the University of the Western Cape two student residences are named after the slain student leaders Colleen Williams and Ashley Kriel. I cannot offhand think of any other memorials to a generation that has made such enormous sacrifices. The imbalance in the Cape is indeed remarkable: On the one hand, there is Robben Island Museum out in Table Bay as a world heritage site which commemorates a brutal history as well as the ability of the human spirit to rise above this history. On the other hand, the terrain of the townships where ordinary people resisted in many different ways, and suffered in many more ways is almost unchanged: still impoverished, without resources and largely unrecognised for having carried the brunt of the resistance struggle. Here, too, there is a triumph of the human spirit which still waits to be acknowledged and celebrated. Is this going to be left to idealists on a shoestring budget, like Yazir with his tours? Or will more recognition and support follow in the wake of pioneering initiatives such as his?

We continue on the tour, listening to Yazir's concise, informative synthesis of history, urban planning, political geography and anthropology as we cross physical and ideological boundaries into and out of different township areas. In Langa we visit another project of the group: the re-upholstery workshop where broken and discarded furniture is restored and refurbished. The aim is not only to create desperately needed jobs, but also to enable people to buy good furniture cheaply, without falling into the trap of crippling hire-purchase rates which so often lead to repossession.

A visit to an African herbalist is a 'first' for us all. A myriad *muti* ingredients ranging from python skin to bark, herbs and indefinable substances in hundreds of bottles. Testimony to a thriving practice which obviously fulfils an important need, physical and spiritual, that is not addressed by Western medicine.

In the midst of a sea of shacks we enter a small shebeen, run by a group of women, where ceremonial beer is served. We gingerly sit down on rickety benches and pass a large tin brimful with foaming beer from one to the next: the slightly sour taste is strange, not unpleasant. Our pipe smoking hostess is amused to notice that we cover our slight nervousness with emphatic bonhomie.

In Bonteheuwel we are welcomed into the home of 'Auntie Miena', the mother of activist Farid (also known as Donovan) Ferhelst. She apologises for her small space – while we are embarrassed to have kept her waiting through the delay caused by some of our group. She is graciously welcoming and generous as she shares her story with us. She tells of years of police harassment, ostracism by neighbours and fear for her activist son who was imprisoned under Section 29. She realised that he was being tortured when she was given his bloodstained clothes to wash. Then, like so many, he was released without ever having gone to trial – a changed and disturbed young man robbed of his childhood and youth. We are deeply moved not only by her story, but by the way it is told: simply, sincerely, without a shred of pathos or self-pity.

We understand why Nkhululeko, our genial Umkhonto guide, affectionately calls her 'the mother I go to when I have problems'. It must have been thus for many of the far too young BMW and Umkhonto cadres, to whom women like Auntie Miena gave unstinting support and comfort, at a cost to themselves which they never counted. And the giving and sharing continues even now: to enable others to understand their history, to appreciate their struggles which in the end may yet help us all to live together as one people.

Reconciliation, as Archbishop Tutu said in his introduction to the TRC Report, does not come cheap – but the real miracle is that it is being offered, continuously and in various ways, by so many people who have suffered so greatly.

This, to me, is the great value of the WCAT initiative: the tours open windows into that understanding. Not only are Yazir and his group *Zeitzeugen* who share their own history, they also facilitate communication with others who have lived and shaped that history: ordinary people whose sacrifices still remain unacknowledged, except when their experiences are claimed and appropriated in political rhetoric – which has yet to deliver tangible and useful results.

During a tour around the shack settlements of Philippi and Crossroads Yazir informs us about the huge forced removal projects which gave rise to these settlements – and about the ways in which people opposed these forces. Here important rights of sojourn and citizenship were eventually won – at enormous cost to those who resisted orchestrated state violence and the myriad forms of *divide et impera* which the apartheid state used to secure its own power base. Small brightly painted brick houses are springing up, a site-and-service scheme in the sandy wastes – one of the very few signs of improvement that we see on our five-hour tour.

As we return to Cape Town we all realise that these last hours have changed the way we shall see our home city in future. Into our thoughtful silence Yazir reads out the names of his fallen comrades in Umkhonto we Sizwe whom we are asked to remember. It is but a handful of names out of many thousands of young people who were killed.

Western Cape Action Tours (WCAT)	P O Box 3168 Grand Central
9th Floor Ruskin House	Cape Town 8000
2 Roeland Street	Tel: +27(0)21 461 1371
Cape Town	Fax: +27 (0)21 461 4387
	e-mail: wcat@iafrica.com

CENTRE FOR CONFLICT RESOLUTION

HOPE IN HELL[3]

Neither the new democratic order in South Africa nor the peaceful second election in June 1999 have changed the way Gadiedja, 8, and Rafik, 9,[4] go to school: they run as fast as they can, often without having had any breakfast. They hurry across the dusty courtyard and along the pitted gravel road – not because they are eager to get to school, but because they are driven by sheer terror. It is the fear of the gangs that drives them, fear of being beaten up – and to get away merely with a black eye would then be very lucky. Too often the ever-present knives are drawn in such attacks.

Rafik has already decided that he, too, will get a flick knife. 'Surely it is better to defend myself and not to wait until I am stabbed by them,' he muses. Like it happened with the woman whose murder he recently witnessed. Gadiedja remembers that too: 'Yes, the knife got stuck in her back, it broke … and then they jumped on her head. And then a big pink balloon came out of her back … I was so frightened!' She has nightmares and often wakes up in the night, screaming. Rafik is terrified to go to the outside toilet at night. 'I rather pee in my pants,' he says.

It would not be easy for him to get out to the toilet without waking the whole family. There is not much space for Rafik in the small room at night, with eighteen people having to share. It will be difficult later, when he is in high school, to find a space where he can do his homework at night, with people sleeping everywhere. Even the kitchen is occupied then, as his aunt sleeps there with her children. The small house is absolutely crammed. This is not likely to improve, as most of the family are unemployed and Rafik's father is serving a long jail sentence. He remembers the last visit to that cold, formidable and frightening place, and how he saw his father

197

behind a thick pane of glass. Rafik shudders at the memory and hopes that he won't have to go back there.

It is already difficult to do homework even now, when the children are still in primary school. There is constant noise in the house all day, everyone shouting and screaming at everybody else, with more physical violence when frustration and anger cannot be contained by verbal abuse alone. This is normal for the children – they have never known life to be any different.

Then, when they reach school at last, all out of breath but glad to have escaped the gangs, they are expected to concentrate on mental arithmetic, or to know who Marco Polo was. That is very hard. Actually, they often do not really hear the teacher – too vivid are the memories of the terrifying noises in the night, and of Mother's crying in the morning … Or they think of the many dangers lurking on the way home in the afternoon.

Rafik has more urgent worries than to remember the name of England's capital, or to know the difference between fish and reptiles. He has to decide soon which gang he will join and where his best chances for survival lie. Perhaps he can then bring home some money occasionally, and Mother will no longer be so desperate … After all, the neighbours live a little better now that their son Henry has become a member of the Hard Livings. And all these friends that Henry now has – and the cool leather jacket he wears! 'He is not afraid, and I bet it does not worry him to go to the toilet at night,' Rafik thinks.

Rafik is lucky. He has a teacher who will not punish him for being inattentive or for not knowing anything about Marco Polo. Mariman Hendricks knows what it is like to live in a home such as Rafik's. It is, after all, no different for any of the other forty children who cause havoc in her classroom. The noise level is normal too – the children have only ever been able to gain attention by yelling and being disruptive. In one corner two boys are fighting – that is normal too, as the children know no other way of solving conflicts.

But something will change very soon; Mariman and her colleague Michael Davids have just attended a course on conflict resolution in schools at the Centre for Conflict Resolution of the University of Cape Town (see

Laurie Nathan, Chapter IV). Both were determined not to give up in the face of overwhelming problems at their school. Both are committed to bringing about change.

'Before I did the course I was like all the other teachers. I taught my subject, Biology, History or Geography, and then I went home as quickly as possible,' Michael admits. 'Of course I knew even then where the problems are. The children here witness the most brutal forms of violence from an early age. They learn very early that power is gained through violence – whether at home or on the streets. They have never experienced peaceful ways of interacting or the importance of being able to listen to each other. Nobody listens to anyone in their homes. There it is normal to curse, to shout and to inflict physical violence. In that way, conflict and violence seem to be the norm. After all, they have no other role models in their lives. No wonder then that it is so easy to take the next step and to become a member of a gang. From there it is not a long way to jail. I kept asking myself how I could intervene in this vicious cycle, but there seemed to be no way out.

'To be realistic, one has to see that conflict and violence will continue to influence their lives. We as teachers cannot change that. But at the Centre for Conflict Resolution we learnt skills to enable our pupils to deal with conflicts in non-violent ways. After all, conflicts are part of life and should not be something threatening. When you succeed in resolving conflicts in a constructive way, you release creative energy. That can be a liberating and very positive experience, for the individual as well as for the group.

'We have started to practise conflict resolution with our pupils. It is so important to start this training early, while they are still in primary school. Later it is often too late. Children learn that conflicts can be instructive, that we must listen carefully to each other, that it is not necessary to shout to be heard. Now they think about conflicts, and they talk about them. They learn to articulate what it is that offends or hurts them instead of hitting each other. They realise now that they have alternatives. That is a liberating experience.'

'But it is not enough to do such training inside the classroom,' maintains Mariman Hendricks. 'Families must be included. Otherwise there is little point to it. We must reach the entire community. We do this now by conducting workshops for adults on weekends. At first they were very sceptical, but now many parents attend the workshops at the school and they join in with enthusiasm. At last we are able to reach the whole community. Then, perhaps, these children will have a chance to break out of the cycle of violence.'

The Centre for Conflict Resolution at the University of Cape Town aims at developing alternatives to the 'culture of violence' in which children in the townships are trapped. There are a variety of courses, including some that offer intensive training in a few days. Staff attached to the Centre also visit schools to offer support and advice.

In this way, they aim to build a staff of teachers who are committed to peaceful resolution of conflicts and who can be skilled facilitators in the wider community. The overarching task of addressing the ravages of apartheid, especially among the young, can only succeed with an inclusive strategy that is built on an understanding of the structural violence of that system and era. A good example can be found in the field of Aids education. Condoms and lectures about 'safe sex' are ineffective by themselves when overcrowding of housing and breakdown of families contribute to incest and child abuse, or when sex offers the only way out of poverty and social deprivation. Fear of Aids is no deterrent when sex seems to offer the only way of survival – and especially not when adults continue to endorse social taboos around this epidemic.

The Centre is dedicated to finding and implementing realistic, responsible ways to empower the youth to deal with abuse and violence. There is no moralising, no preaching – only a commitment to a common goal: to transform an environment which is often experienced as a form of hell.

Centre for Conflict Resolution
University of Cape Town
Private Bag Rondebosch 7700
e-mail: mailbox@ccr.uct.ac.za

AMY BIEHL
FOUNDATION

'CREATING BARRIERS AGAINST VIOLENCE'

This Foundation has a unique history. On 25 August 1993 the young American Fulbright scholar Amy Biehl gave a lift to Gugulethu township to three black fellow students at the University of the Western Cape. At about 5 o'clock that afternoon the car was stoned by demonstrators and brought to a halt. Amy was injured on the head, left the car and ran to a nearby filling station for help. While running she was hit by more stones, tripped and was knifed to death by four youths. The killers were between eighteen and twenty years old and were members of a youth organisation allied to the PAC. They were caught and sentenced to eighteen years' imprisonment. The murder of the 26-year-old Amercian who had come to South Africa in the early 1990s and was actively working for human rights and for a peaceful democratic transition, was seen as a severe blow on the way to reconciliation. Many South Africans from all walks of life wrote to her parents, Linda and Peter Biehl, in California.

Memories of Amy
The first time we met was at a conference which she helped organise for Jimmy Carter's Institute, the NDI[5] in January 1992. Delegates, almost all from government structures and political parties from nine African countries and the United Nations, met at the luxurious Namibian game lodge Mount Etjo to develop strategies for democratic elections, primarily in Southern Africa. I was then responsible for co-ordinating the Black Sash's voter education and election monitoring programme – which earned me the dubious and highly unwelcome status of being the only woman among fifty delegates at Mount Etjo, a fairly telling reflection of the degree of gender sensitivity in African politics at the time. What joy to find a young American feminist among the organising staff!

My first meeting with Amy was not the only time we commiserated about the invisibility of women in politics ... Her subsequent attachment to my place of work, the University of the Western Cape, gave us many opportunities to caucus and strategise together, but also to laugh and to have fun. More than one dreary political speech was made bearable by Amy's bright blue eyes twinkling the message 'don't take it so seriously' across the room at me.

A few days before she was due to go home to the United States, she breezed into our house in her Rheboks and running shorts to have a drink and a chat with my daughter Kathy – an effervescent meeting of two vibrant, joyful, lovely young women, one fair and one dark, who both lived their lives in the spirit of the renaissance that was yet to come.

Then, only a day or two later, a friend's tear-choked voice on the telephone: 'Karin, I can't bear it ... they have killed Amy ...'

In the sense of horror and unbelief of the next few days, I don't want to think about the parents, Linda and Peter Biehl, I have no way of fathoming what they are experiencing – and words of sympathy seem ludicrously and absurdly inadequate.

Nor do I want to think about the killers as the full horror of the news reports hits Cape Town. Can young people really be brought to such brutality by inflammatory rhetoric? Who, then, is ultimately responsible?

I have no way of understanding or even explaining any of it, just an overwhelming sense of despair and hopelessness. If this can happen to someone like Amy, what hope can there be? And where in God's name is hope to be found? How will any of this ever make sense?

I share this sense of despair at the memorial service for Amy at the University of the Western Cape on 27 August, where I read a statement on behalf of the Black Sash which expresses all the incomprehension I feel:

> *The brutal and senseless killing of Amy Biehl brings us yet another step closer to an abyss of despair and anarchy.*
>
> *It is difficult to sustain hope for peace and justice where there seems no end to the cycle of killings, and where so many innocent lives are lost.*
>
> *Those who died in the killing fields of the East Rand and Natal*

are the very people for whom Amy came to South Africa, and for whose future she worked.

Let the meaning of Amy's death lie in an urgent, absolute commitment to peace.

Racist slogans – from whichever side they come – are clear incitements to murder in these tense times. They should be acted upon with all power of law by the state, and with rigorous authority by political parties.

We believe that Amy herself would remind us that solutions to our nation's suffering lie in an uncompromising and untiring commitment to peace.

Some weeks later a gracious note arrives from Linda and Peter Biehl.

Then the coming election takes all energy and focus.

Until ... eight months after Amy's death, the telephone rings again in our house, and this time it is the one tragedy that overwhelms all others: our daughter Kathy is dead, killed in a head-on collision in Windhoek, not far from the township hospital where she worked with such dedication as the much-loved 'Doctor Kathy'. In the dark days that follow, our new democracy is heralded with an explosion of joy – but it does not touch me. Renewal, rebirth, renaissance – those are only abstract terms, almost irrelevant. They remain so for a long time.

Then the Truth Commission begins. So many children, so many mothers, so many deaths ...

Slowly the pain unfolds, mounts up in words for all of us to hear. To call the hearings a common space would be presumptuous, an appropriation to which we, the privileged, have no right. But slowly, words are starting to shed light, to build bridges, to form themselves into the tentative beginnings of explanations. It is a long way from any understanding, but it is a start.

And the parents who grieve for those children? We share a bond that transcends all differences between us ...

The four young men convicted of Amy's murder applied for amnesty before the TRC. When they had been sentenced four years previously they admitted to nothing. Yet the evidence against them was sufficient for a conviction. Now they confessed their guilt and asked for forgiveness. Amy's parents, Linda and Peter Biehl, who, three years before, in 1994, had started a foundation in memory of their daughter, attended the amnesty hearing in July 1997 in Cape Town. They sat in the same hall as their daughter's killers and their families.

The testimony of Mongesi C Manqina, who was twenty years old at the time of the murder, is given below:

> I, the undersigned Mongesi Christopher Manqina do hereby make oath and state that:
>
> I am twenty-four years old and I am currently serving an eighteen-year sentence at the Brandvlei Prison for the murder of Amy Biehl.
>
> … I confirm having attended the meeting at the Langa High Unit PASO launch at the Langa High School … Political speeches were made at the meeting and we were inspired and motivated by the militant speeches made.
>
> We left that meeting. We were about fifty to sixty people in the group. We ran towards the Langa Station. We got to Heideveld just before five pm. I met a girlfriend. She wanted to know what was happening and I told her that we had been at a meeting and that we were on the lookout for 'targets', by which was meant government and company vehicles.
>
> While I was talking to this girl I saw that a beige Mazda 323 was being stoned. The car stopped and the driver, Amy Biehl, stumbled out of the car and started running towards the Caltex petrol station. We chased after her and I tripped her and she fell down next to a box with the name 'Caltex' inscribed on it. I asked one of the persons in the crowd for a knife. I got the knife and moved towards Amy Biehl as she was sitting down in front of the box facing us. I sat in front of her, probably a foot or two away, I took the knife and stabbed her once in front on her left-hand side. I only stabbed her once. Seven or eight others armed with knives also stabbed at her.

I heard the evidence that she was stabbed once and that this blow was fatal. I accept that it must have been the wound which I inflicted. As I stabbed her some people were still throwing stones at her and some of these stones struck me on the shoulder. However, I only suffered some minor injury which did not require any treatment.

After I stabbed her the police came and I saw people running away and that is when I also decided to run away. I stabbed Amy Biehl because I saw her as a target, a Settler. I was highly politically motivated by the events of that day and by the climate prevailing in the township.

I have always been inspired by the slogan 'One Settler, One Bullet'. When the political leaders ordered us to go out and prepare the groundwork to make the township ungovernable I regarded this as an instruction to also harm, injure and kill white people. When I saw that the driver of the vehicle which we had stoned, and which had come to a standstill was a white person I immediately asked one of the comrades in the crowd for a knife. For me this was an opportunity to put into practice the slogan, 'One Settler, One Bullet' ...

I wish to apologise to my legal representatives and to the Court which found me guilty for not telling them the truth. I am now revealing to this Committee what actually happened. I apologise sincerely to Amy Biehl's parents, family and friends and I ask their forgiveness.

On the same day, Peter Biehl made a statement before the Amnesty Committee:

We come to South Africa as Amy came, in a spirit of committed friendship, and, make no mistake about it, extending a hand of friendship in a society which has been systematically polarised for decades is hard work at times. But Amy was always about friendship, about getting along, about the collective strength of caring individuals and their ability to pull together to make a difference …

In her valedictory high school graduation speech in 1985 Amy quoted biologist Lewis Thomas on the importance of collective thinking. Thomas said, 'The drive to be useful is encoded in our genes, but when we gather in very large numbers, as in the modern nation state, we seem capable of levels of folly and self-destruction to be found nowhere else in all of nature … but if we keep at it and keep alive we are in for one surprise after another. We can build structures for human society never seen before, thoughts never thought before, music never heard before.'

This was Amy at age eighteen. This was Amy on the day she died. She wanted South Africans to join hands to sing music never heard before, and she knew this would be a difficult journey.

On 21 June 1993, just two months before she died, Amy wrote a letter to the *Cape Times* editor; she said, 'Racism in South Africa has been a painful experience for blacks and whites and reconciliation may be equally painful. However, the most important vehicle toward reconciliation is open and honest dialogue.'

Amy would have embraced your Truth and Reconciliation process. We are present this morning to honour it and to offer our sincere friendship. We are all here in a sense to consider and to value a committed human life which was taken without opportunity for dialogue. When this process is concluded we must link arms and move forward together …

At the same time we say to you it's your process, not ours. We cannot, therefore, oppose amnesty if it is granted on the merits. In the truest sense it is for the community of South Africa to forgive its own and this has its basis in traditions of ubuntu and other principles of human dignity. Amnesty is not clearly for Linda and Peter Biehl to grant …

In her 21 June 1993 letter to the *Cape Times* editor Amy
quoted the closing lines of a poem, 'Victoria West', written by
one of your local poets. We would close our statement with
these incredible words: 'They told their story to the children.
They taught their vows to the children that we shall never do
to them what they did to us.'

Later, in a television interview, Linda Biehl spoke of a visit to the mother of
one of her daughter's killers: 'I entered the room and saw a rainbow poster
on the wall. We embraced and I felt a sense of peace, a peace with myself.'
In 1998 the four killers were granted amnesty and were released from prison.

Amy's parents brought the Amy Biehl Foundation to South Africa in
1997. It was constituted by funds from Americans who had heard her story
and wanted to contribute in some way to enable her ideals and her work
to continue. These donations, as well as family investment, brought together
a starting capital of US$500 000, sufficient to start an anti-violence project
in the township where Amy was killed, Gugulethu, under the name
'Weaving Barriers against Violence'. In a brochure the Foundation describes
its aims as follows:

> The initiative of preventing violence is aimed at youths
> between 10 and 15 years. Children and youths of this age are
> especially vulnerable, as they have to make important choices
> – whether or not to join a gang, to become violent, to finish
> school. On a second level, the project is aimed at those in
> charge of this age group. If youths grow up in violent families
> the circle of violence remains unbroken, regardless of other
> circumstances. In addition, initiatives which contribute to the
> safety of the community as a whole are supported.

In concrete terms Peter and Linda Biehl and their co-workers have already
founded a number of after-school youth centres as well as economically
viable skills training projects. A good example is the Amy Biehl Foundation
bakery in Gugulethu where six thousand loaves are produced daily and

youths acquire basic skills as bakers within six months. After that they can
have their wages paid out or invest them in further training. The bread is
nourishing and is sold within the township at a very reasonable price.

In the interview mentioned above Linda Biehl reports: 'In one of the
after-school centres a little girl once asked me, "Are you Amy's mother?"
When I said, "Yes, and who are you?" she answered, "I am Mongesi's sister,"
and smiled shyly at me. Mongesi had stabbed our daughter to death. When
I saw his little sister so happy and relaxed among the other children I felt
how right and justified all our work had been. My husband and I now feel
at home in South Africa because here we feel very close to Amy.'

Amy Biehl Foundation
11th Floor
Heerengracht Centre
45 Adderley Street
Cape Town
Tel: +27 (0)21 425 0094
Fax: +27 (0)21 425 0323
e-mail: abftrust@iafrica.com

EPILOGUE

Since the first edition of this book was published in Germany in November 1999, some questions and issues we raised have become more sharply focused, and some additional information has come to light.

The looming Aids catastrophe only became an urgent public concern towards the end of Nelson Mandela's term of office. Educational and community projects were launched, targeting especially the young, who are most at risk, and women, who are most vulnerable. The progress of these campaigns has been slowed and in parts reversed by the confusion and obfuscation around the relationship between HIV and Aids for which the present government must take full responsibility. Where there are no unequivocally clear and forceful messages to the contrary, young people will continue to be very much at risk through unprotected sex and risk-taking behaviour – and the task of parents and educators to stem this tide will be made immeasurably more difficult. At present there are between 2000 and 2500 new infections a day. (Rob Dorrington, Professor of Actuarial Science, UCT, quoted in the *Cape Times* of 13 October 2000.) It is also very clear that the infection rate is highest in the age group below twenty-five.

Of particular concern in this connection is the sharp increase in rape, especially of children and girls. Both the threat and the reality of sexual violence are seriously undermining the rights of children and young people to be protected and safe – whether at school or in their homes.

Fundamental economic problems, of which high unemployment is but one, will have to be addressed by all at the helm of economic power, whether black or white. More than half of all young South Africans between the ages of eighteen and twenty-five are unemployed, with the figure being much higher in rural areas. During the period from 1994 to 1999, only 500 000 jobs were created while three million people over the age of eighteen entered the job market during that period.

There is disappointment and disillusionment among the young who see little change for the better in their own circumstances, especially in the rural areas. One of the most urgent tasks of the government is to enable those youths to take charge of their future. The relatively low voter registration in this age group (only 50% registered for the 1999 elections) is an ominous sign for the future.

Economic experts point to a number of promising initiatives particularly in the small business realm, where entrepreneurs with detailed knowledge of local markets and opportunities have created new ventures. Nothing is more futile than to wait for a miracle from above! The modest and as yet precariously balanced project of the Western Cape Action Tours, described in this book, is an initiative which springs from intimate knowledge of local people and history – and a shrewd assessment of an expanding tourist market. Often such initiatives cannot get off the ground or cannot sustain themselves for a lack of finance and specific skills training. The South African government has started the initiative 'Khula' to gather funds that will be invested as starting capital in small businesses. Khula itself is still in its infancy – but the idea can inspire others to follow suit.

Many young people who testified before the TRC mentioned educational opportunities as their most urgent concern. The legacy of an appalling education system under apartheid cannot be erased in a few years. No new curriculum can be implemented by underqualified teachers in overcrowded schools, some of which lack the most basic equipment. There is also a national crisis around the funding of higher education. That the malaise in school education goes deeper and involves teacher training and motivation as well as parent and community support is also evident from many reports, but a start could be made with a national bursary scheme to provide a level of security for deserving students. That would give high school students a realistic goal and could, over time, also ensure that teacher training improves.

Through indoctrination, censorship and an authoritarian 'Christian National' education system, white conscripts were drafted into a war against their fellow citizens in the townships – or in neighbouring countries that defended their freedom against illegal occupation by the SADF.

Relatively few of these youths had the benefit of a wider vision and the strength and support necessary to resist conscription and consequent courts martial and imprisonment or exile. We feature some of these personal conflicts in our book. At the time of the TRC hearings, the debate around the morality of conscription had not really begun in public among young Afrikaners, though there are many private stories of tragedy which still need to be told. Since the first publication of this book, public challenges have been made by young Afrikaners who feel betrayed by the generation of their elders:

'Julle was die eerste geslag Afrikaners wat julle kinders afgevaardig het om vir julle te gaan sterf. Dié wat nie jul gek drome wou verdedig met die wapens wat julle aan ons uitgereik het nie, is tronkstraf opgelê; of, erger, mal verklaar," wrote Chris Louw who sparked a lively public debate in Beeld. ('Boetman is die bliksem in "Baie jammer, ek is genoeg verneuk, en boonop gatvol".' Beeld, 5 May 2000)

[You were the first generation of Afrikaners who delegated your children to die for you. Those who refused to defend your crazed dreams with the weapons you issued to them, were sentenced to jail; or, worse, were declared insane.]

A hidden story which was simmering within the SADF at the time but which we were not able to bring into the open sufficiently to include an interview in our book in 1999, is the treatment of homosexuals in the military under apartheid. Some evidence surfaced in the medical hearings of the TRC, but too much remained secret. Only in July and August 2000 did the Mail and Guardian go public with stories that began to reveal the extent of persecution, torture and horrendous mutilation to which young homosexuals were subjected in the SADF during apartheid. Stories such as these remind us that the liberal Constitution which we as South Africans now enjoy is built on immense suffering.

During the writing of this book we were under the impression that the new government would honour its obligations to implement a reparations policy recommended by the TRC. The 'deafening silence', as Alex Boraine puts it, on this question since the Final Report was submitted leaves us deeply disturbed.

Some of the unique characteristics of the South African Truth and Reconciliation Commission are that the hearings were held in public, that both victims and survivors gave evidence on an individual basis and that amnesty hearings were included as part of the proceedings.

The continuing credibility and moral force of the TRC rests on a crucial balance between amnesty and reparations. The Promotion of National Unity and Reconciliation Act of May 1995 which brought the TRC into being allows only for restorative justice and prevents other forms of justice once amnesty has been granted. In cases where perpetrators have successfully applied for and been granted amnesty, their victims' normal rights to pursue justice through the courts and to achieve such reparations or at least such satisfaction as may be possible in the criminal justice system have been taken away by the Act. Under the Act, the victims and survivors have to trust that the moral commitment made by the state (and its legal obligation under the Act) will indeed be honoured by the implementation of a comprehensive and effective reparations policy.[1]

It has become more and more clear in recent months, both through blatant non-action of the government and through the pronouncements of its representatives (for instance at the conference hosted by the Institute for Justice and Reconciliation in Cape Town on 4 October 2000) that there is little, if any, political will to honour the commitment to reparations this same government made when the TRC was established. While Alex Boraine admits that there were weaknesses in the Reparations Committee and delays in dealing with the complex issues around formulating a policy on reparations, the TRC fulfilled its mandate when it presented the necessary recommendations in the Final Report in October 1998. Since then, there has been no move on the part of the government to debate and implement these. Except for urgent interim reparations, which in themselves took an inordinately long time (as our story of Ishmael Rantsieng illustrates) and which consisted of minimal amounts, there has been no effective engagement with this crucial area of the TRC's work. As Boraine states: 'I think the model proposed by the Commission can assist in the international debate concerning reparation. We have, in my view, a contribution to make, but no one is going to take us seriously unless the government responds to the Commission's recommendation. … the heavy demands on the fiscus may make it impossible for all the recommendations to be accepted. But both in terms of individual and corporate reparations, there are many possibilities which should be open to the government.'[2]

There is clearly a rising tide of anger and disillusionment among those who testified before the TRC. While the opportunity to tell one's story and to have one's suffering acknowledged is indeed a form of reparation, it cannot remain the only one. The government's apparent refusal to honour its commitments on reparations is inflicting more injuries on those who have already suffered, ironically in the general cause of putting this very government into power. This failure of government erodes the very trust in a new democracy which has enabled so many people to come forward to tell their stories. Those embittered people may well now question the priorities of a government which is ready to spend R32 billion on defence but balks at an estimated reparations budget of R5 billion.

The lack of political will to drive a searching national debate on reparations and to create an efficient and credible infrastructure for implementation has consequences not only for the victims and survivors. It also becomes alarmingly easy for those who benefited from apartheid policies (mainly, but not only whites) to deny collective responsibility for the past. While the number of assassins and torturers who served the regime is relatively small, apartheid could not have survived for as long as it did without the support of those who actively voted for it – or who at the very least benefited from its skewed social and power relations.

Whether the TRC will make a lasting contribution towards moral reconstruction and renewal in South Africa hinges also on the acceptance of responsibility for the past by those who benefited from apartheid. Karl Jaspers, in his essay *The Question of German Guilt*, makes the point that it is only the acceptance of culpability which provides the opportunities for a national new beginning and that we are required to accept responsibility for the history of which we are a part. In terms of the moral trajectory of the TRC, this shifts the responsibility of acknowledgement to the nation as a whole.

Throughout the TRC process it could be observed that white South Africans took relatively little interest in the proceedings. Perhaps this is the shadow side of the tremendously good fortune which South Africa enjoyed by having a transition without large-scale loss of life and an all-out civil war. It is possible for someone who was privileged under the previous regime to go on living as though nothing much has happened. Against this background it becomes explicable why, especially to the more privileged South Africans, the rising crime rate is generally of greater concern than the legacy of gross human rights violations under apartheid. It is a frame of mind which, while identifying one of the major national problem areas, also precludes insight into some of the roots of urban crime. By equating systematic and judicially entrenched violations of human rights with violent urban crime, it somehow seems to absolve the perpetrators and the beneficiaries of the former from any responsibility for restorative justice.

Difficult tasks lie ahead. Where, for example, will be the space for the stories of those who maintained apartheid, either in good faith or in full knowledge of the evil it wrought? It is too easy to dismiss the relatively few prominent evil-doers as 'some bad apples', as former president FW de Klerk did before the TRC, thus absolving even himself from responsibility. The TRC process itself has ensured that 'we did not know' will never in future be a shield behind which South Africans can hide. What is needed is not accusation but genuine dialogue: to create ways in which all South Africans can communicate with each other and where the minority who still control economic power can be brought to use this for the benefit of all. There are still enormous separations created by privileges rooted in the past. These are barriers which, like 'walls in the head' make it almost impossible for young people to meet and live together on an equal basis.

In a moving and surprising submission to the TRC Amnesty Committee, a group of young black South Africans applied for amnesty for apathy. In their application they argued 'that we as individuals can and should be held accountable by history for our lack of necessary action in times of crisis, that none of us did all of what we could have done to make a difference in the anti-apartheid struggle, that in exercising apathy rather than commitment we allowed others to sacrifice their lives for the sake of our freedom and an increase in the standard of living.'

Ways will have to be found to create a culture of acknowledgement, acceptance, and of national reconstruction. There is no doubt that many South Africans, in a corporate as well as in a private capacity, would actually like to contribute to reparation in concrete ways. The building of new schools with corporate funding through the patronage of former President Nelson Mandela is one example. Appeals for donations from a well-administered and audited reparation fund, perhaps controlled by a body of trustees who enjoy credibility across the nation, would certainly also find much support.

Recently, there has been some talk of re-introducing military service in South Africa, to rejuvenate an ageing defence force. Fortunately this met with fierce resistance from human rights groups in the country. How much better than to return to the militarisation of old would it be if there were a national young Peace Force of all school leavers and all who have benefited from tertiary education, doing service in the many disadvantaged communities in our country. That could harness the idealism and the energy of youth which has already once shown the way towards liberation. There will only be lasting peace in South Africa when the poverty of the vast majority of its people is addressed effectively. Negotiating the existing discrepancies in wealth and power in order to build a stable future for all is a formidable task which faces all South Africans. The youth of this 'beautiful and blessed country' will play a key role in its achievement.

Karin Chubb
Lutz van Dijk
Cape Town and Amsterdam
October 2000

APPENDIX I

THE TRC

STRUCTURE AND COMPOSITION

The Truth and Reconciliation Commission was set up by Parliament and was subject to the authority of the Supreme Court. It consisted of three committees and two subcommittees or special units:

HUMAN RIGHTS VIOLATIONS COMMITTEE

From April 1996 to June 1997 human rights violations hearings, some of them with a special theme or focus, were held throughout the country. More than 20 000 people gave evidence at these hearings though not all of them spoke in public.

REPARATION AND REHABILITATION COMMITTEE

After careful investigation, about 22 000 people were found eligible and were proposed for reparations. The suggested amounts were fixed payments of between R17 000 and R18 000 per person per year for a maximum of six years. The recommendation was made that the national budget should reserve approximately R500 million per annum for this purpose. The committee favoured the payment of fixed amounts in order to avoid or at least minimise bureaucratic delay.

AMNESTY COMMITTEE

The working life of this committee had to be extended to cope with the flood of amnesty applications. Its work was to be concluded early in the year 2000 and its report was to be incorporated in the Final Report. By the time the Final Report was published and handed over to President Mandela on 29 October 1998, the Committee had investigated 4 443 applications for amnesty and granted amnesty in 122 of these cases. A total of 2 684 applications were still pending at that time. Applicants who were refused amnesty should, according to the recommendation of the TRC, now face criminal prosecution. In cases where applicants have already been tried and sentenced, these sentences should now take their course.

The two subdivisions had the following tasks:

- The Research Unit was responsible for the research and document-ation which would enable the publication of a comprehensive and detailed Final Report. A particular task was the assimilation and incorporation of the many and diverse testimonies at the hearings into a coherent whole. In addition, it was necessary to create a contextual framework within which some of the broader issues which emerged from this diversity could be presented coherently and made accessible to a wider audience.

- The Investigation Unit: In essence, the task of this subcommittee was to probe all testimony, whether from victims or perpetrators, as thoroughly as possible and also to look for corroborating evidence. This unit was empowered to subpoena witnesses in the course of their investigations.

COMMISSIONERS

The TRC consisted of seventeen commissioners under the chairmanship of Archbishop Desmond Tutu. They were supported by a staff of secretarial, administrative and research assistants. In his introduction to the Final Report, Bishop Tutu has this to say on the subject of the selection procedure of the commissioners (Volume 1, Chapter 1, p9):

> The Commission has also been harshly criticised for being loaded with so-called 'struggle'-types, people who were pro-ANC, SACP or PAC. We want to say categorically we did not choose ourselves, nor did we put our own names forward. We were nominated in a process open to anyone - whatever their political affiliation or lack of it. We were interviewed in

public sessions by a panel on which all the political parties were represented. Moreover, when the President made his choice from a short list, it was in consultation with his Cabinet of National Unity, which included the ANC, the IFP and the National Party. No one, as far as we know, objected publicly at the time to those who were so appointed. Indeed, many of us were chosen precisely because of our role in opposing apartheid - which is how we established our credibility and demonstrated our integrity. I am, myself, even today not a card-carrying member of any political party. I believe, on the other hand, that some of my colleagues may have been chosen precisely because of their party affiliation, to ensure broad representivity.

CENTRAL CONCEPTS

UBUNTU

The African concept of *ubuntu* is often translated as 'humaneness'. In more metaphorical language it is defined thus in Xhosa: *'umuntu ngumuntu ngabantu'*, which is translated as 'people are people through other people'. It is a more radical concept than that of Christian charity or neighbourly love, where the boundaries between individuals remain sharply defined. The African idea of *ubuntu* embodies a different ethic of 'being there for each other', which does not require specific contexts for implementation. On one occasion, when a child was injured in a township confrontation with soldiers of the SADF, a man tried to go to the aid of the wounded youngster. He was stopped because he could not prove that it was his child who was injured. His cry of pain and indignation was captured on camera at the time: 'Any child is my child!' The true meaning of *ubuntu* cannot be illustrated more profoundly.

Ubuntu rests on the premise that every life is to be respected and every life is valuable. In essence, this philosophy is universally accessible, as a white witness before the TRC demonstrated on 23 September 1996 in Klerksdorp. Mrs Susan van der Merwe spoke on that occasion about the abduction and murder of her husband in 1978 by a group of fighters from

, the ANC military wing[1]: 'The Tswanas have an idiom which I learned from my husband which goes "a person is a person by other people, a person is only a person with other people". We do have this duty to each other. The survival of our people in this country depends on our co-operation with each other. My plea to you is, help people throw their weapons away … No person's life is a waste. Every person's life is too precious.'

TRUTH

Only in dictatorships and under authoritarian regimes is there ever only one truth. In principle, the work of the TRC is characterised by the fact that it distinguishes between four different levels of truth, each of them given equal significance.

- Factual or forensic truth: The level of accurate information and corroborated evidence, of objectively verifiable facts relating to for example time and place, evidence of the kind which is uncontestable and can be used in court.

- Personal and narrative truth: Truth on a subjective level, where different people can experience the same event entirely differently and can relate it as such, without any attempt at deceit or subterfuge.

- Social truth: A level of truth which is actively constructed through dialogue, debate and interaction, especially where people or groups have not previously communicated with each other.

- Healing and restorative truth: It is not enough merely to record facts, opinions or disputes. Dignity is restored through acknowledgement of what is known in a specific context. It is on this level that truth can be healing, restorative and transforming - both for the victim who has hitherto been silenced, and for the perpetrator. Restorative truth also encompasses a willingness to analyse or explain the conditions, motives and reasons which drove perpetrators to commit their crimes. This is vital to ensure that they do not happen again.

RECONCILIATION

This concept is probably the most misunderstood, and it has been furiously contested, with reactions ranging from scorn to angry rejection.Yet, it is precisely this 'miracle of reconciliation', as Commissioner Mary Burton called it, which has happened on occasion, in the face of scorn and ridicule. Certainly it could neither be predicted nor planned, but when it happened, it was unexpected and completely credible, for the protagonists concerned as well as for the spectators.

An all but inconceivable scenario: The notorious leader of the Vlakplaas death squads, Eugene de Kock, confesses his crimes before an audience in Port Elizabeth. The widows of the men who were murdered by his trained killers are among the spectators. De Kock confesses his crimes, apologises for them and asks for forgiveness – and after a moment of deep silence the listeners applaud …[2]

Inherent in reconciliation is strength as well as weakness: It cannot be a theoretical construct or an imposed ideology. Reconciliation can only be generated in specific and concrete situations, whether between two individuals or between groups in a deeply strife-torn society. All strategies have to take cognisance of that. Reconciliation is an open process and is always undertaken freely and without force. That reconciliation can liberate the victim in a profound, life-changing way is a realisation which can only come with experience. Only after reconciliation has been accomplished can the victim escape the bondage which is inevitably imposed by the perpetrator and the deed. Their power over the victim remains for as long as the desire for revenge is stronger than that for reconciliation.

A discussion of Amnesty and of Reparation as measures which support a process of reconciliation would also be appropriate in this context. However, they will essentially remain little more than crutches, for perpetrator and victim alike, as long as there is no fundamental and vigorous reorientation towards social justice generally. Only when society as a whole realises at all levels that apartheid between white and black is essentially as evil and as dangerous as apartheid between above and below, between the haves and the have-nots, will reparations be more than Band-Aids. Only then will reparations not perpetuate victimhood so that amnesty is experienced as an affront to one's sense of justice. Both reparations and amnesty might then be understood as necessary measures, promoting patience and insight in view of a common goal.

Perhaps the oldest person ever to testify before the Commission is William Matidza, born in 1895. Bolt upright, with a trimmed white goatee, he walks onto the stage without assistance. He is here, not because the police arrested him from time to time for political reasons and threw him in jail. Not because he was already eighty the last time he was detained. But because all his things have been confiscated. He doesn't care about the house and the furniture and the livestock, these losses he can deal with – but it's his trees, you see. He wants his trees back ... He wants reparation for that. The Commissioners explain somewhat uncomfortably that they don't really have the power, that they can only submit suggestions to the President, that it will all take time. 'Doesn't matter,' says Matidza. 'I know waiting.' [3]

APPENDIX II

EXTRACTS FROM THE TRC'S FINAL REPORT*, 29 OCTOBER 1998[1]

DESMOND TUTU

'True reconciliation is not easy; it is not cheap ...'

Desmond Mpilo Tutu, born in 1931 in Klerksdorp, South Africa; married to Leah in 1955; studied to be a teacher until 1958; studied theology 1958-1960; ordained to the priesthood in Johannesburg and studied in London 1960-1967; returned to South Africa in 1967; from 1972-1975 studied and taught abroad; was Associated Director of the Theological Education Fund of the World Council of Churches; in 1976 became Bishop of Lesotho; General Secretary of the South African Council of Churches, 1978-1985; has received several honorary doctorates in the United States, Great Britain and Germany; awarded the Nobel Peace Prize in 1984; Archbishop of the Anglican Church in Cape Town 1986-1996; from 1995 to 1998, Chairman of the Truth and Reconciliation Commission in South Africa.

Our Recent History

All South Africans know that our recent history is littered with some horrendous occurrences. (...)

Our country is soaked in the blood of her children of all races and of all political persuasions.

It is this contemporary history – which began in 1960 when the Sharpeville disaster* took place and ended with the wonderful inauguration of Nelson Mandela as the first democratically elected President of the Republic of South Africa – it is this history with which we have had to come to terms. We could not pretend it did not happen. Everyone agrees

---

that South Africans must deal with that history and its legacy. It is how we do this that is in question – a bone of contention throughout the life of the Commission, right up to the time when this report was being written. And I imagine we can assume that this particular point will remain controversial for a long time to come.

ON PREPARING THIS REPORT

One of the unique features of the South African Commission has been its open and transparent nature. Similar commissions elsewhere in the world have met behind closed doors. Ours has operated in the full glare of publicity. This means that some of the information contained in this report is already in the public domain. None the less, some significant and new insights are included in the pages that follow.

The work of the South African Commission has also been far more extensive than that of other commissions. The volume of material that passed through our hands will fill many shelves in the National Archives. This material will be of great value to scholars, journalists and others researching our history for generations to come. From a research point of view, this may be the Commission's greatest legacy.

The report that follows tries to provide a window on this incredible resource, offering a road map to those who wish to travel into our past. It is not and cannot be the whole story; but it provides a perspective … that is more extensive and more complex than any one commission could, in two and a half years, have hoped to capture.

Others will inevitably critique this perspective – as indeed they must. We hope that many South Africans and friends of South Africa will become engaged in the process of helping our nation to come to terms with its past and, in so doing, reach out to a new future.

CONSTRAINTS AND DIFFICULTIES

This report has been constrained by a number of factors – not least by the extent of the Commission's mandate and a number of legal provisions contained in the Act. It was, at the same time, driven by a dual responsibility. It had to provide the space within which victims could share the story of their trauma with the nation; and it had to recognise the importance of the due process of law that ensures the rights of alleged perpetrators. (...)

Despite these difficulties, however, we can still claim, without fear of being contradicted, that we have contributed more to uncovering the truth about the past than all the court cases in the history of apartheid.

Ultimately, this report is no more than it claims to be. It is the report of a commission appointed by Parliament to complete an enormous task in a limited period. Everyone involved in producing this report would have loved to have had the time to capture the many nuances and unspoken truths encapsulated in the evidence that came before us. This, however, is a task which others must take up and pursue.

However, the Commission has not been prepared to allow the present generation of South Africans to grow gently into the harsh realities of the past and, indeed, many of us have wept as we were confronted with its ugly truths. However painful the experience has been, we remain convinced that there can be no healing without truth. My appeal to South Africans as they read this report is not to use it to attack others, but to add to it, correct it and ultimately to share in the process that will lead to national unity through truth and reconciliation.

Transitional Options

We could not make the journey from a past marked by conflict, injustice, oppression, and exploitation to a new and democratic dispensation characterised by a culture of respect for human rights without coming face to face with our recent history. No one has disputed that. The differences of opinion have been about how we should deal with that past.

There were those who believed that we should follow the post-World War II example of putting those guilty of gross violations of human rights on trial as the Allies did at Nuremberg. In South Africa, where we had a military stalemate, that was clearly an impossible option. Neither side in the struggle (the state nor the liberation movements) had defeated the other and hence nobody was in a position to enforce so-called victor's justice.

However, there were even more compelling reasons for avoiding the Nuremberg option. There is no doubt that members of the security establishment would have scuppered the negotiated settlement had they thought they were going to run the gauntlet of trials for their involvement in past violations. It is certain that we would not, in such circumstances, have experienced a reasonably peaceful transition from repression to democracy. We need to bear this in mind when we criticise the amnesty provisions in the Commission's founding Act. We have the luxury of being able to complain because we are now reaping the benefits of a stable and democratic dispensation. Had the miracle of the negotiated settlement not occurred, we would have been overwhelmed by the bloodbath that virtually everyone predicted as the inevitable ending for South Africa.

Wounds and Truths

'Those who forget the past are doomed to repeat it' are the words emblazoned at the entrance to the museum in the former concentration camp of Dachau. They are words we would do well to keep ever in mind. However painful the experience, the wounds of the past must not be allowed to fester. They must be opened. They must be cleansed. And balm must be poured on them so they can heal. This is not to be obsessed with the past. It is to take care that the past is properly dealt with for the sake of the future.

In our case, dealing with the past means knowing what happened. Who ordered that this person should be killed? Why did this gross violation of human rights take place? We also need to know about the past so that we can renew our resolve and commitment that never again will such violations take place.

Amnesty for Truth

For all these reasons, our nation, through those who negotiated the transition from apartheid to democracy, chose the option of individual and not blanket amnesty. And we believe that this individual amnesty has demonstrated its value.

One of the criteria to be satisfied before amnesty could be granted was full disclosure of the truth. Freedom was granted in exchange for truth. We have, through these means, been able to uncover much of what happened in the past. We know now what happened to Steve Biko, to the PEBCO

Three,* to the Cradock Four* … We have been able to exhume the remains of about fifty activists who were abducted, killed and buried secretly.

The lies and deception that were at the heart of apartheid – which were indeed its very essence – were frequently laid bare. We know now who bombed Khotso House.* We can recall how Mr Adriaan Vlok, a former Minister of Law and Order, lied publicly and brazenly about this; how he unashamedly caused Shirley Gunn to be detained with her infant son as the one responsible for this act. It must be said to his credit that Mr Vlok apologised handsomely to Ms Gunn during his amnesty application.

Thus, we have trodden the path urged on our people by the preamble to our founding Act, which called on 'the need for understanding but not for vengeance, a need for reparation but not retaliation, a need for *ubuntu* but not for victimisation'.

CRITICISMS

It would have been odd in the extreme if something as radical as this Commission had met with universal approval and acceptance. It would have been even more odd had we been infallible and made no mistakes as we undertook the delicate task of seeking to help heal the wounds of a sorely divided people.

Some of the criticism levelled against the Commission has been legitimate. However, there has been much which was merely political point scoring, ignoring the facts in favour of taking up cudgels against us. There were those who decided from the outset, long even before the Commission had begun its work, to discredit us by trying to paint the Commission as a witch-hunt of, especially, Afrikaners; by claiming that we were biased in favour of the ANC; and as having failed in the end to advance the course of reconciliation. This latter kind of criticism was a clever ploy to seek pre-emptively to discredit the Commission and hence its report.

Those who have cared about the future of our country have been worried that the amnesty provision might, amongst other things, encourage impunity because it seemed to sacrifice justice. We believe this view to be incorrect.

The amnesty applicant has to admit responsibility for the act for which amnesty is being sought. Furthermore, apart from the most exceptional circumstances, the application is dealt with in a public hearing. The applicant must therefore make his admissions in the full glare of publicity. Let us imagine what this means. Often this is the first time that an applicant's family and community learn that an apparently decent man was, for instance, a callous torturer or a member of a ruthless death squad that assassinated many opponents of the previous regime. There is, therefore, a price to be paid. Public disclosure results in public shaming.

We believe that there is another kind of justice – a restorative justice which is concerned not so much with punishment as with correcting imbalances, restoring broken relationships – with healing, harmony and reconciliation. Such justice focuses on the experience of victims; hence the importance of reparation.

The Granting of Amnesty

Others have taken us to task because they were unhappy when the Amnesty Committee gave amnesty to certain perpetrators – such as those responsible for the St James' Church killings or the murder of Amy Biehl. Clearly these people have forgotten the *raison d'être* for amnesty. Amnesty is not meant for nice people. It is intended for perpetrators. There are strict criteria to be met and we believe that the Committee has used those criteria to determine whether or not amnesty should be granted.

Amnesty is a heavy price to pay. It is, however, the price the negotiators believed our country would have to pay to avoid an 'alternative too ghastly to contemplate'.[2] Sadly, in almost all cases, there was an outcry only when the victim was white and the perpetrator black. As a matter of fact, the Amnesty Committee has granted only about 150 amnesties out of 7 000 applications, with a further 2 000 still to be dealt with. This can hardly be described as an avalanche of reckless decisions.

Judgements and Prejudices

Some have criticised us because they believe we talk of some acts as morally justifiable and others not. Let us quickly state that the section of the Act relating to what constitutes a gross violation of human rights makes no moral distinction – it does not deal with morality. It deals with legality. A gross violation is a gross violation, whoever commits it and for whatever reason. There is thus legal equivalence between all perpetrators. Their political affiliation is irrelevant. If an ANC member tortures someone, that is a gross violation of the victim's rights. If a National Party member or a police officer tortures a prisoner, then that is a gross violation of the prisoner's rights.

We have sought to carry out our work to the best of our ability, without bias. I cannot, however, be asked to be neutral about apartheid. It is an intrinsically evil system. But I am even-handed in that I will let an apartheid supporter tell me what he or she sincerely believed moved him or her, and what his or her insights and perspectives were; and I will take these seriously into account in making my finding.

I do believe that there were those who supported apartheid who genuinely believed that it offered the best solution to the complexities of a multiracial land with citizens at very different levels of economic, social and educational development. I do believe such people were not driven by malicious motives. No, I do not call their motives into question. I do, however, condemn the policy they applied.

TRUE RECONCILIATION

The trouble is that there are erroneous notions of what reconciliation is all about. Reconciliation is not about being cosy; it is not about pretending that things were other than they were. Reconciliation based on falsehood, on not facing up to reality, is not true reconciliation and will not last.

We believe we have provided enough of the truth about our past for there to be a consensus about it. There is consensus that atrocious things were done on all sides. We know that the state used its considerable resources to wage a war against some of its citizens. We know that torture and deception and murder and death squads came to be the order of the day. We know that the liberation movements were not paragons of virtue and were often responsible for egging people on to behave in ways that were uncontrollable. We know that we may, in the present crime rate, be reaping the harvest of the campaigns to make the country ungovernable. We know that the immorality of apartheid has helped to create the climate where moral standards have fallen disastrously.

The truth can be, and often is, divisive. However, it is only on the basis of truth that true reconciliation can take place. True reconciliation is not easy; it is not cheap. We have been amazed at some almost breathtaking examples of reconciliation that have happened through the Commission.

APPEAL TO WHITE SOUTH AFRICANS

I want to make a heartfelt plea to my white fellow South Africans. On the whole we have been exhilarated by the magnanimity of those who should by rights be consumed by bitterness and a lust for revenge; who instead have time after time shown an astonishing magnanimity and willingness to forgive. It is not easy to forgive, but we have seen it happen. And some of those who have done so are white victims. Nevertheless, the bulk of victims have been black and I have been saddened by what has appeared to be a mean-spiritedness in some of the leadership in the white community. They should be saying: 'How fortunate we are that these people do not want to treat us as we treated them. How fortunate that things have remained much the same for us except for the loss of some political power.'

Can we imagine the anger that has been caused by the disclosures that the previous government had a Chemical and Biological Warfare Programme with projects that allegedly targeted only black people, and allegedly sought to poison President Nelson Mandela and reduce the fertility of black women? Should our land not be overwhelmed by black fury leading to orgies of revenge, turning us into a Bosnia, a Northern Ireland or a Sri Lanka?

Dear fellow South Africans, please try to bring yourselves to respond with a like generosity and magnanimity. When one confesses, one confesses only one's own sins, not those of another. That is why I still hope that there will be a white leader who will say, 'We had an evil system with awful consequences. Please forgive us.' Without qualification. If that were to happen, we would all be amazed at the response.

APPRECIATION

I am honoured to express our gratitude to all those over 20 000 persons who came forward to tell us their stories – either at the public hearings of our Human Rights Violations Committee or in the statements recorded by our statement takers. They were generous in their readiness to make themselves vulnerable; to risk opening wounds that were perhaps in the process of healing, by sharing the often traumatic experiences of themselves or their loved ones as victims of gross violations of human rights. We are deeply in their debt and hope that coming to the Commission may have assisted in the rehabilitation of their human and civil dignity that was so callously trampled underfoot in the past.

My appeal is ultimately directed to us all, black and white together, to close the chapter on our past and to strive together for this beautiful and blessed land as the rainbow people of God. The Commission has done its share to promote national unity and reconciliation. Their achievement is up to each one of us.

APPENDIX III

CHILDREN AND YOUTH UNDER APARTHEID[✧]

GROWING UP UNDER APARTHEID

The South African social fabric was shaped by apartheid laws and structures that exposed the majority of South Africa's children to oppression, exploitation, deprivation and humiliation. Apartheid was accompanied by both subtle and overt acts of physical and structural violence. Structural violations included gross inequalities in educational resources along with massive poverty, unemployment, homelessness, widespread crime and family breakdown. The combination of these problems produced a recipe for unprecedented social dislocation, resulting in both repression and resistance.

Many white children, on the other hand, were raised in an environment which condoned racial prejudice and fear of the 'other', while demanding unquestioning submission to the authority of family and state. The structural and legislated segregation of apartheid ensured that young white people were isolated and separated from their peers in other race groups. in their homes, schools, communities and every other aspect of their lives.

These conditions led to the recognition by many of South Africa's children that they were being denied opportunities to take up their rightful place as South African citizens. Many of South Africa's children did not stand passively by, but actively disputed the legitimacy of the state. In doing so, they contributed to the dismantling of apartheid.

THE HISTORY OF YOUTH RESISTANCE

The role of youth in resisting apartheid dates back to the formation of the militant African National Congress (ANC) Youth League in 1943. The

---

militancy of the youth provided the impetus for the Defiance Campaign*
of 1952 and the drafting of the Freedom Charter* in 1955. In the 1960s,
students were amongst those who rose up in their thousands to protest
against the pass laws. The state's response to these peaceful protests was
mass repression. Many youth saw no option but to leave the country in
order to take up arms and fight for liberation. *Umkhonto we Sizwe* (MK),
formed in 1961, drew many of its recruits from the ranks of the youth.

Children and youth faced the full force of state oppression as they
took on their role as the 'foot soldiers of the struggle' – as what were called
the 'young lions'. Youth challenged the state by organising and mobilising
their schools and communities against illegitimate state structures.

In June 1976 the student revolt that began in Soweto transformed the
political climate. One hundred and four children under the age of sixteen
were killed in the uprising and resistance spread to other parts of the
country. Classrooms became meeting grounds for organisations such as
the Congress of South African Students (COSAS), which was formed in
1979 and ultimately boasted a membership of over a million students. The
security police clampdown on COSAS resulted in the arrest of over five
hundred of its members by the time of the declaration of the state of
emergency in July 1985.

In the 1980s, in particular, student and youth organisations were
banned, as were the possession and distribution of their publications. From
1976 to 1990 outdoor political gatherings were outlawed. From 1986 there
was a blanket ban on indoor gatherings aimed at promoting work
stoppages, stay-aways or educational boycotts.

RECRUITING INFORMERS

The security establishment engaged in the informal repression of children
by hunting down 'troublesome' youth and developing an informer
network. This latter had dire consequences for youth organisations. Stories
are told about the transfer of detained children to rehabilitation camps
where it is thought that they became informers.

Until 1985 casualties were mainly the result of security force action.
From 1987, however, vigilantism* began to make an appearance. Vigilantes

were recruited from the ranks of the homeland authorities*, black local authorities, black police officers and those who wished to protect existing social hierarchies. The state colluded with vigilante organisations in order to destabilise resistance organisations. As migrant hostel dwellers were drawn into the conflict with youth, vigilante attacks came to reflect class, ethnic and geographic differences.

Many vigilante attacks were rooted in intergenerational conflicts. Some men saw the dramatic surge of women and youth to political prominence as a threat to the patriarchal hierarchies of age and gender. Young people were perceived to be undermining the supremacy of traditional leaders who saw it as their duty to restrain them. Vigilantes mobilised around slogans such as 'discipline the children', and frequently described themselves as 'fathers'.

Large numbers of youth, whether politically active or not, were affected by the violence, especially those who lived near the hostels. In many cases, the responsibility for protecting their homes and streets fell on children. Some young people turned their attention to the defence of their communities, redirecting their energies into the formation of Self-Defence Units that were, in their view, justified by vigilante attacks.

In the 1990s the conflict between the ANC and the Inkatha Freedom Party (IFP) intensified and vigilante attacks increased. In KwaZulu-Natal, in particular, young people were forced to flee to the cities in fear of their lives. Some young people were recruited into vigilante activities by, for example, being offered money to attack the homes of activists. Young people were also manipulated by state projects such as the Eagles, which was founded in the early 1980s and came into conflict with organisations like the South African Youth Congress (SAYCO*). Groups like the Eagles were involved in activities such as assisting the police to identify activists, launching arson attacks and disrupting political meetings. In 1991 the Eagles were exposed as an official state project.

Young White Soldiers
Through government control of the national media and strategies such as SADF visits to white schools, young white people were subjected to

propaganda. Fear of the 'other' was implanted in children under the guise of an imminent 'Communist' plot, articulated through slogans such as 'total onslaught'. All this contributed to a situation in which most white males concluded that it was their obligation to serve in the armed services.

White children were offered few alternatives to being part of the white élite. They had virtually no contact with black children and lived largely in the racially protected environments of school, family and church. Some white youth who fought in defence of a white South Africa were convinced by their military and political masters that both their own suffering and the acts of violence committed in the process were undertaken for a just cause. Others faced the dilemma of being conscripted to fight a war in which they did not necessarily believe. A minority became conscientious objectors, condemned as traitors to the nation and faced with the choice of leaving the country or being sentenced to six years' imprisonment.

Some white youth joined the struggle against apartheid through membership of and participation in resistance organisations such as the End Conscription Campaign, student movements, such as the National Union of South African Students, or by joining political organisations. Like other activists, they became targets of state violence.

FIGURES AND STATISTICS

Our figures do not reflect a universal experience of violations, only those that were reported to the Commission. Many South Africans who experienced human rights violations did not come to the Commission and are therefore not represented. Many parents testified on behalf of their children. Significant, too, was the fact that many women and girls chose not to testify about violations they themselves had experienced. They spoke instead of the violations committed against others, notably their fathers, sons and brothers.

Figure 1 represents the number of killings reported to the Commission. The left side reflects female victims and the right side male victims. It shows that few children under the age of twelve were killed. The majority of victims of killings reported to the Commission were young men between the ages of thirteen and twenty-four.

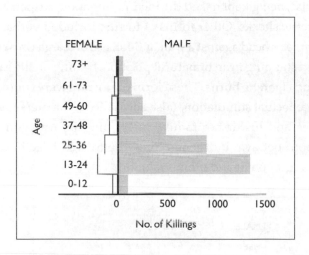

Figure 1

DETENTION AND IMPRISONMENT

In large-scale and often arbitrary police action, thousands of children, some as young as seven years old, were arrested and detained in terms of South Africa's sweeping security and criminal legislation. Sometimes, entire schools were arrested en masse.

All the available figures indicate that the largest numbers of children and youth were detained between 1985 and 1989, during the two states of emergency. Of 80 000 detentions, 48 000 were detainees under the age of twenty-five.

Upon release from prison, many young people were subjected to bannings and other restriction orders, turning the young person's home into another kind of prison. They were forced to report to police stations once a day and were prevented from participating in political and social activities.

TORTURE

Torture usually occurred at the hands of the security forces whilst children and youth were in detention. Types of abuse reported by children included food and sleep deprivation, solitary confinement, beating, kicking, enforced physical exercise, being kept naked during interrogation, suspension from poles, and electric shocks. Other forms of torture included verbal insults, banging a detainee's head against a wall or floor, use of teargas in a confined space, enforced standing in an unnatural position, beating on the ears, near suffocation, and cigarette burns. These forms of torture were compounded by a lack of intellectual stimulation, false accusations, threatened violence to the detainee and his or her family, misleading information, untrue statements about betrayal by friends, pressure to sign false documents, interrogation at gun point and other violations.

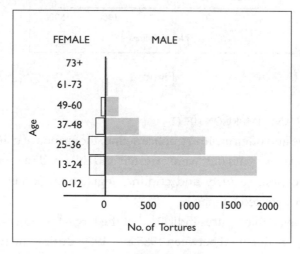

Figure 2

Children and Youth in Exile

In the face of mounting repression, many young people or their family members left the country to reside in other countries or to join liberation movements.

Exile is often experienced as a brutal rupture in an individual's personal history, resulting in a lack of continuity that frequently becomes a serious obstacle to the development of a meaningful and positive sense of identity. They were unable to contact family and friends in South Africa because of the risk of reprisals against their loved ones living there. The conditions to which they were subjected included exposure to disease and hunger.

It is not clear how many young people and members of their families died in exile, either as combatant members of the liberation movements, or from natural or other causes. Some died as a result of South African cross-border raids into neighbouring countries.

The Commission's documentation shows that children and youth were the dominant victims in all categories of gross human rights violations described in the Act. For almost every adult who was violated, probably two or more children or young people suffered. Family life was often damaged, making it difficult for parents to take care of their children and to be emotionally available to listen to them. Many children became alienated from their parents and the trust, faith and communication that should have existed between the generations was sorely tried.

VICTIMS AND FREEDOM FIGHTERS AT THE SAME TIME

This chapter of the Report concerns the statements and testimonies of deponents who were defined as victims in terms of the legislation. This focus on victims is not, however, intended to diminish the active role of children and youth. Children were agents of social change and harnessed vast amounts of energy, courage and resilience during the apartheid era. For many young people, active engagement in political activity resulted in the acquisition of skills such as analysis, mobilisation and strategising, as well as the ability to draw strength from friends and comrades in times of hardship. Many of today's leaders come from a politically active history and have displayed a remarkable capacity for forgiveness and reconciliation.

DISILLUSIONMENT

For many, the new South Africa has not proved to be the land of opportunity that they expected and this has generated deep-seated feelings of resentment. Children who are physically injured, especially if the injury results in permanent disability, suffer extreme stress as they attempt to reconstruct their identity and come to terms with the disfigurement or disability.

Children and youth were prepared to sacrifice their education by joining liberation movements and participating in mass mobilisation under the slogan of 'Liberation before Education'. Fifty-seven per cent of those who reported a disruption to their education also reported that they were suffering from psychological problems of anxiety, depression and an inability to cope; 51 per cent also referred to losses of income as an outcome of violations.

CONCLUDING REMARKS

Those who grew up under conditions of violence will carry traces of their experiences into adulthood. Many have suffered the loss of loved ones. Many carry physical and psychological scars. The life opportunities of many have been compromised through disruptions to their education. Some have transplanted the skills learnt during the times of political violence into criminal violence, as they strive to endure ongoing poverty.

However, perhaps the most disturbing and dangerous aspect of this legacy for the future of the nation is the fact that those who sought to transform the country, and in the process gave up so much, see so little change in their immediate circumstances.

The period of struggle, however, also nurtured resilience, wisdom, leadership and tolerance. Many young people rose above the suffering they experienced. Some defiantly and bravely saw themselves as fighting for the freedom of their people – sacrificing education and opportunities for self-improvement and joining liberation armies and resistance movements.

Many of these young people have become men and women of outstanding calibre.

Despite their suffering, they have shown extraordinary generosity and tolerance and have reached out to their former oppressors in a spirit of reconciliation.

NOTES

CHAPTER I

1. Several months after Germany's surrender, in August 1945, the United States, Britain, France and the Soviet Union formed an international Military Tribunal to try the leaders of the Nazi regime. It was agreed by the Allies that those individuals and organisations guilty of the most appalling crimes against basic human rights which the world had ever seen should be punished, but that they should also have a fair and public trial. The Nuremberg Trials began in October 1945. Only a very small minority of war criminals were prosecuted and convicted at that time – most were able to escape prosecution by going into hiding either in Germany or abroad. No attempt was made in Nuremberg either to indict the German people as a whole – contrary to the opinions of some revisionist historians – or to involve them in the process of truth finding. The Nuremberg trials can be seen only as an attempt at retributive justice, certainly not at restorative justice and even less as reconciliation with the millions of victims.

CHAPTER II

1. The use of these racially defined categories is a very sensitive political issue in post-apartheid South Africa. However, in the interest of achieving equity, such classification is at times necessary, at least until a much greater measure of social justice has become a reality.
2. The TRC investigated the death of Stompie Sepei and came to the following conclusion: 'The Commission finds that Stompie Sepei was last seen alive in the house of Mrs Winnie Madikizela-Mandela and that she is responsible for his abduction from the Methodist manse. She has neglected to act with due responsibility to prevent his death.' (TRC Final Report Volume II, Chapter 6, p. 570).
3. Krog, Antjie. 1998. *Country of My Skull*. Johannesburg 1998, pp 144-5.
4. The reference is to a song featured in the film *Goodbye Mr Chips*.
5. He is referring to F W de Klerk, the former State President, and Magnus Malan, then Minister of Defence.

CHAPTER III

1. 'Commissioner' denotes any questions or comments made by Commissioners or their staff.
2. Grade 7 according to the new system.
3. The 'Trojan Horse' case refers to a shooting in Cape Town on 15 October 1985, when police shot at demonstrating children and youths from wooden crates in which they had concealed themselves on the back of a truck. On that occasion three were killed. This tactic was used in other parts of the country as well, e.g. in Despatch (Eastern Cape) on 15 April 1985, when four youths were killed; in Uitenhage (Eastern Cape) when one youth was killed and in Steynsburg (Eastern Cape) on 27 December 1985 with three youths killed.
4. Std 8 in the old educational system, i.e. before 1997, was the tenth year of school. In the new system it is known as Grade 10. Std 9 would then be Grade 11. Leaving school at this stage is regarded as particularly critical because it is just a year before the final qualifying examination, the Matriculation Examination/Matric.
5. In the Final Report of the TRC, the SDUs are assessed as follows: 'Although it was not official ANC policy, the SDUs contributed to a spiral of violence. Lacking an appropriate infrastructure and in the face of orchestrated state violence, the SDUs often took the law into their own hands and committed serious human rights violations. 'Final Report Volume 5, Chapter 6, pp 242-3.
6. In the transcript of the hearing of 12 June 1997 her name is erroneously given as 'Marwezu'.
7. Addresses in townships are commonly given in such letters and numbers, in the absence of 'real' street names.
8. A Xhosa girl's name meaning 'all of us together'.
9. He is referring to the fight against the British in the Anglo-Boer Wars 1880-81 and 1899-1902.
10. Affirmative action is a process of appointment in which an applicant of colour is given preference over a white applicant, where both generally meet the requirements. In Europe this is also known as 'positive discrimination'.

CHAPTER IV

1. The key concept of President Thabo Mbeki's vision for the future.
2. Government schools which were originally for whites only but were later permitted to enrol black children.

3. Mayor of Cape Town at the time of writing.

4. *Detention and Torture in South Africa*. Cape Town: David Philip, 1987.

5. MK cadres whose murder was clumsily disguised as a grenade explosion; see also WCAT in Chapter V.

6. Literally 'grandfather'. In the Xhosa tradition this means the great wise father or elder who advises and mentors the young boy.

7. A prestigious ultra-marathon run on Easter Saturday over 56 kilometres around the Cape Peninsula.

8. A mixture of Afrikaans and English, especially to achieve rhyming, is a typical feature of Cape Afrikaans.

9. For demarcations and divisions of the city along racial lines, see also Chapter V: Western Cape Action Tours.

10. In September 1989 police in Cape Town used a water cannon with purple dye against demonstrators. The idea was that all who were marked with that colour, which did not wash off for days, would be arrested as demonstrators. This worked for a while, until a courageous young man jumped on to the cannon and turned the purple spray around so that it drenched the police! Most of Greenmarket Square in the centre of the city was coloured purple for days.

11. It is widely accepted that South Africa has the fastest growing HIV infection rate in the world, with more than 1 800 new cases daily in a population of 38 million.

12. See also the letter from the then 19-year-old Tim Ledgerwood in Chapter II.

13. Manenberg has a particularly high level of gang violence.

CHAPTER V

1. Ndebele, Najabulo. Memory, Metaphor and the Triumph of Narrative. In Nuttall, S and Coetzee, C (eds), *Negotiating the Past: The Making of Memory in South Africa*. Cape Town: Oxford University Press, 1998, p27.

2. A huge settlement outside Cape Town incorporating both informal and more structured housing.

3. The film on which this story is based may be obtained from the Centre for Conflict Resolution at the address given in Chapter V.

4. All names have been changed.

5. The National Democratic Institute for International Affairs.

EPILOGUE

1. This is clear in Judge Didcott's pronouncement in the case which AZAPO brought to the Constitutional Court, arguing that the granting of amnesty would violate the constitutional right to justice, when he stated that there was no doubt that the state was to shoulder the national responsibility for reparations. Similar statements were made by the then Minister of Justice, Dullah Omar, in Parliament on 27 May 1994, when he announced the decision of the ANC government to set up the TRC.

2. Alex Boraine: *A Country Unmasked: Inside South Africa's Truth and Reconciliation Commission*. Oxford University Press, Cape Town 2000, p430

APPENDIX I

1. Van der Merwe, Susan, quoted in TRC Report Vol 1, chap 5, p128.

2. Described in Winslow, Tom. Reconciliation: The Road to Healing?. In *Track Two*. Cape Town 3-4 1997, p26.

3. Krog, Antjie. *Country of my Skull*. Johannesburg 1998, pp195-196.

APPENDIX II

1. Subtitles added.

2. Archbishop Tutu is here referring to a service which he conducted in September 1977 after Steve Biko (1946-1977) had been murdered in police custody. On that occasion he said to the angry mourners: 'Let us avoid the alternatives which are too ghastly to contemplate.' He was in fact quoting former President B J Vorster.

GLOSSARY

Compiled by Karin Chubb, Dot Cleminshaw and Lutz van Dijk

The sign→ directs the reader to a further reference in this Glossary

ANC: African National Congress. Founded in 1912; Africa's oldest liberation movement; banned in 1960, which led to the adoption of the armed struggle. After the imprisonment of leaders Mandela, Sisulu and Govan Mbeki (father of Thabo Mbeki), Oliver Tambo led the movement from exile in London and Lusaka. Since its unbanning in 1990, the ANC has been the majority party in SA, and became the majority party in Parliament in 1994. In 1999 the ANC was voted in with almost a two-thirds majority, 266 of 400 seats in Parliament.

APLA: Azanian People's Liberation Army. Armed wing of the PAC →. See also Azania →.

Askari: Resistance fighter or MK → soldier who was turned by the Security Police and worked for them against his former Comrades. Sometimes also used to describe a traitor.

Azania: Ancient name for south-east Africa, probably from Arabic; favoured by Black Consciousness supporting groups such as AZAPO → as new name for a liberated South Africa. The ANC does not use this name.

AZAPO: Azanian People's Organisation. Black Consciousness organisation founded in April 1978 to spread the idea of a future socialist republic of Azania to the masses.

Black Sash: Women's organisation of volunteers, formed in 1955 in protest against the exclusion of coloured voters from the voters' roll. Membership originally only drawn from enfranchised (ie white) women; later open to all race groups. It derives its name from the distinctive black sash worn by members in protest actions against state repressions and human rights abuses; it became known for leading campaigns to stop forced removals and pass laws→. Through a nationwide network of advice offices, the organisation conducted monitoring of human rights abuses, gave assistance to victims, campaigned against detention without trial and the death penalty, highlighted deaths in detention and other human rights violations nationally and internationally, and worked in alliance with other liberation forces. Since 1990 the main focus has been on legislation watch, social welfare policies, gender discrimination, and securing access to rights through advice offices. After the democratic elections in 1994 the Black Sash was dissolved as a volunteer organisation. It still functions today under a Trust, with the advice offices staffed mainly by paid employees.

BMW: Bonteheuwel Military Wing. Militant resistance group drawn from schools in the township of Bonteheuwel, Cape Town. Responsible at first only for organising 'unrest incidents' in the streets of Bonteheuwel in order to tie up police manpower and deflect attention from resistance work at schools, the youths became more organised as many received military training in the underground, at first with homemade and then with more conventional weapons. The BMW was singled out for brutal treatment and torture when its members were captured, their youth offering them no protection. Close links existed with ANC and MK→ underground structures.

Casspir: Armoured personnel vehicle used by the SAP→ and the SADF →.

CCB: Civil Co-operation Bureau. A good example of apartheid's obfuscating nomenclature, this body had nothing to do with either civil or co-operation, but was actually a secret assassination squad, responsible amongst other things for the killing of Wits academic and UDF→ activist David Webster.

Ciskei: Territory in the Eastern Cape declared a homeland→ under apartheid policies in 1951 and an 'independent state' in 1981. Site of severe human rights violations during the 1980s and early 1990s.

COSAS: Congress of South African Students. Militant charterist (ie

ANC-orientated) student organisation formed in 1979, influential in student and school politics in the 1980s.

Cradock Four: Cradock, a small town 300 kilometres north of Port Elizabeth, became a centre of well-organised resistance under the UDF→, the structures of which were set up by activists under Matthew Goniwe, a schoolteacher. After harassment and detentions by the security police, the four leaders Matthew Goniwe, Sparrow Mkonto, Fort Calata and Sicelo Mhlauli were abducted and assassinated outside Port Elizabeth on 27 June 1985. An inquest in 1987 found that they had been killed by 'unknown persons'. In 1993 the inquest was reopened after the disclosure of a top secret military signal calling for the 'permanent removal from society' of Matthew Goniwe. It was found that security police were responsible for their deaths, but at that stage no names were mentioned. In January 1997 six members of the Port Elizabeth security police applied for amnesty for the killing of the Cradock Four. At the time of completion of this manuscript a decision is still awaited.

Defiance Campaign: Reference is here made not to the Defiance Campaign of the 1950s but to a UDF-led initiative, started in February 1989, which united a broad alliance of political and human rights organisations as well as trade unions in a campaign against apartheid laws. Civil disobedience strategies were used which specifically targeted apartheid segregation laws and state of emergency restrictions, culminating in a march through Cape Town on 13 September 1989 by an estimated thirty-five thousand demonstrators led by Archbishop Desmond Tutu.

District Six: A district within the inner city of Cape Town, so named in 1867 when the areas of the city were delineated. Long the home of a flourishing community of about 55 000 mainly coloured people, this crowded residential and commercial area near the harbour was often described as the soul of Cape Town. Known as much for its shady characters and high crime rate as for its strong sense of community, District Six was celebrated in songs, poetry and prose. In 1966 it was declared a white group area, and over the next 15 years the soul of the city was gutted by demolition and forced removals. The once close-knit community was dispersed widely throughout the new townships of the Cape Flats. For many years only a desolate and barren hillside near the city centre remained as silent reminder of one of the most brutal acts of destruction and dislocation under the Group Areas Act. Land restitution to former residents has now been started.

Dompas: Derogatory term (*verdomde pas* in Afrikaans) for the pass (identification document) which every black person over 16 was forced to carry at all times under the pass laws →.

ECC: End Conscription Campaign. Following a call by the Black Sash→ National Conference of 1983 to end military conscription, a national campaign was launched which united about fifty human rights organisations around the issue of resisting conscription in the ECC. By the end of 1983 there were branches in Cape Town, Johannesburg and Durban. Three years later the ECC was represented in all major cities and on most English-speaking university campuses. The ECC was finally banned in August 1988, the first 'white' organisation to be banned in 25 years. Only white males were eligible for conscription.

Enoni: Security Force establishment which became notorious for brutality. Compare also Vlakplaas →.

FEDSAW: Federation of South African Women. Women's political organisation of mostly black and coloured women with close links to the ANC underground. Founded in 1961, it became more or less dormant for some years until its revival in 1981 (Transvaal) and 1986 (Cape).

Freedom Charter: In 1953 and 1954, under the auspices of Albert Luthuli and the ANC →, a charter which represented the aspirations of the South African people was drawn up after consultations with people across the country. The Freedom Charter was drafted on the basis of thousands of submissions made at grassroots level. It was adopted at the Congress of the People, a gathering of almost 3 000 delegates from across the country in Kliptown, Soweto, in June 1955. The charter was subsequently ratified countrywide, although police broke up the Congress at Kliptown and arrested hundreds of delegates and charged them with treason. The Freedom Charter is essentially a moderate document which, in ten clauses, emphasises a non-racial society, liberty and individual rights.

Homelands: Designated areas for resettlement along tribal lines under Verwoerd's policy of 'self determination' for black South Africans. These areas became 'independent' with governmental and civil service structures authorised by Pretoria, an exercise which bled the country's fiscal resources to bolster white supremacy.

Hostel: Accommodation for migrant workers in townships offering neither any degree of basic comforts nor privacy. A myriad social problems resulted from this way of enforced living. In the 1990s vigilante → action often originated or was supported from these hostels

IFP: Inkatha Freedom Party. The ruling party in KwaZulu-Natal →. Formed in 1975, it started out by having close links with the then-banned ANC →. The two organisations fell out, however, and, under the leadership of Chief Mangosuthu Buthelezi, the IFP became more marked by nationalism and ethnocentrism. In this, it served as a moderate alternative to the ANC in the eyes of Pretoria as well as of large sections of the international community. Since 1991 revelations have emerged of the close links between the IFP and the security police and military intelligence in KwaZulu-Natal. Since the 1999 elections the IFP has been represented in Parliament with 34 seats.

Immorality Act: Legislation to prohibit extra-marital sexual intercourse between whites and blacks had existed since the 1927 Immorality Act No. 5, which was extended to include coloureds and Indians in 1950. In 1957 the legislation was replaced by the Sexual Offences Act which made it an offence for a white person to have intercourse with a black person or to commit any 'immoral or indecent act'. Repealed in part in June 1985. In the decades of its application, countless families were destroyed by this legislation, especially where one or more children could 'pass as white' but the parents – or one parent – could not. Investigations invaded personal privacy in particularly brutal ways, often with traumatic results.

ISCC: Inter-Schools Co-ordinating Committee. Co-ordinating body in which representatives from schools met and planned resistance activities on a regional level.

June 16, 1976: See entry under Soweto →.

Kangaroo courts: Street justice outside the law.

Khotso House: Headquarters of the South African Council of Churches and of the Black Sash →.

KwaZulu-Natal: Province incorporating Kwa-Zulu, the 'homeland' of the Zulu people and the former province of Natal. See also KZP →.

KZP: KwaZulu Police. A force of about 4 000 police formed in 1980 under Chief Mangosuthu Buthelezi as its Minister of Police. This force was seen by critics as functioning as the private army of the IFP and being responsible for much of the violence in the province. A commission under Mr Justice Richard Goldstone confirmed in December 1993 that hit squads existed within the ranks of the KZP and that KZP members had received military training at the hands of the SADF →.

Madiba: Clan name of Nelson Mandela, used by friends and admirers as a sign of affection and respect.

MK: *Umkhonto we Sizwe* (Xhosa), literally 'The Spear of the Nation'. Military wing of the ANC, established soon after the organisation was banned in 1960. See also Young Lions →.

NP: National Party. Political party formed by JBM Herzog in 1914 to represent Afrikaner interests. Finally came to power in 1948, when it immediately started to set out a system of racial separation. A series of racist Acts followed which codified the division of South Africa along racial lines and further disempowered and dispossessed black and coloured people, culminating in the grand apartheid plan of Hendrik Frensch Verwoerd. The latter led South Africa out of the British Commonwealth to realise the Afrikaner ideal of an independent republic. The increasingly harsh racist laws led to South Africa's international isolation and to increased resistance internally. When international pressure began to find its mark, the National Party pushed through some limited reforms of apartheid laws. In the main, they were rejected by blacks. In 1989 FW de Klerk, then known as a conservative member of the NP caucus, took over as President. In February 1990 he unbanned the ANC, the PAC and the SACP → and a process of negotiation began which resulted in South Africa's first free and democratic election in 1994, where the NP gained 82 of 400 seats in Parliament, compared with the 252 seats of the ANC. In the 1999 election the 'New' National Party could only win 28 seats.

NUSAS: National Union of South African Students. Association of mainly English-speaking liberal student bodies founded in 1924.

PAC: Pan Africanist Congress. Africanist movement formed in 1959 and led by Robert Sobukwe when a faction of the ANC grew suspicious of growing white, Indian and Communist Party influences within the ANC. The PAC, which also ran an armed wing, Poqo, after it had been banned, survived in exile and was unbanned in South Africa, with the ANC →, in February 1990. In the 1994 elections it won 5 seats in Parliament and 3 in 1999. See also PASO →.

PASO: Pan Africanist Students' Organization. Student wing of the PAC →.

Pass Laws: While legislation controlling the movement of blacks had existed long before the NP → came to power in 1948, the carrying of passes was made compulsory only in 1952 when the Bantu Laws Amendment Act No. 54 was passed. All black persons, men and women, over the age of sixteen were to carry passes at all times and were not allowed to stay in urban areas for longer than 72 hours unless they had permission to do so. The pass laws were designed to maintain a pool of labour without citizenship rights in the white areas, and to force into the Bantustans (later homelands) all who were not productive or were declared 'undesirable'. These laws split families and prevented wives from living with their husbands, parents with their children. They also effectively curtailed people's rights to sell their labour, as leaving a job almost certainly led to 'endorsement out' of an urban area. The failure to carry a pass was declared a criminal offence, and within a few years of the enactment of these laws arrests were averaging two thousand a day. The pass laws were repealed in July 1986, though indirect controls remained.

PEBCO Three: Three members of the UDF-affiliated Port Elizabeth Black
    Civic Organisation (PEBCO) were abducted and killed on 11 May
    1985 by members of the Port Elizabeth Security Branch. Their bodies
    were thrown into the Fish River. Askaris from Vlakplaas → assisted
    in the operation which was carried out after a visit, a short time
    before the murder, of Prime Minister PW Botha and Ministers Vlok
    (Police) and Malan (Defence), during which it was emphasised that
    all measures were to be taken – with no holds barred – to stabilise
    the Eastern Cape. Activists were to be 'neutralised'.

SACP: South African Communist Party. The Communist Party of South
    Africa (CPSA) was formed in 1921 to promote Marxist socialism;
    outlawed under the Suppression of Communism Act of 1950, it
    was driven underground where it was re-formed as the South
    African Communist Party (SACP) in 1953. It was unbanned in
    February 1990.

SADF: South African Defence Force, now the South African National
    Defence Force (SANDF).

SAP: South African Police, now the South African Police Service (SAPS).

SAYCO: South African Youth Congress. Youth wing of the UDF.

SDU: Self Defence Units. Militarised groups loosely allied to the ANC,
    established by youths in the violence-torn townships of the East
    Rand to protect local communities. They themselves were found to
    have carried out militant and brutal actions.

Section 29: Notorious section of the Internal Security Act of 1982 which
    allowed for the detention without trial of any suspects for 30 days
    and longer, at the Minister's discretion. Only the Minister could
    release such a detainee. After six months (180 days) the police were
    obliged to furnish 'adequate reasons' for continued detention.

Section 51: Legislation to control illegal gatherings. Under this law,
    especially during the States of Emergency, any two people who
    publicly made any political comment or held a placard could be
    arrested.

Sharpeville: A countrywide, sustained and non-violent campaign planned
    by the PAC → against the pass laws → turned into a massacre on

21 March 1960 when police opened fire and killed 69 people and wounded 180 in the township of Sharpeville in the Vaal Triangle. No warnings were given by the police, who later claimed that they had been in desperate danger because the crowd was stoning them. Three policemen were in fact reported to have been hit by stones.

Soweto: Acronym for South Western Townships. A contiguous group of African townships south-west of Johannesburg. Historically, the name is indelibly linked to the Soweto Uprising, the youth revolt of 1976, starting on 16 June in Soweto, and triggered by protests against Afrikaans as medium of instruction in African schools. It soon became a revolt against Bantu education in general and an uprising against the whole system of apartheid.

SOYA: Students of Young Azania. Student organisation linked with AZAPO →.

SPU: Self Protection Units. Loosely linked to the IFP.

SRC: Students' Representative Council. A democratically elected form of pupil representation in schools, often a rallying point of student activism.

Ubuntu: An ethos of humaneness and mutual responsibility and connected-ness, rooted in Xhosa culture.

UCT: University of Cape Town. Traditionally liberal English-speaking university.

UDF: United Democratic Front. Extra-parliamentary, non-racial political alliance of various organisations striving for a democratic South Africa, established in August 1983. Charterist in orientation, it spearheaded the mass campaigns of the 1980s which were largely instrumental in bringing about the unbanning of the ANC and other organisations.

Umkhonto we Sizwe (Xhosa, 'Spear of the Nation'): Underground army of the ANC; MK.

UWC: University of the Western Cape about 25 kilometres from the centre of Cape Town. Orginally established as a coloured university under apartheid, it was a centre of resistance politics in the 1980s.

Vigilantism: Vigilantes are people who take the law into their own hands. The term is usually used to designate conservative and militant blacks in townships who with or without support from the police acted against liberation forces (ANC, PAC). During the 1980s several groups of vigilantes operated with different aims. Some protected NP-supported people and structures in townships from the liberation movements. Others functioned in the 'homelands' to protect puppet 'governments'; other vigilante groups operated as a third force against the liberation movement, probably with covert support from the security establishment.

Vlakplaas: Unit of the Security Branch of the SAP → which took its name from the farm on which it was housed. Ostensibly a place where turned 'terrorists' were rehabilitated, it was in fact, according to evidence before the Truth Commission, a killing machine which targeted enemies of the regime. The last and most notorious head of the unit (1985-1993) was Colonel Eugene de Kock, now serving life sentences for murder in a maximum security jail.

Young Lions: Militant youth, most of them aligned towards the ANC and MK.

ACKNOWLEDGEMENTS

Our most sincere gratitude goes to all those South Africans, adults and youths alike, whose experiences are at the heart of this book. We are grateful for their trust and hope that we have been able to honour it in these pages. May this book become a contribution to the building of peace and understanding in South Africa, and may it help to focus attention on the human rights of children and young people.

We thank Archbishop Desmond Tutu for his interest in this book and for his contribution.

Special thanks for criticism, advice and encouragement in the different phases of our work on this manuscript are due to: Professor Denise Ackermann, Cape Town; Anthony Chubb and Peter Chubb, Cape Town; Dr Jenny Clarence, Pietermaritzburg; Dot Cleminshaw, Cape Town; Lionel Davies, Robben Island; Sheena Duncan, Johannesburg; Professor Carl-Heinz Evers and Micha Evers, Berlin; Hans Hartmann (KAIROS), Utrecht; Dr Glenn Hawkes, Vermont; Dorothea Ihme, Berlin; Dr Wolf Kaiser, (Wannsee-Villa Memorial Site), Berlin; Lenny de Koker, Cape Town; Azim Koning, Madeleine Maurick and Anton Dekker (Nederlands Instituut voor Zuidelijk Afrika), Amsterdam; Gerard Kosse, Amsterdam; Aki Krieger, Bonn; Menno Metselaar (Anne Frank Foundation), Amsterdam; Deirdre Prins, Robben Island; Rudolf Rode, Cape Town; Colleen Scott, Amsterdam; Frank Stevens (Amnesty International), Amsterdam; Frank Strickstrock, Marianne Sparr and Uwe Naumann (Rowohlt Verlag), Reinbek; Professor Charles Villa-Vicencio, Cape Town; Reinhard Widera, Cape Town; Gisela Wiese, Hamburg.

The staff of the Black Sash Advice Office, Grahamstown, especially Rosemary van Wyk-Smith and Jonathan Walton, for their help with research.

Special thanks to the pupils and staff of Cape Town High, School.

We thank the Goethe-Institute, Munich for financial support and Mr Stefan Huesgen of the Goethe Institute, Johannesburg for his advice.

PHOTOGRAPHS

FOREWORD
Archbishop Desmond Tutu
photographed on Robben Island in 1997

TRUTH
The Berlin Wall comes down

CHILDREN AND THE YOUTH
Township children celebrate as a building goes up in flames

SOMEONE WHO LISTENS
Dr Ivan Thoms gives his
full attention to a small patient

GETTING ON WITH LIFE
Riefaat Hattas, pictured with his niece,
is one of many youths whose story needs to be heard

REMEMBRANCE AND THE FUTURE
Peace education in action: children sing the peace song